PETER ACHINSTEIN

CONCEPTS OF SCIENCE
A Philosophical Analysis

THE JOHNS HOPKINS PRESS
BALTIMORE, MARYLAND

In memory of my mother,
Betty Achinstein

PREFACE

This book is concerned with concepts important for understanding the nature of science. Those to be discussed are not themselves scientific concepts, they are not ones scientists usually examine in the course of their work, nor are they concepts appropriate for one science but not another. Rather, they are very general ones applicable to all sciences, and would be invoked in talking about, rather than within, these sciences. They are the province of the philosopher of science. Those to be treated in this book might be placed in three broad categories: definitions, theories, and models.

I begin by examining various types of terms in science and the relationships between the information presented in their definitions and the terms themselves. The main thrust of the discussion is to introduce and develop the notion of relevance, especially semantical relevance, and to show how, in many important cases, this concept, rather than traditional ones of logical necessity and sufficiency, must be invoked to understand the nature of definitions in science. The conclusions reached will be applied to recent philosophical theories on the meaning of scientific terms. One, contemporary Logical Positivism, using formal techniques of symbolic logic, proposes what it regards as an ideal way to reconstruct scientific systems to guarantee all terms empirical meaning. Another, defended by those more influenced by the history of science, emphasizes the theory-dependence of scientific terms and eschews formalizing procedures of Positivism as failing to account for such dependence. Both positions will be criticized in the light of the theory of definitions I shall develop.

Turning to the second category, theories, I ask what conditions must be satisfied for something to be classified as a theory. What is the nature of the speculative character of theories? What sort of coherence must the principles of a theory display? What elements can be distinguished when a theory is presented? What are the different kinds of presentations in science and the advantages of each? I also consider several accounts of theories that have become standard, for example, the "hypothetico-deductive" account and the view of theories as "conceptual organizers." I then turn to the distinction between theoretical and nontheoretical terms widely assumed in the philosophy of science. Why is such a distinction necessary, and can it be drawn by invoking concepts such as observation, theory-dependence, conjecture, precision, and degree of abstractness? How should these concepts themselves be explained, and what importance do they have within the philosophy of science?

Finally, the concept of the scientific model will be treated. I characterize various types of models employed in the sciences, indicating their functions, how they differ from one another and from theories, and how each is subject to quite different standards of evaluation. I also examine a widespread doctrine, supported by contemporary Positivists, which attempts to provide a unifying scheme for all the models distinguished. I try to show how this doctrine fails to characterize these conceptions adequately or supply a new concept of value to the sciences.

Philosophers of science are often tempted toward one of two extremes. Some, using techniques and concepts of modern formal logic, construct abstract and extremely general schemes for describing and unifying science. As a result they may disregard actual cases in the sciences, many of which fail to fit their schemes, or may propose new schemes of little value in actual use. At the other extreme, some, approaching science from the historical point of view, consider individual cases in depth, emphasize differences, and avoid generalization. As a result they may provide valuable "case histories" but little appreciation for what is common to these cases. Still another temptation, combining elements of the first two, is to offer a detailed case history and then generalize from the one case with little concern for others. Steering a course between these extremes is often difficult, and at some points I too have yielded to one of these temptations. However, by the use of numerous examples, mainly from physics, I have tried to maintain contact with at least one science and at the same time to say something general and, I hope, revealing about the concepts I have chosen to discuss.

It is my pleasure to acknowledge the institutions and individuals who helped make this book possible. To The Johns Hopkins University I am grateful for a leave of absence of three semesters in 1965 and 1966, during which much of the writing was done. Preliminary research was supported by a three year grant from the National Science Foundation, and later by a fellowship from the John Simon Guggenheim Memorial Foundation. Support for the final stages of work was provided by a faculty research grant from Johns Hopkins. I have used as a basis for parts of several chapters the following publications: "Theoretical Terms and Partial Interpretation" and "Theoretical Models," *British Journal for the Philosophy of Science,* 14 (1963), 89–105, 16 (1965), 102–20; "The Problem of Theoretical Terms," *American Philosophical Quarterly,* 2 (1965), 193–203; "Models, Analogies, and Theories," *Philosophy of Science,* 31 (1964), 328–50; "Rudolf Carnap," *Review of Metaphysics,* 19 (1966), 517–49, 758–79. To the editors and publishers of these journals I am grateful for permission to use parts of this material.

The manuscript served as a basis for graduate seminars at Johns Hopkins, M.I.T., and Stanford, and I benefited from many suggestions and criticisms offered by students in these seminars. I must also mention the following persons, discussions with whom affected points in the book: Asher Achinstein, Stephen Barker, Sylvain Bromberger, Roderick Firth, Carl G. Hempel, Jerrold Katz, Marvin Levich, Maurice Mandelbaum, Ernest Nagel, Hilary Putnam, Israel Scheffler, Abner Shimony, Marshall Spector, James Thomson, and Judith Thomson. To my colleague Stephen Barker I am further indebted for reading the entire manuscript and offering important criticisms. Above all, I want to thank my wife for her constant encouragement and invaluable aid in final preparation of the manuscript.

CONTENTS

CONTENTS

CONCEPTS OF SCIENCE

CHAPTER ONE

DEFINITIONS, I

A science characteristically develops general principles and employs a variety of terms for expressing them. Many of these terms will be new ones coined for particular purposes; others will be everyday ones used in technical senses, some will be everyday ones used in everyday senses. The subject of definition is broad and includes questions concerning the nature of terms in science, meaning, the empirical or a priori status of laws and principles, the operational character of terms, changes in scientific concepts, and many others. Philosophers usually approach such questions armed with distinctions between nominal and real definitions, contextual and noncontextual, or explicit and partial ones. Although I will discuss various sorts of definitions, my main concern is different.

To explain what it is, let me begin by saying that the word "definition" will be used to cover the sort of information contained in dictionary entries. For example, in the case of a term such as "copper," I am concerned with the following sort of information that a dictionary might provide: "A reddish metal of atomic number 29, which is malleable, ductile, and a good conductor of electricity and heat; density 8.92g/cc; found in abundance in its natural state; used for wiring, coins, piping, pottery; has been used since ancient times." I will speak of this as a definition for the term "copper" and use the word "property" in a very broad way to refer to any single fact about an item that might be included in such a definition.

The central question I raise can be put as follows: What is the relationship, or what are the various relationships, between the properties cited in a definition and the term defined? Answering this question will put us in a better position to understand the nature of definitions and

1

the considerations that prompt the selection of properties for them. It will also put us in a better position to consider alternative philosophical theories about definitions in science.

A definition for a term may vary considerably from one dictionary to another. The *International Dictionary of Physics and Electronics* (1956) provides the following entry for "copper": "metallic element. Symbol *Cu*. Atomic number 29." The entry for "copper" in the *Condensed Chemical Dictionary* (1942) runs to a full page and includes a wealth of specific information under headings such as color and properties, constants (specific gravity, melting point, etc.), soluble in, derivation, methods of purification, forms available, etc. *Webster's New International Dictionary* (1929) contains a small part of the same information. Despite these differences I will try to show that general claims about such definitions can be made and will develop a theory about terms in science and the sorts of definitions they have.

The terms to be considered can be divided into three types, as follows:

A	B	C
copper	conservative system	kinetic energy
metal	diatomic molecule	velocity
electron	Newtonian system	length
atom	reversible process	temperature
acid	Carnot cycle	entropy
sulfuric acid	rigid body	density
oxygen	Bohr atom	specific gravity
electroscope	quadruped	force
insect	fermion	potential energy

These are not meant to exhaust the types of terms in science; nor is the division perfectly sharp. Roughly speaking, we might say that terms on list A designate physical objects or stuffs; those on list B express somewhat more abstract concepts applicable to physical objects, stuffs, phenomena, and so forth, provided the latter satisfy certain necessary and sufficient conditions; terms on list C designate quantities capable of numerical degree. What I will show is that terms on list A receive definitions of different sorts from those on B, and that some terms on C are defined similarly to those on A, whereas others are defined like those on B. The first list will be discussed in the present chapter; the others, in Chapter Two.

1. LOGICAL NECESSITY AND SUFFICIENCY

Different persons, even within the same linguistic community, may use the same term differently. They may differ over what they regard as standard cases to which it applies and over the criteria in virtue of which it is applicable. The semantical categories I shall introduce for describing the various possible relationships between properties of X and the term "X" do not require agreement in use from speaker to speaker. What is required is that there be something to be called *a use* of a term, whether this is attributable to a single speaker or a group of speakers; also, that for a given speaker or group there be something that might be called normal, standard, or typical use (or uses) of a term by contrast with special uses (for example, stretched, metaphorical, or other figurative uses). Deviations from normal use, except for special circumstances, can be misuses of the term, although this will be a matter of degree depending on the extent of the deviation. Moreover, a normal use to which a scientist puts a term may differ from a more popular use of the same term, and use may change over time. In what follows I shall be concerned with a normal use which a term has for a scientist or group of scientists at a given time.

The first category to be introduced is logical necessity. By saying that a property P is logically necessary for being an X I mean that, as the term "X" is used, an item lacking P cannot correctly be classified as an X no matter what other properties it has. The matter should be closed if the property is known to be lacking.[1] My first general claim about terms on list A is this: As these terms are used by many scientists, properties that a dictionary attributes to X are, for the most part, not logically necessary for being an X. This claim rests on two facts.

[1] Some properties of certain items on list A are attributable to the substance X as well as to all or most individual X's or chunks of X (for example, boiling point, in the case of copper). Others are attributable only to X but not to all or most individual X's or chunks of X (for example, used in wiring, in the case of copper). And for some properties attributable to X, it may not be clear whether they are attributable to particular X's (for example, having the atomic number 29, in the case of copper). In the above characterization of logical necessity, I speak of an item lacking a property P. "Item" here can be used to refer to both a type and a particular sample. If P is a property attributable only to X but not to all or most particular X's, then if "item" is used to refer to a sample, by "item that lacks P" I shall mean "a particular sample of a type that lacks P." Thus, if we are considering whether use in wiring is logically necessary for copper, and the item in question is a particular sample S, the issue will be not whether S itself happens to be used in wiring, but whether S is a sample of a type (of substance) so used.

First, some properties cited in dictionary entries are not possessed by all actual items classified as X's. Among the properties of metals frequently cited are hardness, high conductivity, high melting point, metallic luster, solid at room temperature, ductility, malleability, and opacity. Yet mercury, a metal, is a liquid at room temperature, and the alkali metals (lithium, sodium, and so on) are soft and have low melting points. Dictionaries will often employ terms like "most," "generally," and "typically," when listing properties possessed by many, though not all, types of items to which the term is actually applied. The more general the term on list A ("metal" by contrast with "copper"), the greater the exceptions likely to be found. For certain terms on list A (for example, "insect"), not only may types of X lack properties cited but also atypical individual X's of types with such properties may lack them. If actual exceptions to "X's have P" are recognized, P cannot be logically necessary for X.

Second, even if actual exceptions do not exist one must consider possible ones. The term may be used in such a way that although known X's have P, if a type of object were discovered which lacked P but was sufficiently like X in other respects, it would be classified as an X. As many physicists and chemists use the term "copper," having a melting point of 1083°C. is not a logically necessary property. If some substance were discovered sufficiently like copper but with a lower melting point, they would still classify it as copper (though perhaps as low-melting copper).

In this connection, consider the property of atomic weight. It used to be thought that an element was composed of atoms with the same mass and that atomic weights gave the relative masses of atoms. The discovery of isotopes changed this. For example, although most of what was being classified as carbon consists of atoms of atomic weight 12, about 1 per cent was found to consist of atoms of atomic weight 13. Yet the latter were sufficiently similar in their chemical and spectrographic properties to warrant the classification "carbon," and were recognized as different isotopes of carbon. In short, atomic weight 12 was not treated as logically necessary for carbon.

Or, to invoke a hypothetical case, consider atomic number. Construed in its modern sense, this indicates the position of the element in the periodic table, determined solely by reference to the number of electrons outside the nucleus of a neutral atom of the element. Suppose that atomic theory comes to be discredited. It might be that a new and more powerful theory is developed according to which, for certain elements, varying numbers of extranuclear electrons are possible and are responsible for the same macroscopic chemical and physical properties; or it might be a more radical theory, exorcising electrons altogether. In such a case, if, as seems reasonable to suppose by analogy with the case of atomic weight, elements retained their present classifications (on the basis of macroscopic chemical and physical properties) despite modifications in, or even an elimination of, the concept of atomic number, then having a certain atomic number would not be a logically necessary property of elements.

Similar remarks can be made for most properties attributed to items designated by terms on list A. There are actual or possible cases in which such properties are not attributable to something still classifiable as an X. In short, terms on this list tend to be used by scientists in such a way that most properties cited in a dictionary entry will not be logically necessary for their application. In some cases none of the cited properties will be. There is one important type of exception, which might be called "substance" classifications. Properties of this type will often be logically necessary, depending upon their level of generality. Being a chemical substance would normally be treated as logically necessary for being an acid, being an instrument as logically necessary for being an electroscope, though being an element might not be considered logically necessary for being copper.

This is not to deny that a definition for a term on list A might give logically necessary conditions in the following sense: although no single property cited may be logically necessary for being an X, some disjunction of properties might be. A term would be inapplicable to an item possessing none of these properties. Some dictionaries, however, indicate only a few properties for terms on list A even the disjunction of which is not logically necessary. Nor is this to deny that scientists could change the use of a term by stipulating that a certain property is now to be considered logically necessary. (Cases of this sort will be considered in the next chapter.)

Let me turn to logical sufficiency. When I speak of a property as logically sufficient for being an X, I mean that, as the term "X" is used, an item possessing this property is correctly classifiable as an X no matter what other properties it has. The matter should be closed if the property is known to be possessed. Terms on list A tend to be used by scientists in such a way that no property cited in dictionary entries for these terms is logically sufficient for their application.[2] This claim, like the one for logical necessity, rests on an appeal to actual as well as possible cases. Some of the properties of X cited in dictionary entries are also possessed by actual non-X's. Thus, having the melting point 1083°C. is not logically sufficient for being copper, since deoxidized arsenical copper, an alloy of copper, phosphorus, and arsenic, has the same melting point. Similar claims could be made about properties of copper such as reddish color, high conductivity, and metallic luster. In the case of certain properties, however, appeal to possible cases would need to be made. As the term "copper" is used by many physicists and chemists, having the atomic number 29 would not be logically sufficient for being copper. Cases could be envisaged (involving modifications in atomic theory) in which a substance possessing this property, but lacking a large number of others cited in a definition for "copper," would not be classifiable as copper.

2. RELEVANCE

If the relationship between a property of an item on list A and being an item of that sort is, in general, not one of logical necessity or sufficiency, how can it be described? Here I must introduce the concept of relevance and speak of a property as relevant for being an X. By this I mean that if an item is known to possess certain properties and lack others, the fact that the item possesses (or lacks) the property in question normally will count, at least to some extent, in favor of (or against) concluding that it is an X; and if it is known to possess or lack sufficiently many properties of certain sorts, the fact that the item possesses or lacks the property in question may justifiably be held to settle whether it is an X.

Consider the term "metal." The property of high (electrical and thermal) conductivity is relevant though neither logically necessary nor logically sufficient for being a metal. If an item is known to possess certain other properties (for example, hardness and metallic luster), then the fact that it does have high conductivity will normally count, to some extent, in favor of concluding that it is a metal (though the possession of other properties may count against such a conclusion). And if it is

[2] Nor, for reasons to be explained in sec. 6, will the *conjunction* of properties typically cited in a dictionary entry for "X" be logically sufficient for X.

known to possess sufficiently many properties of certain sorts, the fact that it has high conductivity might be taken to settle the matter. If it does not have high conductivity, this does not necessarily preclude it from being a metal; some item might be discovered which lacks this property but has sufficiently many others of appropriate sorts to be classifiable as a metal. However, the fact that an item lacks high conductivity will normally count as some reason against concluding that it is a metal; and if it lacks certain other properties as well, this fact may be taken to settle the question.

Again, having a melting point of 1083°C. is relevant for copper, though not logically necessary or sufficient. The fact that an item with certain other properties has this melting point will normally count as some reason in favor of concluding that it is copper (without necessarily settling the matter); and, if the item has sufficiently many other properties cited in the dictionary, the fact that it melts at 1083°C. might justifiably be held to settle the question of its classification. Other relevant, though not logically necessary or sufficient, properties of copper would be reddish color, having the atomic number 29, being a good conductor, and so forth.

In classifying properties with respect to relevance, we must, as indicated, consider what would *normally* happen. There might be circumstances in which the fact that an item lacks high conductivity would not count at all against its being a metal (or copper); but these would be special—for example, if the item were to be heated to an extremely high temperature, thus radically decreasing its electrical conductivity.

Two distinctions are now possible. The first is between positive and negative relevance. If the fact that an item has P tends to count more in favor of concluding that it is an X than the fact that it lacks P tends to count against it, P can be said to have more positive than negative relevance for X. The second distinction is between semantical and nonsemantical relevance and is applicable only to certain cases of relevance.

Suppose one is asked to justify the claim that the reddish metallic element of atomic number 29, which is a good conductor and melts at 1083°C., is copper. One reply is that such properties tend to count in and of themselves, to some extent, toward classifying something as copper. By this I mean that an item is correctly classifiable as copper solely in virtue of having such properties; they are among the properties which constitute a final court of appeal when considering matters of classification; such properties are, one might say, intrinsically copper-making ones. Suppose, on the other hand, one is asked to justify the claim that the substance constituting about 10^{-4} per cent of the igneous rocks in the earth's crust, that is mined in Michigan, and that was used by the ancient Greeks, is copper. Among the possible replies is *not* that such properties tend to count in and of themselves, to some extent, toward something's being classifiable as copper—that is, it is not true that something is classifiable as copper solely in virtue of having such properties. These properties do not constitute a final court of appeal when considering matters of classification. They are not intrinsically copper-making ones. Rather, the possession of such properties (among others) counts in favor of classifying something as copper solely because it allows one to infer that the item possesses other properties such as being metallic and having the atomic number 29, properties that are intrinsically copper-making ones, in virtue of which it is classifiable as copper.

How can we determine whether, for a given scientist or group, properties are of one sort or the other? We must look to what scientists do in actual situations of classification and to what, in fact, they say about such situations; we must also determine what they would do and say about hypothetical ones. The following considerations are pertinent. (1) When attempting to identify an X, are these the properties scientists look for and accept as settling questions of classification most decisively? (2) In actual disputes over classification, when it is known that a given item has the properties in question, how do scientists defend the claim that it is an X? Do they argue that the possession of these properties means that it must have other properties which make it an X? Or do they treat such properties as "ultimate," speaking of them as "defining" properties, as ones which make it an X, in virtue of which it is an X, or something similar? (3) How do they answer corresponding questions about hypothetical contexts in which items are to be classified and justifications given? What properties do they say they would look for as determining proper classification most decisively, and what sorts of justifications do they say they would give for claims that items with such properties are X's? To decide whether properties count in and of themselves toward classifying something as an X, questions such as these must be answered.

Suppose $P_1, \ldots, P_n$ constitutes some set of relevant properties of X. If the properties in this set tend to count in and of themselves, to some extent, toward an item's being classifiable as an X, I shall speak of them as *semantically relevant* for X. If the possession of properties by an item tends to count toward an X-classification solely because it allows one to infer that the item possesses properties of the former sort, I shall speak of such properties as *nonsemantically relevant* for X. This distinction is not meant to apply to all relevant properties of X, for there will be cases on or near the borderline not clearly classifiable in either way.[3]

What sorts of properties will be semantically relevant for items on list A? No general answer can be given, but something can be said about various classes of items on this list, for example, chemical compounds. Before the seventeenth and eighteenth centuries, classification of chemical compounds was based on a few physical properties such as color, taste, smell, consistency, solubility, and method of preparation.[4] Properties of these sorts were treated as ones which in and of themselves tended to count in favor of an X-classification, and not as mere indicators of properties more fundamental. Indeed, such properties were often appropriated as part of the names given to compounds. Magnesium carbonate and manganese dioxide were distinguished by color and called *magnesia alba* and *magnesia nigra*, respectively. Similarly, if two different methods of preparation existed, this counted in and of itself, to some extent, in favor of classifying substances differently. *Spirit of nitre* and *aqua fortis* were distinguished as separate compounds because they were prepared in different ways, though both are what we now call nitric acid.[5] However, in the latter part of the eighteenth century, with the systematic chemical nomenclature of Bergman and Lavoisier, the chemical composition of compounds began to be treated as semantically relevant; and, indeed, properties such as color, taste, and consistency were generally treated as mere indicators of chemical composition; it was the latter that provided the basis for classification of compounds.

I have used the labels semantical and nonsemantical relevance because X's semantically relevant properties have something to do with the meaning or use of the term "X" in a way that X's nonsemantically relevant properties do not. Exactly what this is will be discussed in section 9. The next two sections will consider ways of further developing this distinction. They will propose a somewhat idealized set of concepts, ones that lie behind the rather intuitive distinction just drawn and represent one fairly natural way of extending and explaining it.

[3] See sec. 4, pt. (*a*).
[4] See Maurice P. Crosland, *Historical Studies in the Language of Chemistry* (Cambridge, Mass., 1962).
[5] *Ibid.,* p. 90.

Some may want to omit these sections at a first reading and turn to section 5, where the main thread of the argument continues.

3. SEMANTICAL RELEVANCE

Let us turn to the kinds of cases that will be useful for developing the distinction between semantical and nonsemantical relevance. Essentially, I want to consider substances having relevant properties of X except for P and then ask: Does lack of P in and of itself count, to some extent, against classifying them as X's? In virtue of lacking P, do we (i.e., members of the linguistic community using the term "X") think of such substances as not the best examples of X, not the most typical or standard cases of X? I also want to consider substances described as having some of the relevant properties of X, without an indication of whether they have others as well; or else described as having some of the relevant properties of X but also as lacking others, so that they might be thought of as borderline cases of X. Now suppose we are informed that in addition these substances have P. Then I want to ask: Does the possession of P in and of itself count, to some extent, in favor of classifying them as X's (without necessarily settling the matter)? In virtue of possessing P, do we think of them as closer to typical or standard cases of X?

Some of these substances may be actual ones, and if so, in order to answer these questions, we must consider what in fact is done in actual situations of classification. For example, when substances are found that have relevant properties of X except for P, do those using the term "X" take the fact that these substances lack P to be a decisive reason against considering them the most typical cases of X? Is lack of P decisive in this way if disputes arise regarding classification, when appeal may need to be made to the most typical cases of X?

Other substances, however, will be hypothetical ones. We might consider, for example, a hypothetical substance as similar as possible to copper, except that its melting point is 500°C., not 1083°C. Suppose this is not specially treated copper and that the atmospheric conditions have not suddenly changed. The question is: Would the fact that it melts at 500°C. count in and of itself as some reason (though possibly not a conclusive one) against classifying it as copper? Furthermore, we might consider a substance described as having some of the relevant properties of copper (for example, reddish color, conductivity, malleability) without indicating whether it has others; or else, as having these properties of copper but lacking certain others. Now, in addition, this substance is described as having the melting point 1083°C. Would the fact that it has this melting point in and of itself count as some reason (though possibly not a conclusive one) in favor of classifying it as copper? We might expect the answers to these questions to be different if, instead of melting point, we chose properties such as being mined in Michigan or being used by the ancient Greeks. When substances are hypothetical ones, to determine whether the possession (or lack) of a certain property counts in and of itself for (or against) an X-classification we must consider two things: what those who use the term "X" would *say* about such hypothetical cases, and what in fact they *do* in actual situations when confronted with substances that are similar in certain ways.

Let me now formulate a distinction between two types of relevance. I shall do so in a series of steps, beginning with a simplified statement.

Formulation A: (1) Suppose that X's normally have properties P_1, . . . P_i . . ., P_n, each both positively and negatively relevant for X. Let us consider a substance with all the properties in this set except P_i. If the fact that this substance lacks P_i counts in and of itself, at least to some extent, against classifying it as an X (though it need not rule out this classification), let us say that P_i is (*negatively*) *semantically relevant* for X. If the latter fact in and of itself counts to no extent whatever against this classification, let us say that P_i is (*negatively*) *nonsemantically relevant* for X. (2) Let us consider another substance which has some of the properties in P_1, . . ., P_n. It may be incompletely described by saying that it has some of these properties but not saying whether it has others. Or, it may be described more completely by saying that it has some of the properties in this set and that it lacks others, so that we can think of it as a borderline case of an X. Now suppose, in addition, we are told that this substance possesses P_i. If the latter fact in and of itself counts, at least to some extent, in favor of classifying the substance as an X (though the lack of other properties may not justify this classification), let us say that P_i is (*positively*) *semantically relevant* for X. If the latter fact in and of itself counts to no extent in favor of such a classification, let us say that P_i is (*positively*) *nonsemantically relevant* for X.

This formulation needs to be altered by mentioning not one but various subsets of properties in the set P_1, . . ., P_n. To determine semantical relevance we must consider various ways a substance might lack P_i and various ways it might be a borderline case of X.

Formulation B: (1) Suppose that X's normally have properties $P_1, \ldots P_i \ldots, P_n$, each both positively and negatively relevant for X. A substance having a subset of properties in a set S, where this subset contains a vast majority of the properties in S, will be said to have a *vast majority* subset of properties in S. Let us now consider various substances, each with a different vast majority subset of $P_1, \ldots, P_n$, where each subset lacks P_i. If the lack of P_i by these substances in most such cases counts in and of itself, at least to some extent, against classifying them as X's, let us say that P_i is (negatively) semantically relevant for X. If the lack of P_i by these substances in most such cases counts in and of itself not at all against classifying them as X's, let us say that P_i is (negatively) nonsemantically relevant for X. (2) A substance described as having a subset of properties in S, where this subset contains quite a few, although not a vast majority, of the properties in S, and where the substance may also be described as lacking properties in S, will be said to have a *partial* subset of properties in S. Let us now consider various substances, each of which is to have a different partial subset of $P_1, \ldots, P_n$ (where none of these includes P_i). The substances may be described as having quite a few of the properties in $P_1, \ldots, P_n$, where the question of whether they have any of the remaining properties is left open; or, they may be described as having quite a few of the properties in $P_1, \ldots, P_n$ and also as lacking certain of the other properties in this set. In either case the properties present and absent are to be those which make the substances borderline cases of X. Suppose, in addition, we are told that each of these substances possesses P_i. If, in most such cases, the latter fact counts in and of itself, at least to some extent, in favor of classifying them as X's, let us say that P_i is (positively) semantically relevant for X. If, in most such cases, this fact in and of itself counts to no extent whatever in favor of such a classification, let us say that P_i is (positively) nonsemantically relevant for X.

The most important factor not accounted for in either Formulation A or B is background information. This presents a problem, for to describe a hypothetical substance as lacking a certain property or set of properties may be to court inconsistency with theories or laws assumed as part of the background. And this may tempt one to ask how such a substance can have other properties attributed to it. For example, if a physicist is told to consider a substance just like copper in all respects, including atomic number, except that it is a nonconductor of electricity, his reply might be: "How could it be a nonconductor if it has the atomic number 29—that is, if its outer shell has one electron? If you ask me to consider this, then you ask me to suppose that my atomic theory is wrong and hence that many other properties I attribute to copper must be dropped. And then you are asking me to change so many things that I don't know what to say."

Two extreme views are possible. One is that any hypothetical substance can be considered, with any combination of properties, independently of background information; and we can decide in every such case whether the possession of a certain property by the substance counts in favor of an X-classification. Another is that we can never consider hypothetical cases involving combinations of properties different from those that are actually found. To do so, the background would need to be changed in unknown ways. We can never determine all the consequences of considering an X that lacks certain of its typical properties, and we can never tell whether the lack of these will affect other properties we are assuming X to possess.

Both of these views I reject. Of course we cannot postulate just any change in the properties of X and know clearly whether to say that certain properties are or are not X-making in every case. We must also consider how these postulated changes affect and are affected by background information. Yet it is not true that the background must always be described completely—that we always need to know exactly how the hypothetical changes we postulate could come about. In some cases, even without much background information, there may be strong tendencies to classify items in certain ways; other cases may require a more thorough description; and in all cases, when other information is supplied, it is always possible that the items may be classified differently or defy classification. On the other hand, it is a gross exaggeration to say that because of background information we can never consider hypothetical cases or know how to speak in any such situation. Some hypothetical substances of the sort we are to consider are perfectly compatible with accepted beliefs. These are substances described as having some of the properties of X, where it is not said whether they have other properties as well. Others may be incompatible with certain beliefs but not with accepted theories or laws. However, even if theories or laws are violated, clear description is often possible. Physicists invoke concepts of perpetual motion machines of the first and second kinds (ones, respectively, that create energy from nothing and in which the thermal efficiency is unity). These violate the first and second laws of thermodynamics, respectively. Yet physicists discuss them and attribute to them fundamental physical quantities such as work and heat. Many idealizations employed by the scientist require supposing that X's behave quite differently from the way they actually do, where what is supposed may violate fundamental theories and principles. Yet the similarities with what is actually the case are often sufficient to suggest how classification should proceed.

For each hypothetical substance we might consider, an indefinitely large number of backgrounds is possible. Such backgrounds might be described in minimal terms or in considerable detail; they might be as close as possible to the background now assumed for actual X's or extremely different; and each would be included or presupposed as part of the hypothetical case. This means that the number of hypothetical cases is indefinitely large, possibly infinite, so we cannot speak of how we would classify *most* of them (as we did in Formulation B where the number of possibilities is limited). Moreover, these cases will not be of equal importance or weight with respect to the matter of classification. Suppose, for example, we consider hypothetical substances with different vast majority subsets of $P_1, \ldots, P_n$, where each lacks P_i. In some of these cases it may be more clear than in others whether the lack of P_i counts in and of itself against an X-classification. The clearer cases will carry more weight in deciding whether to say that P_i is semantically relevant for X. In some of these cases the background assumed will be closer to what it is now than in other cases; and the former will carry more weight than the latter with respect to questions of semantical relevance, since they are closer to cases in which questions of classification are already settled. For the same reason, hypothetical substances with vast majority subsets of $P_1, \ldots, P_n$ that are close to those possessed by actual substances will count more than those very different from actual ones.

To reduce proliferation of cases that results from more and more detailed description of the background, let us adopt the following procedure: we are to suppose that for each hypothetical substance only as much background is supplied as is needed to produce a case in which it is more or less clear whether the lack of P_i counts in and of itself against an X-classification; it is assumed that the rest of the background is as close as possible to what it is for actual X's. We consider a series of cases beginning with substances possessing vast majority subsets of $P_1, \ldots, P_n$, where such substances are as close as possible to ones actually to be found, and where the supplied background is as close as possible to what is now assumed for X's. Substances are then considered whose properties and background are less like those assumed for actual X's.

We want to decide whether the lack of P_i by such hypothetical substances counts in and of itself, to some extent, against classifying them as X's. It may not do so in every such case; and we cannot appeal to what happens in the majority of cases because, even with the above method of reducing the number, cases are weighted differently and the class in question may be indefinitely large. Some less precise criterion is needed here. Let us say that the lack of P_i by hypothetical substances *tends* to count in and of itself against classifying them as X's. We shall want to say this if, by considering cases in the manner above, we discover those of sufficient weight in which the lack of P_i counts in and of itself, to some extent, against an X-classification. A similar procedure can be adopted to decide whether the possession of P_i by hypothetical substances with partial subsets of $P_1, \ldots, P_n$ tends to count in and of itself, to some extent, in favor of classifying them as X's. Of course in determining whether the lack of P_i tends to count in and of itself against an X-classification, we shall want to appeal not only to hypothetical substances similar to X but also to actual ones lacking P_i, if such exist, in order to determine how classification in fact proceeds in such cases; the same holds true for determining whether the possession of P_i tends to count in and of itself in favor of an X-classification.

The distinction between semantical and nonsemantical relevance can now be stated as follows.

Formulation C: (1) Suppose that X's normally have properties $P_1, \ldots P_i \ldots, P_n$, each both positively and negatively relevant for X. Let us consider various substances with different vast majority subsets of $P_1, \ldots, P_n$, where each subset lacks P_i. If, considering various backgrounds and appropriate weights, the lack of P_i by these substances tends to count in and of itself, at least to some extent, against classifying them as X's, let us say that P_i is (negatively) semantically relevant for X. If the lack of P_i in such cases in and of itself tends not to count at all against such a classification, let us say that P_i is (negatively) nonsemantically relevant for X. (2) Let us consider various substances, each being a borderline case of an X and having a different partial

creature-with-a-heart-picture
creature-with-kidney picture } *cf Goodman*

*

Similarly, to suggest what differences in meaning exist between the expressions "creature with a heart" and "creature with kidneys" (which apply to the same actual items), one might invoke hypothetical cases. One might construct pictures of imaginary creatures showing their insides to contain kidneys but no heart, or vice versa, and then indicate that one expression but not the other applies.

Sometimes the way we now describe a hypothetical item turns out to be different from what we say when and if it is actually discovered. In speaking of how a person applies a term to a hypothetical item, I mean to indicate as well something about how he would apply it if this item were actualized. What one means by a term is to be ascertained not only by observing how he now applies it to hypothetical cases when these are described to him but also by trying to discover how he would apply it were such cases to become actual. Of course, what he now says about certain hypothetical cases is a fairly reliable guide for what he will say when these cases occur, but asking him to describe hypothetical cases is not the only test for determining how he would apply a term. We must consider also how he now applies the term in actual situations and determine what he now appeals to in settling disputes about its application.

Hypothetical cases are of two sorts. In one, reference is made to an item which does not exist but whose description is compatible with theories or other general principles we may hold; in the other, reference is made to an item whose description is inconsistent with such theories or principles. Some philosophers might object to either sort of hypothetical case; others, only to the second.

A possible objection to the second was noted in the previous section: imagining a substance to have or to lack a certain property, where this is inconsistent with our theories, will make it unclear how it can have other properties attributed to it. In reply, I pointed out that in at least certain cases scientists and others can and do consider hypothetical situations of this sort, keeping other things constant as far as possible.

A second objection to the related notion of possibility is Quine's, and it concerns either sort of hypothetical case.[6] Quine eschews talk about "possibles" for lack of a clear principle of individuation—that is, a principle for deciding whether one possible is the same as or different from another. If, to take Quine's example, *A* speaks of the possible fat man in the doorway and *B* of the possible bald man, there is no way to

[6] W. V. Quine, *From a Logical Point of View* (Cambridge, Mass., 1953), Chap. 1.

18

decide whether one or two possible men are being described. Even if after much further description A's man and B's man turn out to have all the same properties, there is no way of deciding whether there is one possible man or two possible men with the same properties.

Quine's objections are against possible *individuals,* but when I consider hypothetical cases I am concerned only with possible *types.* Here individuation is not as problematic. One can certainly distinguish the type of gas called an ideal gas, defined as satisfying the equation $PV = nRT,$ from that called a van der Waals gas, defined as satisfying the equation $\left(P + \dfrac{a}{V^2}\right)(V - b) = nRT,$ though neither is an actual type of gas; or similarly, a perpetual motion machine of the first type from one of the second type, though neither is an actual type of machine. For present purposes we can say that X and Y are different possible types if and only if they are described in such a way that one has at least some property the other lacks.

5. LINGUISTIC DESCRIPTIONS; CENTRALITY

I have claimed that, in general, properties cited in a dictionary entry for a term "X" on list A are relevant for X without being logically necessary or sufficient; of these, some are semantically relevant, others nonsemantically relevant. In the light of this, let us try to say how terms on list A are used in science. To describe such use I shall proceed indirectly. Suppose, by contrast, we were dealing with a term "X" used by a speaker or group in such a way that $P_1, \ldots, P_n$ are properties logically necessary for X, and their conjunction logically sufficient. Then a description of such a use (what I shall call a *linguistic description*) might be, or at least contain, the following:

D_1: As the term "X" is normally used by . . ., items (both actual and hypothetical) are correctly classifiable as X's if and only if they have each of the properties $P_1, \ldots, P_n.$

Since most of the properties cited in a scientific dictionary for a term on list A will not be logically necessary, a linguistic description for such a term will not be, nor contain, a statement like D_1. How will it differ from D_1? In three respects: (1) A term "X" on list A would apply to a substance even if it lacked some of the semantically relevant properties of X cited in such a description. For the most part, properties that are semantically relevant for X are not logically necessary. (2) There might be circumstances in which the term "X" does not apply, or in which one would hesitate to apply it, to an item with many or even all of the properties cited in the description. (3) The description of a scientific use of a term on list A is much less definite than that suggested by D_1. Before saying how such a description might be formulated, these points need to be expanded. The first will occupy the present section, the others, sections 6 and 7.

For the sake of illustration, let X be copper and suppose that properties such as being reddish, having the melting point 1083°C., and having the atomic number 29 are taken to be semantically relevant. To be classifiable as copper, a substance need not possess all the properties semantically relevant for copper. Which ones and how many it must have will depend upon differences in *centrality* among single properties as well as among sets of properties. With respect to two properties that are semantically relevant for X, to claim that one is more central for X than the other is to claim that the possession (or lack) of the one by an actual or hypothetical item tends to count more in favor of (or against) classifying that item as an X than does the possession (or lack) of the second property by an item. As the term "copper" is used by many physicists, having the atomic number 29 is more central than having the melting point 1083°C. The fact that an actual or hypothetical substance has (or lacks) the atomic number 29 tends to be a stronger reason for classifying it as copper (or for refusing to do so) than the fact that it has (or lacks) the melting point 1083°C. To determine an order of centrality among semantically relevant properties, we may consider which ones scientists do, or would, appeal to as tending to settle the matter of classification, and which they do, or would, appeal to as tending to settle it more decisively. We might describe an item as having certain properties of copper $P_1, \ldots, P_i$. Then we ask whether the addition to this set of the property *melting point 1083°C.* or of the property *atomic number 29* would provide a stronger reason for classifying the item as copper. As we vary the $P_1, \ldots, P_i$, if scientists tend to consider atomic number 29 a stronger reason, this would suggest that atomic number is more central than melting point for copper. To see which properties scientists tend to treat as more decisive in settling disputes about classification, we would rely not only on such tests but also on what they do and say when classifying actual substances.

We can also distinguish positive from negative centrality. If the fact that an item has the melting point 1083°C. tends to count more in favor of the conclusion that it is copper than the fact that it has a different melting point tends to count against it, I shall say that melting at 1083°C. has greater positive than negative centrality for copper. We can also consider differences in centrality among properties that are non-semantically relevant for X and among those that are relevant but not clearly classifiable as semantically or as nonsemantically relevant.

Semantically relevant properties that are the most central for X need not be logically necessary or sufficient for X. Having the atomic number 29 may be the most central of the semantically relevant properties of copper for many physicists and chemists, although it might not be logically necessary or sufficient for them. However, if a property is treated as logically necessary for X, then it has at least a maximum amount of negative centrality; the fact that an item fails to possess that property settles the question of whether it is an X as conclusively as anything can. Positively speaking, however, it need not be among the most central properties.

There are also differences in centrality among *sets* of properties. This cannot in general be determined simply by considering differences among the individual ones. As the term "copper" is used by chemists, the fact that a substance has the melting point and color of copper might tend to count as a stronger reason for classifying it as copper than the fact that it has the melting point and the boiling point of copper, even though boiling point might be considered by chemists more central than color for copper. In this case one must consider the variety and independence of the properties cited.

I have spoken of properties solely as possessed or not possessed by items. However, when properties are capable of degrees, to determine whether an item is classifiable as an X we may also need to consider how closely its properties approximate those central for X (for example, how close is its boiling point, density, or color to that of copper). In short, classification of an item as an X can depend not only on whether it has properties that are sufficiently central for X but also on how similar certain properties it has are to ones typical of X.

6. UNKNOWN PROPERTIES

There is a second respect in which a description of a scientific use of a term on list A will differ from D_1. If all the properties in D_1 are possessed by an item, then the term in question is applicable to it. However, in the case of a term classifiable on list A, there might be circumstances in which most or even all of the semantically relevant (and central) properties that might be cited in a linguistic description are possessed by an item, but in which the term "X" would not be applicable, or in which there would be hesitation in applying it.

One sort of case involves very abnormal items. A substance manifests all or most of the semantically relevant properties of X cited in a linguistic description, but, say, disappears every five minutes, weaves magic spells, and metamorphoses, so that we might be unwilling or hesitant to classify it as an X. A more important type of case occurs where an item has all or most of the semantically relevant properties that might be cited in a description of use, but where the item and situation are not abnormal. Consider the following example suggested by Putnam.[7]

The term "multiple sclerosis" is used to refer to a disease in which various symptoms are displayed. Some think the disease is caused by a virus, although this has not been proven. Suppose in future years a certain virus V comes to be identified as the cause. It is then possible that although certain patients exhibited all the symptoms of multiple sclerosis these symptoms were not caused by this virus. According to Putnam, we would not say that because such patients exhibited all the ("paradigmatic") symptoms of multiple sclerosis they therefore had this disease. Rather we would say that despite the presence of all the symptoms they did not have it. And this, he claims, would not reflect a change in the use of the term "multiple sclerosis."

Putnam seems to suggest that this is the only way to describe such cases. But surely a number of possibilities are open to us. (1) We might deny that virus V is the only cause and say that there are (at least) two types of multiple sclerosis—that caused by virus V and that caused by some different agent(s), perhaps unknown. In fact, something like this has happened with epilepsy. In 25 per cent of the cases, causes are assigned (for example, brain injury, congenital defect, brain tumor). In 75 per cent of the cases, no cause is assigned, though the illness is still

[7] Hilary Putnam, "Dreaming and 'Depth Grammar,'" *Analytical Philosophy*, ed. R. J. Butler (Oxford, 1962), pp. 218ff.

called epilepsy. (The two types are distinguished as acquired epilepsy, where a cause is assigned, and as idiopathic epilepsy, where it is not.) (2) We might restrict the term "multiple sclerosis" to cases in which virus V is the cause and coin a new term for the others—that is, call these another disease. This would be likely if we noticed somewhat different symptoms in the two cases; if there were no differences between the symptoms we would be likely to do (1). In (2), if the choice of the term "multiple sclerosis" for one disease rather than the other was arbitrary, I should want to say that this term is now being used in a more restricted way, and hence that there has been a change in its use.[8] (3) If the symptoms in the virus V cases are at least somewhat different from those in the non-V cases, we might realize that the latter were instances of another previously recognized disease—for example, acute chorea. Here we would not be changing the use of the term "multiple sclerosis." We would simply be recognizing that we were (by our own previous standards) once mistaken in classifying the non-V cases as multiple sclerosis. (4) We might not know what to say. For example, the cases might be isolated ones, "freaks," where no others have been or will be recorded.

However, Putnam's example does suggest something important: some (perhaps most) terms that might be put on list A are such that, when attending to their scientific use, one must consider the question of unknown as well as known properties. Often we can indicate something about these unknown properties or at least about the general category in question—for example, etiology in the case of multiple sclerosis. We might say that as the term "multiple sclerosis" is now used, if the particular cause of the disease were known, it would be treated as semantically relevant. Or, we might say that, as the term "multiple sclerosis" is now used, *cause* is a semantically relevant category although the particular cause is unknown. This fact, expressed in either way, would need to be indicated in a full description of the current scientific use of the term. Moreover, if the particular cause came to be known and were treated (together with certain of the symptoms) as semantically relevant and quite central, this would obviously reflect some change in the use of the term.

Considerations of unknown properties in a given category apply to many of the terms on list A. For example, ancient Romans may have used the term "copper" (or their word *"aes cyprium"* or *"cuprum"*) to

[8] Cf. Chap. Three, sec. 6.

refer to a metallic substance reddish in color, malleable, and a good conductor of heat—where they treated such properties as semantically relevant for copper.[9] Yet, we may suppose, they also believed that the substance had a certain characteristic "inner structure" (for example, an atomic structure) which, if known, would serve as a basis (as a semantically relevant property) for classifying actual and hypothetical substances. If this were so, then a full description of their use of the term "copper" would indicate this fact; or at least it would indicate that "copper," as they use it, is a term for which the category of "inner structure" is semantically relevant, though the nature of this structure is unknown.

Some terms classifiable on list A are like "copper" in this respect; others are not. Some refer to items whose "inner structure" can vary within certain limits. The term "bronze" is used to refer to an alloy of copper, tin, and (sometimes) zinc and phosphorus, in varying proportions. Some terms refer to items classified almost entirely by reference to function, or to behavior, or to shape, size, and "outer structure." As scientists use the term "electroscope," considerations of function and "outer structure" would be semantically relevant, but "inner structure" (for example, molecular composition) would not. And there are terms for illnesses requiring a different analysis from that for multiple sclerosis, for example, terms for psychological disorders applied to persons exhibiting characteristic behavior. "Paranoia" refers to a disorder characterized by behavior involving systematic delusions. As psychologists use this term, the discovery of a variety of different causes for such behavior would not be likely to produce a change in its application.[10] And, of course, categories such as cause and inner structure can vary in degree of centrality from one type of item to another as well as from period to period in the history of science. Thus, in the case of chemical compounds (see section 2), inner structure was considered much more central after the eighteenth century than before.

7. *INDEFINITENESS IN LINGUISTIC DESCRIPTIONS*

The third respect in which a description of a scientific use of a term such as "copper" will differ from D_1 is that such a description

---

[9] See Crosland, *op. cit.,* p. 105.

[10] See Norman Cameron, "Paranoid Disorders," *An Outline of Abnormal Psychology,* ed. G. Murphy and A. J. Bachrach (New York, 1954), pp. 407–34.

would be much less definite. Suppose, as part of this description, we try to include information regarding differences in centrality. The question whether one property is more central than another for copper may have no ready answer. Sometimes centrality can be determined by considering how scientists tend to classify actual substances and what properties they appeal to as carrying the greatest weight in settling actual disputes about classification. In other cases centrality can be determined only by describing hypothetical substances having some of the properties of copper but not others, and then asking questions such as: Which of the two properties, P_1 or P_2, in addition to those already mentioned, would, if substances possessed them, count more in favor of a copper-classification? An appeal to the regularities involving a scientific use of the term "copper" may not settle this question. Although some comparisons may be possible, the regularities involving the use of "copper" do not allow such fine distinctions that, with respect to any two properties of copper, one can determine which is more central or whether they are equally central; the same is true for sets of properties.

Three respects in which a description of a scientific use of a term on list A will differ from D_1 have been recorded in this and the previous two sections. Recognizing these differences, how shall we formulate a description of the former sort? Suppose that as the term "X" is used by a speaker or group of speakers, $P_1, \ldots, P_n$ are properties semantically relevant (both positively and negatively) for X, though not logically necessary or sufficient; suppose also that they are among the most central ones for X. Then we might have:

D_2: As the term "X" is normally used by . . ., items (both actual and hypothetical) are correctly classifiable as X's if and only if they have most or at least many of the properties $P_1, \ldots, P_n$, among others.

This is one way of formulating a partial linguistic description for a term "X" on list A where the properties in question do not constitute a set in which each is logically necessary and whose conjunction is logically sufficient for X. Of course, some semantically relevant properties of X might also be logically necessary for X. If so, this could be indicated in the description. In any case, such a description is quite different from D_1, according to which a term "X" is used correctly to apply to an item if and only if the item possesses certain properties, each logically necessary for X, their conjunction being logically sufficient.

Formulation D_2 has the advantage of simplicity. The difficulty is in knowing how to apply descriptions of this form to determine whether, given this use, something is correctly classifiable as an X; this requires information of the sort noted earlier. We need at least some knowledge of what other properties (not stated) are semantically relevant; which properties are more central than others; which combinations of properties are more central; whether certain unknown properties in a given category (for example, causes or "inner structure") could affect classification once they are known; and what sorts of cases involving items with properties cited in D_2 but still not classifiable as X's to regard as isolated, abnormal cases (tinged with the miraculous).

We might try to include such information in the linguistic description itself, but only at the cost of generating a statement exceedingly involved. However it is formulated, we shall have to recognize its essential complexity, whether this appears in the description or in the considerations required for using this description for classifying items. Where a description provides a set of logically necessary and sufficient conditions (that is, D_1), then, once we know whether these conditions apply, such complexities do not arise.

Variations on each of D_1 and D_2 are possible, for example:

D_1': As the term "X" is normally used by . . ., items (both actual and hypothetical) are correctly classifiable as X's if and only if they have at least one of the properties P_1, . . ., P_n.

Others could specify various combinations of properties whose possession would allow the term "X" to be applied. They would stipulate a set of conditions each of which is (or various conjunctions of which are) logically sufficient for X, their alternation being logically necessary. Such descriptions are of the same type as D_1. In various forms, each supplies combinations of conditions logically necessary or sufficient for X.

Here is a variation on D_2:

D_2': As the term "X" is normally used, by . . ., items (both actual and hypothetical) are correctly classifiable as X's if and only if they have some conjunction of properties in the set P_1, . . ., P_n, some in the set Q_1, . . ., Q_m, and so forth.

Thus, in the case of "copper," one might consider various categories such as atomic properties, thermodynamic properties, color and texture, and so forth, where these would be semantically relevant for copper.

26

Other more complex variations of D_2 could be cited. What makes such descriptions similar is that they allow an item to be classified as an X that does not have all the properties in each combination cited, or perhaps no one in some combination cited; also, that those properties an item must have to be classified as an X will depend upon differences in centrality among individual properties and sets of properties.

My aim here has been to show what descriptions of use are appropriate for terms on list A and what considerations would be relevant in employing them in classification. Now we must ask whether these descriptions can be expressed in a manner that is both simpler and more precise, and what the relationship is between such a description for a term and the meaning or use of that term.

8. MODELS OF LINGUISTIC DESCRIPTIONS

Can descriptions of the use of terms on list A be characterized in a simpler and more precise way? I want to consider models of two sorts which attempt to do just this. The first will seek to characterize such descriptions in terms of logically necessary and sufficient conditions; the other will introduce numerical considerations. A study of these models should afford more insight into the concept of a linguistic description.

Model A. (*a*) For a term on list A there are minimal conjunctions of logically sufficient properties. A conjunction of properties is a minimal conjunction for X if it is logically sufficient for X and if the omission of any property from the conjunction prevents the resulting conjunction from being logically sufficient for X. (*b*) For a term on list A in general there will be more than one such minimal set; accordingly, we can speak of a disjunction of (possibly overlapping) sets, each disjunct being logically sufficient for X, the entire disjunction being logically necessary for X. (*c*) We shall say that any property in any such minimal set is semantically relevant for X. This accords with our earlier characterization of semantical relevance in the following way: if an item, actual or hypothetical, is known to have some of the properties in one of these sets, then the fact that it possesses another one in this set tends to count in and of itself, at least to some extent, in favor of classifying it as an X; and under a certain condition—namely, if all but one property in a minimal set are known to be possessed by an item—the possession of this property can justifiably be held to settle the question. Furthermore, individual properties in these minimal sets need not be logically necessary or logically sufficient for X. On this model, then, a linguistic description for a term "X" on list A would be as follows:

> As the term "X" is normally used by . . ., items (both actual and hypothetical) are correctly classifiable as X's if and only if they have at least one minimal conjunction in the disjunction "$P_1.P_2$ . . . or $Q_1.Q_2$ . . . or . . . or $Z_1.Z_2$ . . .."

This model characterizes semantical relevance as well as linguistic descriptions for terms on list A in a way that is obviously simpler and more precise than that given in the previous section. Yet it has several disadvantages. It fails to account for differences in centrality among single properties or among sets of properties and thus provides no way of deciding whether the possession of certain properties (or sets of them) counts more toward an X-classification than others. Also, the model is too rigid. For a term "X" on list A, it is unrealistic to suppose that there is a set of properties such that the addition of just one property will make the set logically sufficient for X, whereas its omission prevents the set from being logically sufficient. Indeed, as indicated in section 6, it is unrealistic to suppose that any set will be logically sufficient for X. The model is also too rigid in supposing that for every single property P we can decide, in a Yes-or-No manner, whether P is semantically relevant for X—that is, whether P is to be included in some such minimal set. Let us turn to a second model.

Model B_1. (*a*) For a term on list A there is a set of properties, each member of which is assigned a numerical weight. (*b*) There is a rule to the effect that to be classifiable as an X an item, actual or hypothetical, must have properties the sum of whose numerical weights is at least some specifiable number.

On this model, in general, the possession of no single property will be necessary or sufficient for an item to be an X. Moreover, under certain conditions (if an item is known to have certain properties), the fact that it possesses P may count in favor of an X-classification, insofar as the possession of P adds to the total points required for X; and under some conditions (if sufficiently many other properties with high numerical measures are possessed), the possession of P may give the item the number of points required to be classifiable as an X. This model, unlike model A, accounts for differences in centrality among properties, but it fails to do so for sets of properties. So we might construct the following variation.

Model B₂. (*a*) Properties are divided into general categories, each considered semantically relevant. For example, in the case of copper (and other metals) these might be atomic properties, thermodynamic properties, color and texture, and so forth. To each category a (possibly different) numerical weight is assigned. If an item is reported to have one (or a few) of the properties in a given category (but it is not yet reported whether it has others as well), assign a fairly large percentage of the weight of that category to this property (or subset of properties) so that the possession of other properties in this category will not increase the numerical weight very appreciably. However, assign percentages in such a way that differences in centrality among properties are recognized. (*b*) There is a rule that to be classifiable as an *X* an item must have properties the sum of whose numerical weights is at least *N*. This number will be such that an item may be required to have properties in more than one category (thus taking account of variety).

We need not list all the properties in any given category, but since we know that the numerical weight for each category is fixed, the discovery that an item possesses more and more properties in a certain category will not continue to increase the point count indefinitely. This model lacks some of the rigidity of model A. We need not suppose that for each *X* there is a class of properties such that adding just one property to this class will provide a score sufficient to make the term *"X"* applicable, whereas omitting it will provide a score insufficient for this purpose. We can, however, suppose that there exist sets of properties the possession of which provides a score sufficient to make the term *"X"* applicable, whereas the removal of a few properties no longer makes the score sufficient.

Another aspect of model A's rigidity, we recall, lies in supposing that one can always decide in a Yes-or-No manner whether a given property is semantically relevant for *X*. B₂ avoids this by making relevance a matter of degree. If the weight assigned to a property is sufficiently high, we might say that it is semantically relevant; and here we can countenance borderline cases. Still, B₂ might be criticized for requiring some precise minimal number of points for an item to be classifiable as an *X*. If so, we could liberalize it as follows.

Model B₃. This is like B₂, except that in place of (*b*) we substitute a rule that to be classifiable as an X an item (actual or hypothetical) must have properties the sum of whose numerical weights is *approximately* N (or $N \pm \epsilon$).

Although an improvement, even this model is too rigid. True, it does not require a Yes-or-No answer for each property with respect to the question of semantical relevance; but it does require definite numerical weights to be assignable to each property and to each set of properties, thus allowing precise comparisons to be made. If the model reflected scientific use of a term *"X"* on list A, then by careful attention to this use with respect to actual cases, and by careful preparation of questions about hypothetical cases (Would you still be willing to call it an X if it lacked P? How much less willing would you be to call it an X if it lacked P than if it lacked Q but still had the other properties of X?), we would be able to arrive at numerical measures for each property (and category). This is unrealistic. Even the most careful attention to actual use will not enable us to assign precise numerical values in the manner proposed by model B_3 (or B_1 and B_2). Even the most carefully formulated hypothetical cases may produce the response, "I don't know what to say in such a case" (see sections 3–4).

There are three other respects in which some or all of these models are idealized.

a) It may be unrealistic (in the case of B_1–B_3) to assign even an approximate number of points for something to be classifiable as an X. Scientific use of terms on list A may sanction only some vague requirement that an item have *many* or *most* of a certain group of properties. Accordingly, there would be a fairly large range of borderline cases if items were discovered or imagined that had many of these properties but also lacked quite a few.

b) All these models fail to account for the fact, noted in section 5, that the classification of an item as an X can depend not only on whether it has certain properties but also on how close some of its properties come to those typical of X (for example, how close its boiling point is to copper's).

c) When an item is classifiable as an X, certain assumptions noted in section 6, but not accounted for in any of these models, will need to be made. It will need to be assumed that the item (the sample) is in relevant respects normal (untouched by monstrosity and so forth). Otherwise even a maximum point total will not be sufficient for an X-classification. It may also need to be assumed that certain unknown properties of X will, when they become known, affect the classification of X's and that these properties are shared by X's. For example, in the case of certain *stuffs* (copper, acids, and so on) the category of "inner structure" may be considered semantically relevant.

We might try to construct a new model, taking into account all or some of these factors. However, I think that model building here reaches the point of diminishing returns. Whatever necessary-and-sufficient condition or numerical model we construct, the actual situation can be understood by considering both the model and the ways it is idealized. Any such model we are likely to devise will introduce more structure than actually exists or will omit something relevant, and then our job will be to point this out.

9. SEMANTICAL RELEVANCE, MEANING, AND USE

In section 7, I formulated the following type of linguistic description for terms on list A, where the properties cited are semantically relevant for X.

D_2: As the term "X" is normally used by . . ., items (both actual and hypothetical) are correctly classifiable as X's if and only if they have most or at least many of the properties P_1, . . ., P_n, among others.

We should now like to know whether semantically relevant properties of X are part of the (or a) meaning of "X." More precisely, when we cite properties semantically relevant for being an item denoted by "X" (in short, when we cite a description such as D_2), are we saying something about the meaning of the term "X"?

To begin with, for terms on list A, we do not normally ask, "What is the meaning of (the term) 'X'?" We do not ask, "What is the meaning of (the term) 'copper'?" Nor do we normally say that "copper" means a metal with such and such characteristics. The more natural question would be, "What is (an) X?" Furthermore, if someone does ask for the meaning of "copper," the most natural reply would not be " 'copper' means ———," but "copper is ———."

Paul Ziff distinguishes *having a meaning* from *having meaning* and, choosing as his example the word "tiger" (which I would place on list A), suggests that this does not have a meaning though it has meaning.[11]

---

[11] Paul Ziff, *Semantic Analysis* (Ithaca, N.Y., 1960), Chap. 5.

He explains this by saying that words which have a meaning have associated with them a set of conditions each of which is necessary and the conjunction of which is sufficient. The reason that the conditions associated with the term "tiger" (being a large, carnivorous, quadrupedal feline, tawny yellow in color with blackish transverse stripes and white belly) do not say what the word "tiger" means is because they are not necessary conditions.

It is doubtful that Ziff's proposal supplies a sufficient condition for speaking about the meaning of words or expressions. As I shall argue later, terms on list B are terms for which logically necessary and sufficient conditions can be given. Yet where "X" is a term on this list, one would normally not ask for the meaning of "X," but rather, "What is an X?" (What is a conservative system, a Bohr atom, a fermion?) What must be added to Ziff's requirement is that the necessary and sufficient conditions be given by *single words* or *short phrases* (that are in use). Short phrases (supplying necessary and sufficient conditions) can be given for terms like "bachelor" and "brother" but not for terms like "fermion" and "conservative system," though necessary and sufficient conditions can be given for the latter pair as well as for the former. Since the single word or short phrase requirement is relevant, the oddness associated with speaking of the meaning of a certain term may be a matter of degree, depending on the length of the necessary and sufficient condition definition.

From the fact that we do not normally ask for the meaning of a term like "tiger" or normally say, " 'tiger' means ———," it does not follow that we never speak this way. But when we do, there are special reasons for it. Ziff notes that a foreigner first learning English might ask, "What does 'tiger' mean?" because he doesn't know enough about English to ask the right question. Ziff also notes that one could answer, " 'Tiger' in English has the same meaning as ——— in your language." When we consider equivalent words from different languages we can speak of "having the same meaning as," or even of "the meaning" of the words, in raising questions such as "Is the meaning of the word 'tiger' in English the same as the meaning of the word ——— in your language?" Here we have something like the necessary and sufficient conditions required by Ziff: X is a tiger if and only if it is a ——— (or, something is, or would be, called a tiger in English if and only if it is, or would be, called a ——— in your language); furthermore, these "conditions" are given by single words or short phrases.

One might also ask for the meaning assigned to the term "tiger" by the lexicographer. This, however, seems to be a stretched use of the expression "the meaning." Although a lexicographer does many things in a dictionary, it is useful to refer to what he does in a shorthand way, by saying that he gives the meanings of words. For many words and entries this is true, for some it is not. The assumption that it is correct to speak about the meaning of terms on list A may also derive from a tendency to confuse what a person means when he uses these terms (which is perfectly legitimate) with the meaning of the term (which may not be). We might say that by "copper" the physicist means (to be referring to) a metal of a certain sort, not a policeman (another use of "copper"). But it does not follow that the meaning of "copper" is a metal of a certain sort.

Finally, there may be some tendency to speak of the meaning of terms on list A because, when certain changes occur with respect to these terms, we may speak of a change in their meanings. Suppose the word "tiger" is used in future years to mean any ferocious animal. Here we might say a change has occurred in the meaning of the word "tiger." This is because the word "tiger" now has a meaning, namely, ferocious animal. This would be a necessary and sufficient condition for being a tiger, and one given by a short expression. It does not follow that we can say what the meaning of the word "tiger" once was, although we can say that the word "tiger" once did not have this meaning. Or, suppose that in the future the words "lion" and "tiger" become interchanged so that whatever was once called a lion is now called a tiger and vice versa; and suppose there has been no change "in the world." We might say that the word "lion" now means tiger and "tiger" now means lion. But this is analogous to the case of translation from one language to another. In the new language the word "lion" has the same meaning as the word "tiger" did in the old language (and here we have something like necessary and sufficient conditions and ones given by single words or short expressions).

I began this section by asking: When we cite properties that are semantically relevant for being an item denoted by "*X*," are we indicating something about the meaning of the term "*X*"? Because the concept of *the* (or *a*) *meaning of a term* is not completely appropriate for terms on list A, except in special circumstances, I want to shift to the corresponding question about *use*. Doing so should not avoid the issue that needs to be discussed but perhaps put it in a more felicitous way.

33

Wittgenstein was the philosopher who first emphasized the importance of thinking about use.[12] And George Pitcher, offering an explanation and expansion of Wittgenstein's position, considers several different aspects of use in the case of terms.[13] There is the "grammatical" aspect. One who knows this can recognize and construct grammatically correct as well as grammatically deviant sentences or expressions containing the term. For example, in the sentence-schema "I saw a _____ tiger," one who knows the grammatical aspect of the use of "tiger" will know that the blank can be filled by "beautiful" or "fierce" but not by "beautifully" or "not" without grammatical oddity. There is also the "speech-act" aspect of use. Words and expressions are used to do, or in the course of doing, a multitude of things such as describe, report, explain, predict, question, request, demand, propose, express, and so forth. One who knows how to use a word will know how to perform, and recognize performances of, various speech-acts with the word. One who knows how to use the term "tiger" will be able to use, and recognize uses of, sentences like "A tiger will be present tonight" to report, predict, warn, promise, request, ask a question, and so forth.

Most important for present purposes is the "semantical" aspect of use. Knowing the use of, or how to use, the term "tiger" involves knowing more than how to recognize grammatically correct and deviant sentences with this word and what speech-acts can be performed using it. To put the matter simply, it involves knowing what a tiger is. But what information about X would be included in a description of the semantical aspect of the use of the term "X"? Suppose someone does not know how to distinguish tigers from other things or to describe or even recognize standard or paradigm cases of tigers. We might say that in an important respect he is unable to use the term "tiger." In general, in the case of a term "X" on list A we might say that one who knows the semantical aspect of the use of such a term knows how to (1) distinguish X's from other things and (2) recognize paradigm cases of X; and he will be able to do these things by observing X's (if such there be) in appropriate contexts, or at least from suitable descriptions of X's.[14] Moreover, he knows how to (3) apply the term "X" to ap-

[12] Ludwig Wittgenstein, *Philosophical Investigations* (New York, 1953).

[13] George Pitcher, *The Philosophy of Wittgenstein* (Englewood Cliffs, N.J., 1964), Chap. 10.

[14] Cf. Ziff, *op. cit.*

propriate items noted in (1) and (2).[15] These criteria are applicable as well to terms on list B. For example, one who knows the semantical aspect of the use of the term "diatomic molecule" knows how to distinguish such molecules from others and from items that are not molecules; he knows how to recognize standard cases; and he knows how to apply the term to appropriate items so distinguished and recognized. We can also extend this to quantities on list C (kinetic energy, velocity), provided that (2) is construed as meaning: recognize, in standard cases, when one is dealing with a given quantity Q. Of course, there may be differences in degree regarding the extent to which one knows how to do (1), (2), and (3), and hence differences in the extent to which one knows the semantical aspect of the use of a term.

I have mentioned several aspects of *use*. When we cite properties that are semantically relevant for being an item denoted by the term "X" are we indicating something about the use of "X"? Obviously we are. Citing properties semantically relevant for being an item denoted by "tiger" will provide at least some information about the types of sentences into which the term "tiger" can enter with and without grammatical oddity (the "grammatical" aspect). It will also provide at least some information about the sorts of speech-acts we might expect the term to be used to perform or in the course of performing (the "speech-act" aspect). On the other hand, these things are also true when non-semantically relevant properties are attributed to tigers. It is to the third aspect of use, the semantical one, that we must then turn.

Suppose you learn the semantically relevant properties of items denoted by the term "X." Then you will know those properties a possession of which by actual and hypothetical substances in and of itself tends to count in favor of classifying them as ones to which the term "X" is applicable. If you know this, you know how to do three things mentioned above in connection with the semantical aspect of use. You know how to distinguish X's from other things: simply determine that the semantically relevant properties are not present in other things. You know how to recognize paradigm cases of X: simply determine whether the object in question (one produced or described) has the semantically relevant properties of X. You also know how to apply the term "X" to

---

[15] This condition is obviously needed, since one unfamiliar with English might know how to distinguish tigers from non-tigers and recognize paradigm cases, but still not know the use of the word "tiger."

the appropriate items, since you know what properties are semantically relevant for being an item denoted by the term "X." And you know how to do these things even though you don't know any or very many properties of X that are not semantically relevant. For example, you can distinguish tigers from other items, recognize paradigm cases, and apply the term correctly without knowing that tigers are native to most of Asia, that they kill 32,000 head of cattle annually in India, and so on (properties that are presumably nonsemantically relevant for tigers). Furthermore, if you do not know which properties of X are semantically relevant —that is, those which in and of themselves tend to count in favor of classifying items as X's and may, under certain conditions, settle this question—then you will not know very much, if anything, about how to distinguish X's from non-X's. You will not know what it is about X's that would normally be appealed to as most clearly and decisively distinguishing them from any other things. Nor will you be able to go very far toward recognizing paradigm cases of X, since you won't know in virtue of what they are paradigm cases. *A fortiori,* you won't know how to apply the term "X" to appropriate items. So if you know only non-semantically relevant properties of X, then, unless a knowledge of these will indirectly provide information about the semantically relevant ones, you won't know how to do (1), (2), and (3) very well, if at all. Equally important, if you know what properties are semantically relevant for X, then (even though you don't know those that are not semantically relevant) you will know how to do (1), (2), and (3) for hypothetical as well as actual cases. This, as previously emphasized, is part of knowing how to use a term. To know how to use the term "tiger" (in the semantical sense I want to recognize) is to know how to identify tigers in pictures and stories as well as in zoos and jungles. To acquire this sort of knowledge means acquiring knowledge of semantically relevant properties of tigers.

10. LINGUISTIC DESCRIPTIONS AND USE

Knowing a linguistic description of the sort D_2 for a term "X" involves knowing that as the term "X" is used, properties such as $P_1, \ldots, P_n$ are semantically relevant for X. One with such knowledge need not be able to verbalize it, but he must be able to use his knowledge of what properties are semantically relevant in classifying items as X's. Suppose someone lacks such knowledge. How shall such a person be described? Several different situations might be considered.

1) Suppose a speaker of English knows none or very few of the semantically relevant properties of tigers. For example, he knows only that they are animals, but does not know (or believe) that they are four-legged, striped, of such and such size, and so forth. (He might of course know the properties of tigers and simply not know that creatures with such properties are called tigers in English; but this is not the case I want.) If he does not know these things he does not know how to recognize tigers; he does not know how to distinguish them from lions or even from baboons.

Can we say that he doesn't know what tigers are? Not necessarily, for the question "What are X's?" is often answerable simply by providing some quite general category in which to place X, for example, a metal, a gas, something investigated by the scientist, or (in the present case) an animal. Accordingly, if the person does not know any or very many of the semantically relevant properties of tigers, then (even if he can provide some answer to the question "What are tigers?") a better way to describe him is to say that he knows very little about tigers.

Does he know the meaning of the term "tiger"? As previously noted, "tiger" is not the sort of term to which we would normally attribute a meaning. But suppose the question arises whether "tiger" in English has the same meaning as the term T in some different language. This question, we recall, might very well be asked. And suppose the person is told that T in this other language refers to an animal having such and such properties. Then, if he does not know the semantically relevant properties of tigers (if he does not know a D_2 for "tiger"), we could say that he does not know whether "tiger" in English has the same meaning as T in the other language. This is one way we can tie knowledge of descriptions such as D_2 to knowledge of meanings.

Can we also say that the speaker does not know how to use the term "tiger"? Since the concept of use is so broad, perhaps the answer is not a clear Yes or No. For example, he knows how to use the term in the sense that he can use it in sentences in English that are grammatical (and many of which are true), and he can correct others that are not grammatical. He also knows, in a general way, what sorts of speech-acts the term can be used to perform or in the course of performing. Furthermore, he can give an answer to the question "To what is the term 'tiger' in English normally used to refer?" He may say, "A certain sort of animal," but he does not know what sort of animal. So although he knows how to distinguish tigers from things that are not animals, he does not know how to distinguish them from other animals or recognize paradigm cases. He knows something, though very little, about the semantical aspect of the use of the term.

In sum, one who knows few of the properties that would be cited in a linguistic description of the sort D_2 for "tiger" cannot *without qualification and explanation* be said to be ignorant of a standard use of the term "tiger." In some respects he is ignorant of this use, in others, not.

2) Suppose someone in appropriate conditions for observation is confronted with a rabbit but calls it a typical tiger. And suppose he does not have knowledge of strange happenings and means to be using the term in a standard sense. I think we should say here that he is *misusing* the term "tiger." In such a case we would suppose he thinks that tigers are creatures with rabbit properties—that is, that properties $P_1, \ldots, P_n$, among others, are those which are semantically relevant for tigers. If so, we would inform or remind him that as the terms "tiger" and "rabbit" are used, these properties are semantically relevant for rabbits, not tigers. That is, we would appeal to D_2, or something like it, for the terms in question.

3) Suppose someone confronted with a jaguar calls it a typical tiger (jaguars being similar to tigers in certain respects); and suppose he means to be using the term in a standard sense. Here we might imagine two cases. (*a*) When afterward he is confronted with a tiger and shown the differences, he recognizes his mistake. (*b*) When afterward he is confronted with a tiger and shown the differences, he does not recognize his mistake but continues to call both of them typical tigers (though he would not call rabbits or baboons tigers). In the latter case, I would say that he is misusing the term "tiger"; in the former, that he is simply mistakenly identifying something as a tiger.

4) Suppose that someone confronted with actual tigers correctly identifies them as such and is able to distinguish them from other animals. Yet he believes they can fly, although they do so only when people are not watching. Is his use of the term "tiger" different from the standard one? We must ask how this belief affects his classification of hypothetical as well as actual tigers.

a) Suppose he would refuse to classify as tigers hypothetical beasts imagined to be in every possible respect like what he calls tigers except that they are nonflying; or suppose he would consider the fact that they do not fly a strong reason—though perhaps not a conclusive one—against a tiger-classification. For this person the capability of flying is semantically central, and possibly logically necessary, for tigers. Accordingly, his use of the term differs somewhat from ours, though this difference would be difficult to detect if we considered only actual cases. The difference would be reflected in somewhat different linguistic descriptions we could give for our respective uses of the term "tiger."

b) Suppose, on the other hand, his belief that tigers fly is such that he would have no hesitation in classifying hypothetical nonflying beasts as tigers—that is, the fact that they cannot fly would be considered by him as no reason against classifying them as tigers. For this person the capability of flying is a nonsemantically relevant property of tigers. His use of the term does not differ from ours, though he has certain beliefs about tigers that we do not share.

I have noted four cases in which someone might not know semantically relevant properties of X. Others could be described, but these should be sufficient to show that questions concerning the relationships between semantically relevant properties of X and the use of the term "X" are complex ones. Even if someone is ignorant of many or most of these properties, it may be misleading to accuse him of being ignorant of the use of the term "X," for he may know certain important aspects of its use. We can accuse him of ignorance of, or at least of not knowing very much about, the *semantical aspect* of the use of the term. And, I believe, this is something we cannot say about someone ignorant only of many of the nonsemantically relevant properties, or of the relevant properties not happily classified as semantically or as nonsemantically relevant. A knowledge of a linguistic description D_2 for a term on list A is, therefore, a knowledge of one important aspect of use in a way that a knowledge of only relevant properties that are not semantically relevant is not.

11. ANALYTICITY

If P is logically necessary for X, then sentences of the form "X's are P" ("Vixens are female") would normally be used to express statements philosophers call *analytic*. If P is not logically necessary for X, then sentences of the form "X's are P" ("Copper is mined in Michigan") would be taken by most philosophers to express synthetic (and empirical) statements. Can sentences attributing semantically relevant (though not logically necessary) properties of X to X ever be used to express statements that could be construed as analytic in any reasonable sense? The term "analytic" has been used by philosophers in several ways. Of these, I want to suggest the following (which includes the sense in which if P is logically necessary for X, then "X's are P" is analytic). A person might be construed as making an analytic statement using a given sentence if he is making a statement that he would defend, and that it would be proper for him to defend, solely by appeal to the use of certain terms in that sentence; more particularly, by appeal to the semantical aspect of use, for example, by appeal to linguistic descriptions of types D_1 or D_2.

Analytic

Consider the sentence "Vixens are female." Someone could use this to make a statement that he would defend, and that it would be proper for him to defend, simply by pointing out that as the term "vixen" is normally used, items, both actual and hypothetical, are correctly classifiable as vixens only if they are female. Such a defense would appeal to a linguistic description of type D_1.

Now consider the sentence "Copper is a reddish metallic substance, of atomic number 29, which is a good conductor, and which melts at 1083°C." This sentence *might* be used by someone to make a statement that he would defend, and properly so, solely by pointing out that, as the term "copper" is normally used by scientists, items, actual and hypothetical, are correctly classifiable as copper if and only if they have many or most of a certain set of properties among which these are semantically relevant and quite central. Similarly, consider the sentence "Copper is the element of atomic number 29" (where having the atomic number 29 is treated as semantically relevant but not logically necessary for copper). This might be used to express a statement that would be defended, and properly so, solely by pointing out that, as the term "copper" is normally used by scientists, items, both actual and hypothetical, are correctly classifiable as copper if and only if they have many or most of a certain set of properties among which atomic number 29 is semantically very central. In short, such sentences, which attribute semantically relevant properties of X to X, could be construed as expressing analytic statements if they are construed as expressing statements appropriately defended solely by appeal to linguistic descriptions of the sort D_2. On the other hand, sentences which attribute nonsemantically relevant properties of X to X could not be used to express statements defensible in this manner. It is not true that, as the term "copper" is normally used in science, actual as well as hypothetical items are correctly classifiable as copper if and only if they have many or most of a certain set of properties among which being mined in Michigan is semantically central.

Statements attributing to X a semantically relevant (though not logically necessary) property of X are different in two important respects from those (such as "vixens are female") which philosophers have traditionally called analytic. First, a traditional analytic statement would be construed as one defensible solely by appeal to linguistic descriptions of the form D_1 rather than D_2; it would be construed as one ascribing a logically necessary property to X. Second, a statement expressed by a sentence of the form "X's are P_1, . . ., P_n" (or "X's are P"), if defensible by appeal to D_1, means or implies that all X's are P_1, . . ., P_n (or P); whereas a statement expressed by a sentence of this form, if defensible by appeal to D_2, means or implies something weaker—namely, that, other things being equal (characteristically, normally), X's will be P_1, . . ., P_n (or P). Whether or not such statements are called analytic, the important point is that statements of both sorts are alike in the following respect: they can both be defended solely by appeal to (the semantical aspect of) the use of constituent terms.

Now it is possible for a *sentence* of the form "X's are P" ("Copper is the element of atomic number 29"), where P is semantically relevant for X, to be used to express two different *statements*. One is a statement defensible solely by appeal to the use of the terms in the sentence. Another is a statement defensible not solely in this manner but by appeal to experiment and observation or to theories and principles confirmable by experiment and observation. For example, the sentence "Copper is the element of atomic number 29" might be used to express a statement that would be defended, and properly so, by appeal to a D_2 for "copper." However, it might also be used to express a different statement defensible by appeal to experiment and observation and to theories supported by these. When so construed, the question of the truth of the statement can be raised in the following way: does that substance which is metallic, reddish in color, a good conductor, and so on (that is, which has the other properties typical of copper) also have

41

the atomic number 29? *This* question is decidable by empirical means and is the one envisaged when sentences of the above sort are said to express empirically verifiable statements.

But, it might be objected, how is it possible for the sentence "Copper is the element of atomic number 29" to be used to express an analytic statement at one time and an empirical one at another, unless the term "copper" has a different definition on each occasion? Suppose I say, "Copper is the element of atomic number 29," and defend this empirically; but suppose when asked for the definition of "copper" I say, "the element of atomic number 29 which has such and such other properties." Then, it would seem, I cannot give an empirical defense of my statement that copper is the element of atomic number 29, because this, by my own admission, is part of the definition of the term "copper."

To raise this objection is to ignore the fact that in offering an empirical defense of the statement that copper is the element of atomic number 29 I am adopting the following procedure. I am temporarily "withdrawing" this property from those semantically relevant for copper, and I am appealing to the fact that the element with such and such other properties (perhaps central enough to make it classifiable as copper) can be shown, by empirical means, to have the atomic number 29. I temporarily ignore one central aspect of its definition and concentrate on the others.

It is not my claim that sentences of the form "X's are P_1, . . ., P_n (or P)," where these properties are semantically relevant for X, are *for the most part* actually used to make statements meant to be defended solely by appeal to normal or standard use of the term "X." I think this happens sometimes in science, especially when the scientist is coining a new term or when he first introduces into his writings a term already in use. In his *Treatise on Electricity and Magnetism,* James Clerk Maxwell begins his section entitled "The Electric Field" with the following sentence: "The Electric Field is the portion of space in the neighborhood of electrified bodies, considered with reference to electric phenomena." I would here take Maxwell to be making a statement that he would defend, and properly so, by saying that as the term "electric field" is used in physics, items, actual and hypothetical, which are the portions of space in the neighborhood of electrified bodies, and so forth, are correctly classifiable as electric fields. In short, I would be taking him to be making an analytic statement.

Sometimes a sentence can be construed as expressing two statements at once. An introductory chemistry text contains the following sentence about germanium which appears under the heading "Properties and Uses": "Germanium is a hard, brittle, grayish white metal which is resistant to tarnish. . . ." [16] This might be construed as making two statements: an empirical one that would be defended by showing that there are substances with this conglomeration of properties, or by showing that items classified as germanium by physicists and chemists actually have these properties; and a nonempirical one, that would be defended solely by pointing out that substances, actual and hypothetical, with these properties are correctly classifiable as germanium—that is, that this is a standard scientific use of the term.

On the basis of my characterization of analyticity there will be many statements not happily classifiable as analytic or as nonanalytic. For a statement to be clearly classifiable one way or the other, two conditions must be satisfied. The person who makes it must intend that it be defended in a certain way, and it must actually be defensible in that way. So, two things may prevent a definite classification. The author of the statement may not make it clear (or be clear himself) how he intends it to be defended; or the sentence involved may attribute to X a property that is not clearly classifiable as semantically or as non-semantically relevant. If so, then even if its author intends that it be defended in the manner of an analytic statement, it is not clearly classifiable as analytic—that is, it is not clearly classifiable as a statement that can legitimately be defended solely by appeal to the use of the terms involved.

No philosopher has so sharply criticized the concept of analyticity as Quine.[17] His attack focuses on several attempts to define this concept that are somewhat different from the one I have been suggesting. One problem he finds is that the definitions he criticizes fail to indicate empirical tests for analyticity. The definition I have urged appeals to the concept of semantical relevance. The question of the application of this concept on the basis of what a speaker does in actual situations of classification as well as what he would say about hypothetical ones was

[16] H. H. Sisler, C. A. Vander Werf, and A. W. Davidson, *General Chemistry* (New York, 1949).

[17] *From a Logical Point of View,* Chap. 2. See also "Carnap and Logical Truth," *The Philosophy of Rudolf Carnap,* ed. P. A. Schilpp (LaSalle, Illinois, 1963), pp. 385–406.

discussed in sections 2–4 and so will not be pursued here. I do, however, want to comment on some other points Quine raises that are relevant to the present discussion.

Those who invoke the concept of analyticity usually think of analytic statements as expressing truth by linguistic convention, a notion of which Quine is critical. With respect to a system of statements, he argues, there are two types of conventions. One involves "a mere selection, from a preëxisting body of truths, of certain ones for use as a basis from which to derive others, initially known or unknown." [18] This Quine calls *discursive postulation.* It occurs, for example, when the geometer selects certain truths as axioms. But it is not *truth* by convention. The other type of convention, *legislative postulation,* does "hint" of truth by convention, since by convention certain sentences (not preëxisting truths) are instituted as truths. Thus, Quine says, the scientist may introduce a new term "for a certain substance or force" by an act of legislative postulation.[19] The reason this only *hints* at truth by convention is because conventionality lies only in the immediate act of postulation and does not linger after the sentence becomes part of our "fabric of sentences." When other facts are learned about the substance or force, the original postulation is treated on a par with these as something revisable in the light of further evidence. Accordingly, given our fabric of sentences, the division of these into analytic and synthetic (true or not true by convention) has been assigned no clear meaning.

Suppose a scientist engages in an act of legislative postulation and says that by "curium" he shall mean the element of atomic number 96. When he adopts this postulate, the scientist can claim that the statement that curium is the element of atomic number 96 is true because that is the way he proposes to use the term "curium." Once he has so postulated and the statement becomes part of his scientific corpus, he can no longer defend it by saying that he so decides to use the term "curium" this way (he has already been through that). Nor can he defend it by saying that he once so decided (after all, he could have changed his mind in the interim). Moreover, if it is true that curium is the element of atomic number 96, then the scientist cannot change the truth of that statement by convention. From these facts, it seems, Quine concludes that once the scientist has so postulated, then, with respect

[18] "Carnap and Logical Truth," p. 394.
[19] *Ibid.,* p. 405.

to *truth,* the statement becomes like any other in his corpus, revisable only in the light of further experience.

But there is an alternative. The scientist can defend the statement that curium is the element of atomic number 96 not only on the ground that once upon a time he decided to use the term "curium" this way, but on the ground that this is the way he continues and intends to continue to use the term. (This, of course, does not presuppose some sort of continuous act of postulation.) If with respect to the question "Why is it true that curium is the element of atomic number 96?" Quine accepts the answer "It is true only because I have now decided to use the term 'curium' in this way," he should also be willing to accept the answer "It is true only because I once decided to use the term in this way and continue to use the term this way." Of course, in the latter case truth is not *created* (solely) by convention; but, one might say, it is *sustained* (solely) by convention. The mere fact that a statement is already accepted as true does not prevent its being *defended* by appeal solely to normal use of its terms. (I have preferred to speak of linguistic *use* rather than *convention* and to say that analytic statements are those which would be properly defended solely by appeal to the semantical aspect of normal use.)

With reference to Quine's claim that a sentence whose truth is once created by convention may be subjected to the tribunal of sense experience, I have two comments. (1) One must distinguish sentence from statement, recognizing that a given sentence can be used to express two different statements: one, defensible solely by appeal to normal use of the words in it; another, by appeal to experiment and observation. (2) The fact that any sentence may be revised in the light of experience does not suffice to blur the distinction between analytic and nonanalytic, for two different types of revision are possible. There is revision where the terms involved retain their meanings and the statement expressed is simply *refuted* by experience or shown to be implausible. There is revision where experience suggests the need for changes in definition, for new or modified rules governing the terms involved. (For example, experience may present new and odd borderline cases; it may uncover new areas where broader or narrower concepts are needed.) In the latter case, the sentence may formerly have been used to express an analytic statement, while now it is used to express a synthetic (and possibly false) one. Accordingly, the mere fact that a statement is defended solely by appeal to the semantical aspect of normal use does not prevent that use itself from being defended, or changes in that use from being defended, at least in part, by reference to certain facts of experience. The important claim of those defending the concept of analyticity is that, given the normal use, one can distinguish statements defensible solely by appeal to this use from others not so defensible.

12. CONCLUSIONS ON LIST A

This chapter began by asking: What is the relationship, or what are the various relationships, between the properties of X cited in a definition and the term "X" defined? With respect to terms on list A, my answer has been that properties cited will not be logically sufficient for X, nor, for the most part, logically necessary, though they will be relevant. In composing a definition for a term on list A, a lexicographer will consider properties that are semantically relevant for X and will make rough distinctions among these as to centrality. He will also consider sets of semantically relevant properties that are more central than others (and thus will often cite varied and relatively independent properties). Limitations of space may necessitate choosing a small set of properties that has maximum centrality where each member has considerable centrality. Longer dictionary entries may include properties that are less central and ones that are relevant but not semantically relevant.

This is not to say that shorter dictionaries will include only the most central properties and longer ones less central ones. Here one must consider as well the type of dictionary and the level of sophistication of the intended readers. If an understanding of the most central properties of X requires considerable sophistication, the dictionary may cite a number of facts that are not the most central for X. Moreover, even the shortest dictionary entry of the most sophisticated sort may include information that is not semantically relevant for X although quite useful for the scientist (for example, the fact that the chemical symbol for copper is Cu). My only claim is that appeal to semantical relevance and centrality is important in deciding what to include in a definition for a term on list A and how to understand the nature of definitions that are proposed.

46

CHAPTER TWO

DEFINITIONS, II

At the beginning of the previous chapter three lists of terms in science were presented. Attention has so far been focused on the first. In the present chapter I turn to the others and consider whether and how the semantical categories already introduced are applicable.

1. LIST B

On list **B** we have terms such as "conservative system," "rigid body," and "Bohr atom." They are defined by citing conditions to be satisfied if they are to apply in a given case. For such terms a dictionary entry will include a condition that is both logically necessary and logically sufficient; or, in some cases, a set of conditions each of which is logically necessary and the conjunction of which is logically sufficient. For example, "conservative system (of particles)" is defined as a system in which the work required to move particles from one position to another depends only on the positions of the particles and not on the paths chosen; "rigid body," as a body in which the distance between any two points remains constant; "Bohr atom," as one satisfying the postulates of the Bohr theory; and so forth. In each case the condition is logically necessary in the sense that if an item, actual or hypothetical, fails to satisfy it, the term cannot be applied, no matter what other conditions are satisfied. A set of conditions is logically sufficient in the sense that if an item, actual or hypothetical, satisfies them, then, no matter what others it satisfies, the term in question applies to it. Terms on list B, then, are used in accordance with linguistic descriptions of type D_1 (Chapter One, section 5).

Such a term is considered defined even though in the definiens a term of the definiendum reappears. For example, "diatomic molecule" is defined as a *molecule* consisting of two atoms. The point of the definition is to state what conditions a molecule must satisfy to be diatomic, not the conditions something must satisfy to be a molecule (a term I would place on list A). Notice, then, that although a definition for a term on list B may include a condition that is logically necessary and sufficient, the latter may contain terms for which there are no such conditions.

For some terms on list B dictionaries may cite an alternative condition which is both logically necessary and sufficient. For example, besides the type of definition of a conservative system listed above, the *International Dictionary of Physics and Electronics* gives: "system of particles in which the forces acting on any particle of the system are forces which can be derived from a potential energy function." This can be shown to be mathematically equivalent to the first condition cited, once the notion of potential energy is defined. But not all conditions given are mathematically, or otherwise logically, equivalent. One standard definition of "reversible process" is this: a process is reversible with respect to a system and its surroundings if and only if the system and the surroundings can be completely restored to their respective initial states by reversing the direction of the process. However, in accordance with the second law of thermodynamics, a process is reversible if and only if there is no entropy increase during the process. (This is not entailed by the first definition.) Where the conditions are not logically equivalent, one but not both could be treated as logically necessary and sufficient.

2. *RELEVANCE*

The concept of relevance for terms on this list can be introduced as follows. To say that a condition C is relevant for X is to say that if an item is known to satisfy certain other conditions, then the fact that it satisfies C normally will count, to some extent, in favor of concluding that it is an X; and in certain cases this fact may justifiably be taken to settle the question. Semantical and nonsemantical relevance could be introduced, as in Chapter One, section 3, by reference to vast majority and partial subsets. However, for present purposes the following will suffice. If the satisfaction of a condition C by actual and hypothetical items in and of itself would tend to count, at least to some extent, in favor of classifying them as X's, then C is (positively) semantically relevant for X. If the satisfaction of C in and of itself would tend to count to no extent in favor of such classifications, then C is (positively) nonsemantically relevant, provided that it is positively relevant.

We can also speak of differences in centrality. For terms on list B, if only one condition is cited as the definition, and it is both logically necessary and sufficient for X, obviously the question of differences in centrality does not arise. Nor will it arise (except in one case to be noted), even where several logically independent conditions are given each of which is logically necessary and the conjunction of which is logically sufficient. If each condition is logically necessary but not logically sufficient for X, then each has as much *negative* centrality as any other. The fact that a given item fails to satisfy such a condition settles whether it is an X just as conclusively as its failure to satisfy any of the other conditions. Can some of the logically necessary conditions have more *positive* centrality than others? No condition is such that the satisfaction of it in and of itself counts more than the satisfaction of any other condition toward an item's being classifiable as an X. However, one condition may be more central than another in the sense that the satisfaction of the former makes it more likely that the remaining conditions are satisfied than does the satisfaction of the latter. This would be to say that the former is nonsemantically more central than the latter. In short, where each of the logically independent conditions is logically necessary for X and the conjunction is logically sufficient, some conditions may be nonsemantically, but not semantically, more central than others.

The concept of relevance is important for terms on list B because dictionary entries for these may provide information in addition to logically necessary and sufficient conditions. Properties may be cited that are relevant though not logically necessary or sufficient for being a Carnot cycle (for example, possessing maximum efficiency, something provable by reference to the second law of thermodynamics). There may be information not about individual X's but about the concept X, for example, about its history or its role in a theory. An entry for the term "Carnot cycle" might indicate that the French engineer and army officer Sadi Carnot introduced the concept of this cycle early in the nineteenth century; it might also indicate something about how this concept is employed in thermodynamics. Such information could be taken to provide relevant conditions for a Carnot cycle.

3. LIST A VS. LIST B

The important difference between lists A and B is this. A definition for a term on list B will include a property logically necessary and sufficient for X; or else a set of properties each logically necessary, their conjunction logically sufficient. For terms on list A, on the other hand, no property that is both logically necessary and sufficient will be cited; nor will any set of logically necessary and sufficient properties. Indeed, no single property cited may be logically necessary for X, although some will be semantically relevant and quite central.

There will be terms on or near the borderline between lists A and B, for example, "ion." Is being a charged atom a logically necessary and sufficient condition for being an ion, or is information regarding the production of ions semantically relevant for being an ion though not for being charged? (Is a proton an ion? A negatively ionized hydrogen atom is a proton.) Moreover, with respect to terms on list A, as well as on list B, there will be differences in the degree to which dictionary entries resemble definitions of the logically necessary and sufficient condition type. One standard definition of "electroscope" is an instrument for detecting very small charges of electricity. This comes closer to providing a logically necessary and sufficient condition than does a corresponding standard definition for "copper." (What prevents this definition of "electroscope" from being logically necessary and sufficient is the question of the physical construction of the instrument, which may be semantically relevant to some extent.) How close a term comes to having a definition of the logically necessary and sufficient condition type is reflected in how close its linguistic description comes to D_1 or to D_2 (Chapter One, sections 5, 7).

Finally, there are bound to be some differences among individual scientists. Some physicists may use the term "copper" in such a way that having the atomic number 29 is logically necessary and sufficient for copper (where other properties cited in a dictionary are nonsemantically relevant, or semantically relevant insofar as they are semantically relevant for having the atomic number 29). For them the term "copper" would be placed on list B.

4. CHANGES IN DEFINITION

Changes may occur that will make a term once classified on list A now classifiable on list B. Or a term may be treated in some contexts like a term on list A and in others like a term on list B.

Included under the entry for "acid" in *Webster's New International Dictionary* we find: "any one of a class of substances which typically are soluble in water, sour in taste, and redden vegetable blues, as litmus." Reference might also have been made to corrosive properties of acids and to the fact that they neutralize bases and react with active metals to give, as one product, free hydrogen. None of these properties is treated as logically necessary for being an acid, although at least some are semantically relevant. This reflects the manner in which the term is frequently used and suffices to place it clearly on list A.

However, in 1923 J. N. Brønsted proposed that "acid" be defined as any substance that can donate a proton to any other substance (and "base" as any substance that can receive a proton from any other substance). Brønsted's definition is meant to provide a condition that is logically necessary and sufficient. There is no temptation by those employing the definition to withhold the term "acid" from anything satisfying the definition, even though it lacks properties noted in *Webster's,* or to call something an acid which fails to satisfy it, even though it possesses properties in *Webster's.* In this case items not previously classified as acids now would be (for example, positive ions).

Is there here a change in the use of the term "acid," especially in the semantical aspect of use? In part, the answer depends upon whether, as the term was once used, and still is by many, having a common "inner structure" (though unknown) would have been considered semantically relevant for being an acid, how central it would have been considered, and whether the degree of centrality has changed.[1]

Hilary Putnam, who notes this case, answers that the assumption of a common "inner structure" was always very central, and thinks indeed that properties such as being soluble in water, sour in taste, and

[1] See Chap. One, sec. 6.

turning blue litmus red were treated by eighteenth century chemists as *"crude* ways of detecting a 'natural kind' of chemical." [2] If so, such properties would not be very central at all and indeed would have been considered nonsemantically relevant. In his view we could not say there has been a change in the use of "acid." The term was always used to designate substances assumed to have a common inner structure responsible for properties such as solubility, sour taste, and so forth.

A common inner structure was probably semantically relevant for eighteenth century chemists, though it might not have been as central as Putnam suggests. But more important, it was probably not semantically relevant, or if so, not very central, for chemists prior to the seventeenth and eighteenth centuries, who based classification of chemical compounds mainly on properties such as color, taste, consistency, and preparation, rather than on composition.[3] Accordingly, such a use of the term "acid" does differ from the Brønsted use. Even if the assumption of a common "inner structure" was always semantically relevant, when the actual nature of that structure was discovered and treated as semantically relevant and quite central, the use changed in the sense of being made more specific.

Since the Brønsted definition stipulates a condition logically necessary and sufficient for being an acid, for those using the term in accordance with this definition, "acid" would have to be placed on list B, not list A. (Because the term was not originally employed in this way, and is still employed by many in the original way, I have placed it on list A.) For those who use Brønsted's definition, properties such as sour taste and ability to turn blue litmus red could now be treated as relevant for being an acid if the presence of such properties would constitute some reason for assuming the satisfaction of the condition deemed logically necessary and sufficient.

Some philosophers, such as Carnap, have emphasized that what motivates changes in definition of this sort is the desire to eliminate borderline cases which can give rise to differences in classification among scientists.[4] Perhaps this is one factor. However, notice that although a definition of the necessary and sufficient condition type tends to reduce

---

[2] Hilary Putnam, "Dreaming and 'Depth. Grammar,'" *Analytical Philosophy,* ed. R. J. Butler (Oxford, 1962), p. 221.

[3] See Chap. One, sec. 2.

[4] Rudolf Carnap, *Logical Foundations of Probability,* 2nd ed. (Chicago, 1962), Chap. 1.

the number of borderline cases in one respect (we are no longer faced with the problem of how to classify an item having some but not all properties of X), it by no means eliminates them. We can stipulate that being domiciled in a state is a logically necessary and sufficient condition for being a *resident* of that state, but, unless we further stipulate what is to count as *being domiciled,* borderline cases are possible.

Moreover, contrary to what Carnap suggests, when scientists appropriate a term from everyday speech and redefine it, they may not be citing properties that are logically necessary and sufficient for X. Consider the term "fish," an example invoked by Carnap himself. As used by the ordinary person, it designates any animal living in water only. As used by the zoologist, it designates "any of numerous completely aquatic, water-breathing craniate vertebrates having the limbs (when present) developed as fins, and in the more typical forms an elongated and somewhat fusiform body commonly covered with scales or plates and ending in a broad vertical caudal fin" (*Webster's*). Although the latter definition introduces technical terms and more characteristics, and narrows the range of the former, it by no means provides a set of logically necessary and sufficient conditions. Note qualifying terms like "in the more typical forms" and "commonly."

When definitions of the logically necessary and sufficient condition type are proposed for terms on list A—terms that are already in use—the following is frequently involved. Before such conditions are stipulated a certain property of X's is discovered, for example, that acids donate protons, that metals can replace the hydrogen of an acid, that copper is a collection of atoms with 29 electrons, that a gas is "a state of matter in which the molecules are practically unrestricted by cohesive forces" (*Handbook of Chemistry and Physics,* 36th ed.). Such claims could be defended by pointing out that items with properties given by standard scientific dictionaries also have the properties cited, where this is construed as establishable by appeal to experiment and observation and to theories and principles themselves establishable in this way. The property cited, however, is recognized as more basic than others in the sense that it reflects an underlying structure or condition of X's that can serve to explain other known properties of X; items have these other properties in virtue of this underlying structure. So, scientists may say, an acid is really (just) a proton donor; a metal is really (just) an element that can replace the hydrogen of an acid; and so forth. Such propositions might be said to be partly empirical: they make claims

53

about acids, metals, and so forth, that can be defended by appeal to observation and theory. They might also be said to be partly non-empirical, or empirical in a different sense: they suggest, among other things, that the properties cited can be appealed to in providing explanations of many other properties of the item.

If a property P is explanatory in this manner, it may then be taken to be a definition (sometimes called a "theoretical" definition) of the term "X," in one of two ways: (*a*) P is now construed as logically necessary and sufficient for X. (If so, of course, other properties may still be relevant for X.) This is what happens for those employing the Brønsted definition of "acid." (*b*) P is now construed as semantically relevant and quite central for X, though not logically necessary or sufficient. This, I suggest, is what happens when a definition for "copper" is given by reference to atomic number.

5. LIST C; MATHEMATICAL DEFINITIONS

We have considered terms on list A, whose definitions do not contain logically necessary and sufficient conditions, and terms on list B, whose definitions do. Let us turn now to list C, which contains quantity terms such as "kinetic energy," "velocity," and "length." Before discussing whether the semantical categories already introduced can be applied here as well, I want to say something about two types of definitions scientists and lexicographers actually give for terms on this list: mathematical and operational definitions.

The most familiar type of definition for a quantity is one in which it is defined as some mathematical combination of other quantities. "Kinetic energy" is defined as one-half the product of mass and velocity squared; "velocity," as time rate of change of position; "(average) density," as mass divided by volume; "enthalpy," as internal energy plus the product of pressure and volume. All of these can be expressed symbolically: $k.e. = \frac{1}{2}mv^2$, $v = \frac{ds}{dt}$, $\rho = \frac{m}{V}$, $H = U + pV$. A definition of a related form defines a quantity by considering changes in it. For example, "entropy" is defined by the relationship $S_2 - S_1 = \int_1^2 \frac{dQ}{T}$, where S_1 and S_2 are the entropies of the system in states 1 and 2, dQ is an infinitesimal quantity of heat transferred, T is the absolute temperature, and the integration is over a reversible path from state 1 to state 2.

Such definitions identify the quantity as one whose magnitude (or whose change in magnitude) is identical with the magnitude of a mathematical complex of other quantities. I shall speak of a definition of this type as a mathematical definition of a quantity (and I include here definitions of those quantities that are vectors as well as those that are scalars). Within a theory, or rather within a given presentation of a theory, most quantity terms will be defined in this way. But some will not. In many presentations of classical mechanics, the quantities length, time, and mass are not assigned mathematical definitions. Some authors call them "primitives" and speak of them as undefined. This can be misleading since it suggests that no definition is given for such terms or even that none *can* be given. The most that can be claimed is that within a particular presentation no *mathematical* definition may be given. It does not follow that no definition, or that nothing worthy of being called a definition, is or can be given. (What other sorts of definitions are possible here will be noted subsequently.) Nor does it follow that in other presentations of the same theory no mathematical definition can be given. Mach, for example, showed how to provide a mathematical definition of "mass" in terms of acceleration, using Newton's third law of motion.[5]

Within the class of mathematical definitions two types might be distinguished. Some, such as those for kinetic energy, momentum, and enthalpy, are obtained by deriving a formula from a theory and then stipulating that a certain expression in this formula will be called kinetic energy, momentum, or enthalpy. This is to be contrasted with definitions, such as those for density and velocity, which are not obtained in this way but are proposed *ab initio*. In considering the definition of a term of the former sort, it will often be important to refer to this derivation in order to understand both the concept expressed by the term and why the mathematical definition given by the scientist may change when the theory changes.

For example, in many presentations of classical mechanics the definition of "kinetic energy" as $\frac{1}{2}mv^2$ is arrived at by considering the work done by a force on a particle during the displacement from an initial

[5] Ernst Mach, "Über die Definition der Masse," *Carl's Repertorium der Experimentalphysik,* 4 (1868), 355–59.

position P_0 to a final position P_1. "Work" is defined (in vector notation) as $W = \int_{P_0}^{P_1} \mathbf{F} \cdot d\mathbf{r}$, where $\mathbf{F}$ is force and $d\mathbf{r}$ is an infinitesimal displacement. Taking Newton's second law of motion in vector form, $\mathbf{F} = m\ddot{\mathbf{r}}$, we can derive the result $\int_{P_0}^{P_1} \mathbf{F} \cdot d\mathbf{r} = \frac{1}{2}mv_1^2 - \frac{1}{2}mv_0^2$. This means that the work done by the particle during the displacement from P_0 to P_1 is equal to the difference between the value of the quantity $\frac{1}{2}mv^2$ at the end of the displacement and its value at the beginning, where m is the mass of the particle, v_0 its initial velocity, and v_1 its final velocity. A knowledge of this derivation, or some other like it, is crucial for understanding how the expression $\frac{1}{2}mv^2$ is obtained. Otherwise the choice of this expression would seem perfectly arbitrary. It is also crucial for understanding changes in the definition. In relativity theory "kinetic energy" (of a particle of rest mass m_0 and velocity v) is defined as

$$m_0 c^2 \left[\frac{1}{\left(1 - \frac{v^2}{c^2}\right)^{\frac{1}{2}}} - 1 \right],$$

where c is the velocity of light. This definition is also obtained by considering the work done by a force on a particle during the displacement from P_0 to P_1, that is, $\int_{P_0}^{P_1} \mathbf{F} \cdot d\mathbf{r}$. But in relativistic mechanics,

$$F = \frac{d}{dt} \left[\frac{m_0 v}{\left(1 - \frac{v^2}{c^2}\right)^{\frac{1}{2}}} \right].$$

6. OPERATIONAL DEFINITIONS

Another type of definition scientists and lexicographers actually supply for terms on list C makes reference to operations for measuring the quantity. Such definitions range from those providing only minimal suggestions of operations to those providing a quantitative scale of measurement based on operations.

As an example of the latter, "mass" is sometimes defined by the following stipulations: (i) Given two bodies, A and B, if A balances B on a scale, then the mass of A is equal to the mass of B. (ii) The mass of the body consisting of A and B is equal to the sum of the masses of A and B. (iii) A specific object, the Standard Mass, is designated to have a mass of 1.

Such a definition not only indicates what operational procedure can be used for determining masses but also allows the numerical magnitude of the masses to be determined (to within differences ascertainable by the balance). Shorter definitions of mass found in various texts cite only the operational information (*i*) without including stipulations (*ii*) and (*iii*) as part of the definition. For example, physicists sometimes define "mass" as that quantity which two bodies are said to have in equal amounts when they balance each other on a scale.[6]

At the other extreme there are definitions which make no reference to instruments but provide at least some suggestion of how observations as well as measurements could be made. "Temperature" is frequently defined as that property which two objects have in equal degrees if when brought into contact (provided they do not react with each other chemically or electrically) there are no observable changes in their properties.[7] In this case, when an additional assumption is made, namely, that two bodies at the same temperature as a third are at the same temperature as each other, the notion of a thermometer can be introduced for determining temperature equalities.

Terms defined by reference to operations may also be given mathematical definitions. Physicists sometimes define mass by reference to operations with a balance, sometimes as the ratio of the force acting on the body to the acceleration that results.[8] In short, as definitions for terms on list C are actually presented, some provide only an indication of what operations or observations are involved in measuring the quantity; others cite only a mathematical complex of quantities without any indication of operations for measurement (this may be given separately or not at all); some combine both features.

7. OTHER DEFINITIONS FOR QUANTITIES

Many definitions for terms on list C do not proceed in either of the two ways discussed above. Instead, they select some nonmathematical, nonoperational description of the quantity and identify it as one which satisfies this description.

For example, "entropy" is sometimes defined as a quantity an

---

[6] For references see Max Jammer, *Concepts of Mass in Classical and Modern Physics* (Cambridge, Mass., 1961), p. 105.

[7] Cf. F. W. Sears, *Thermodynamics, the Kinetic Theory of Gases and Statistical Mechanics,* 2nd ed. (Cambridge, Mass., 1953), p. 4.

[8] See James Clerk Maxwell, *Matter and Motion* (New York, 1920).

increase of which is a measure of the loss of energy convertible into mechanical work; "potential energy," as energy due to the position or configuration of a body; "kinetic energy," as "the energy a body possesses because of its motion";[9] the "partition function" in statistical mechanics, as "an expression giving the distribution of molecules in different energy states in a system."[10] In each of these cases we have a quantity introduced in the context of a theory where a certain description is applicable to it, one that does not consist simply of a mathematical complex of other quantities or contain references to operations. A definition is given by identifying the quantity as one satisfying the description. As in the cases above, the quantity may be one that in the particular presentation of the theory is also defined as a mathematical complex of others. Or, it may be "primitive"; thus, many texts define "temperature" as the degree of hotness of a body or as "that property of a body which determines the flow of heat,"[11] and "mass" is sometimes defined as quantity of matter.

There may be alternative definitions using different descriptions for the same term. "Entropy," for example, has several definitions in addition to the one above. In the *Encyclopedic Dictionary of Physics* (1961) we find: "The entropy of a system may be most generally defined as a measure of the capacity of the system to undergo spontaneous change." And in the *International Dictionary of Physics and Electronics*: "Application of the 'second law' of thermodynamics leads to the conclusion that if any physical system is left to itself and allowed to distribute its energy in its own way, it always does so in a manner such that this quantity, called 'entropy,' increases. . . ."

Definitions of the present sort have been roundly criticized by some who write about the foundations of science. According to these critics, if a definition for a quantity provides no indication of how the quantity is to be measured, then statements involving that quantity cannot be subjected to test.[12] Others contend that such definitions are irrelevant and misleading because a quantity is nothing more nor less than what

[9] Henry Semat, *Fundamentals of Physics,* rev. ed. (New York, 1951), pp. 826, 823.

[10] *International Dictionary of Physics and Electronics.*

[11] Arthur L. Kimball, *A College Textbook of Physics,* 3rd ed. (New York, 1923), p. 243.

[12] For a critique of the definition of "mass" as quantity of matter, see Robert B. Lindsay and Henry Margenau, *Foundations of Physics* (New York, 1936), p. 90.

is defined by a set of ordering relationships making reference to operational procedures. For example, Brian Ellis writes:

> The student [of the physical sciences] asks what mechanical energy or entropy is, and he is given a formula—a means of calculating the measure of it from other measurements. Or else he is given a theoretical interpretation of it, when he doesn't yet know what it is he is supposed to be interpreting. He wants to know what he is measuring or interpreting. . . . If I am right the student's demands are based on a misconception of the notion of quantity. To point to a quantity is to do no more than to point to a group of ordering relationships.[13]

I agree that these sorts of definitions are deficient, but only in one respect: in failing to provide a method to test statements involving quantities so defined. It does not follow that such definitions are not useful in any way. They may provide an important and illuminating fact about the quantity, one that might not be evident from a mathematical or operational definition. Moreover, to take issue with Ellis, it is in those cases where the mathematical definition is quite intricate that the student is helped to understand the concept by being given other facts about it (as in the case of entropy and potential energy). This is not to say that all such definitions are acceptable or that any fact cited in the definition of a quantity is as enlightening as any other. The definition of "entropy" as that quantity an increase of which is a measure of the loss of energy convertible into mechanical work is obviously more illuminating than the definition of "mass" as quantity of matter.

8. CONDITIONS FOR QUANTITIES

I have noted three types of definitions actually given in scientific texts and lexicons for terms on list C. It is not my claim that whenever a scientist introduces such a term, or whenever the lexicographer composes an entry for it, he will provide only one type of information. All three may be provided (even though the scientist or lexicographer may call one piece of such information the definition). In the case of "mass," for example, the *Encyclopedic Dictionary of Physics* includes a mathematical definition in terms of the law *"force = mass × acceleration,"* a

---

[13] Brian Ellis, "Fundamental Problems of Direct Measurement," *Australasian Journal of Philosophy,* 38 (1960), 40.

description of it as the "quantity of matter in a body," the fact that it is a concept employed by Newton in his theory of mechanics, information concerning its use in the law of gravitation, some description of methods for measuring mass by means of beam balances, and many other facts.

In short, a dictionary may cite a mathematical definition of the quantity (if there is one), operations required to measure it, the role of the quantity in a theory, facts which follow from its mathematical definition and principles of a theory, its history, and so forth. In what follows I shall say that such entries provide *conditions* for the quantity defined. When considering list B, I said that for an item to be classifiable as an X (conservative system, fermion), it must satisfy such and such conditions. Now I shall speak of the conditions a quantity must satisfy for it to be classifiable as quantity Q. (For example, for a quantity to be classifiable as mass, must it satisfy the relationship *"force = mass × acceleration,"* be measurable by a beam balance, and so on?) The question to be raised concerns the relationship between such conditions and the quantity defined.

Some conditions for a quantity Q might be spoken of as logically sufficient for Q: if a quantity satisfies them, it is classifiable as Q no matter what other conditions it satisfies. Some might be spoken of as logically necessary for Q: a quantity failing to satisfy them would not be classifiable as Q. Some might be relevant for Q: their satisfaction by a quantity would tend to provide some reason in favor of concluding that the quantity is Q, and if other appropriate conditions are satisfied, could justifiably be said to settle the question.

Among the relevant conditions, the distinction between semantical and nonsemantical relevance could be drawn as follows.[14] Suppose that quantity Q satisfies conditions $C_1, \ldots, C_n$, each being positively and negatively relevant for Q. Let us consider various quantities which satisfy different vast majority subsets of $C_1, \ldots, C_n$, where each such subset lacks C_i. If, taking into account various backgrounds and appropriate weights, the failure to satisfy C_i by such quantities would in and of itself tend to count, to some extent, against classifying them as Q, we may say that C_i is (negatively) semantically relevant for Q. If the nonsatisfaction of C_i in such cases in and of itself would tend not to count against classifying them as Q, we may say that C_i is (negatively) nonsemantically relevant for Q. Let us also consider various quantities which satisfy different partial subsets of $C_1, \ldots, C_n$, where none of

[14] Cf. Chap. One, sec. 3, formulation C.

these includes C_i. Suppose, in addition, we are told that each of these quantities satisfies C_i. If the satisfaction of C_i tends to count in and of itself, to some extent, in favor of a Q-classification, we can say that C_i is (positively) semantically relevant for Q. If it does not, we can say that C_i is (positively) nonsemantically relevant for Q.

Now there are quantity terms used by scientists in such a way that of the conditions cited in a definition one or more are logically necessary and sufficient for the quantity, whereas others are semantically relevant without being either. For certain terms no condition cited may be logically necessary or sufficient, though all may be relevant and central in varying degrees. But here we need to treat particular cases and consider the various types of definitions for quantities distinguished earlier.

9. CONDITIONS IN MATHEMATICAL DEFINITIONS

"Velocity" is defined in classical mechanics as instantaneous rate of change of position with respect to time. This provides a logically necessary condition in the following sense: as the term "velocity" is used in classical mechanics, if a quantity satisfies this condition, then, no matter what else is true, the quantity is correctly classifiable as velocity. Consider now the concept of specific heat (at constant volume) in thermodynamics. A definition which provides a logically necessary and sufficient condition is this: $c_v = \dfrac{(dq)_v}{(dT)_v}$, roughly, the ratio of a small amount of heat flowing into a substance, per unit mass, to the rise in temperature, under constant volume conditions. Given this definition, together with the first law of thermodynamics (which implies that $(dq)_v = (du)_v$, where u is internal energy per unit mass), we can derive the following: $c_v = \left(\dfrac{\partial u}{\partial T}\right)_v$, the partial derivative of the internal energy per unit mass with respect to the temperature. In thermodynamics it is the latter formula that is often said to provide the definition of specific heat (at constant volume). The satisfaction of the condition $c_v = \left(\dfrac{\partial u}{\partial T}\right)_v$ is neither logically necessary nor logically sufficient for specific heat, although it is relevant. Shall this be described as semantical or as nonsemantical relevance, or is it not classifiable in either way? Consider vast majority subsets of conditions satisfied by the quantity specific heat at constant volume. If a given subset satisfied by a quantity c_v contains the condition $c_v = \dfrac{(dq)_v}{(dT)_v}$, then the failure of this quantity to satisfy the condition $c_v = \left(\dfrac{\partial u}{\partial T}\right)_v$ in and of itself does not count at all against classifying it as specific heat, since the former condition is logically sufficient. If a given subset does not contain the former condition, then failure to satisfy the latter in and of itself does not count against classifying the quantity as specific heat. It would count against this classification only insofar as it suggests that the quantity fails to satisfy the condition $c_v = \dfrac{(dq)_v}{(dT)_v}$. If this is correct, then the condition $c_v = \left(\dfrac{\partial u}{\partial T}\right)_v$ is negatively nonsemantically relevant for specific heat.

Also, suppose that we describe various quantities, each satisfying a different partial subset of conditions for specific heat; these subsets would have to exclude the condition $c_v = \dfrac{(dq)_v}{(dT)_v}$, since this is a logically sufficient condition for specific heat. Suppose, in addition, we are told that each of these quantities satisfies the condition $c_v = \left(\dfrac{\partial u}{\partial T}\right)_v$ and that we are to assume the background as close as possible to what it is now. The fact that these quantities satisfy this condition would not in and of itself count in favor of a specific heat classification, except insofar as it suggests that the quantities satisfy the condition $c_v = \dfrac{(dq)_v}{(dT)_v}$. If so, the condition $c_v = \left(\dfrac{\partial u}{\partial T}\right)_v$ is also positively nonsemantically relevant for specific heat.

Kinetic energy is another quantity of this sort. In many presentations of classical mechanics the definition of kinetic energy in terms of work ($k.e. = \int \mathbf{F} \cdot d\mathbf{r}$) provides a logically necessary and sufficient condition for this quantity from which, together with Newton's second law of motion, the equation $k.e. = \frac{1}{2}mv^2$ can be derived. Accordingly, that a quantity Q satisfies the relationship $Q = \frac{1}{2}mv^2$ is relevant for its being kinetic energy, though not logically necessary or sufficient. Moreover, under this interpretation, it is nonsemantically relevant. The satisfaction (or nonsatisfaction) of the condition $Q = \frac{1}{2}mv^2$ would tend to count in favor of (or against) classifying Q as kinetic energy only insofar as it allows one to infer the satisfaction (or nonsatisfaction) of the condition

$$Q = \int \mathbf{F} \cdot d\mathbf{r}.$$

I have noted a mathematical definition that provides a logically necessary and sufficient condition for a quantity and mathematical definitions that provide nonsemantically relevant conditions. Are there quantities with mathematical definitions that provide semantically relevant but not logically necessary or sufficient conditions?

Mass can be construed in this manner in some presentations of classical mechanics. A number of facts about this quantity are cited, including Newton's second law of motion. The latter may then be taken to provide a semantically relevant condition for mass though not a logically necessary one. (Mass is that quantity which, among other things, satisfies the relationship *"force = mass × acceleration"*; the fact that a quantity satisfies this relationship tends to count in and of itself as some reason in favor of classifying it as mass.) This does not preclude the second law from also being used to express an empirical statement. Here we must recall the earlier treatment of terms on list A. From the semantically relevant conditions for mass we may temporarily "withdraw" the one in question and ask whether Newton's second law holds when mass is construed as a quantity satisfying the remaining conditions; and this can be an empirical issue (see Chapter One, section 11).

10. CONDITIONS IN OPERATIONAL DEFINITIONS

Consider now definitions given by reference to operations. What might it mean to say that these provide logically necessary conditions for a quantity? Possibly, that if a quantity is classifiable as Q, then it must be correctly measurable by the operations specified. However, if this is construed as requiring operations to be applicable over all ranges of the quantity, it would be an overly strict notion of logical necessity for quantities. The following seems more reasonable. To speak of operational conditions as logically necessary for a quantity Q is to say that if a given quantity is classifiable as Q, then the quantity, within certain roughly specifiable ranges, must be correctly measurable by the operations specified. And to speak of operational conditions as logically sufficient for a quantity Q is to say that if a certain quantity is correctly measurable by the operations, then this quantity is classifiable as Q (and the magnitude of Q is that given by the measurement).

Even in this weaker sense, however, operational definitions do not provide logically necessary and sufficient conditions. Two sorts of cases should be noted. First, those where actual conditions obtain, or where hypothetical ones can be described, that would prevent the quantity from being correctly measurable by the operations specified. There are an indefinitely large number of possible disturbing factors and no operational definition lists them all (thus the *ceteris paribus* clause usually understood at least implicitly). Accordingly, an operational definition does not supply a logically necessary condition for a quantity.

Turning to the second type of case, consider a quantity such as temperature which is measurable by a number of different operational methods. Suppose we discover new substances for which, by measuring their temperatures with mercury thermometers, we arrive at significantly different results from our measurements with constant volume hydrogen thermometers. Suppose that the temperature ranges are those to which both types of thermometer are normally applicable, and that we can discover no disturbing conditions affecting either thermometer. If this happened, and if operational definitions provide logically sufficient conditions, it would follow that both methods give the correct measurements of temperature for these substances; but this, I take it, we should want to deny.

Now suppose that other methods of measuring temperature (for example, using gases other than hydrogen or using a solid-rod thermometer) indicate, together with known or accepted facts about temperature, that the mercury thermometer gives correct measurements. If we accept this value as correct, then it is not logically necessary that temperature be correctly measurable by a constant volume hydrogen thermometer. The same argument can be repeated for the mercury thermometer. In short, these operations, even within appropriate temperature ranges, provide neither logically necessary nor logically sufficient conditions for temperature.

I suggest that operational definitions do supply conditions relevant for quantities. They supply conditions the satisfaction (or nonsatisfaction) of which constitutes some reason for (or against) concluding that the quantity in question is Q, and under certain circumstances, might be taken to settle the issue. Could any such conditions be classified as semantically relevant?

Consider the operation of measuring temperature by means of a solid-rod thermometer, which depends on the principle of the expansion of a solid with increases in temperature. Suppose there are solid bodies described as being in contact with flames, as feeling hotter and hotter, as having changed in color to glowing red, and so forth, but as not expanding; and suppose that these bodies, their surroundings, and the observers are assumed as normal as possible in other respects. I would say that as the term "temperature" is currently used in physics, the fact that such bodies do not expand would in and of itself tend to provide some reason (though by no means a conclusive one) against saying that their temperatures have increased. Again, suppose there are solid bodies described as having as well as lacking some of the properties characteristic of those whose temperatures have increased; then the fact that such bodies have expanded would in and of itself tend to count, to some extent, in favor of saying that their temperatures have increased. If so, expansion of solids (and the thermometric operation based on this) is semantically relevant for temperature.

Contrast my position on operational definitions with two others. One, formulated originally by Bridgman, asserts that an operational definition supplies a logically necessary and sufficient condition for a quantity.[15] Distinct operational definitions mean distinct quantities (which may be related empirically). The other view denies that operational definitions provide logically necessary or sufficient conditions and avers that they are straightforward empirical propositions.[16] Both positions are unduly restrictive. For reasons previously noted, operational definitions do not in general supply conditions that are logically necessary or sufficient, even for a limited range of values of the quantity. Nor must they always be construed as empirical propositions. My view has been

---

[15] P. W. Bridgman, *The Logic of Modern Physics* (New York, 1927).

[16] This is suggested by Rudolf Carnap, Carl G. Hempel, and Arthur Pap, among others, in articles in *The Philosophy of Rudolf Carnap,* ed. Paul Arthur Schilpp (LaSalle, Illinois, 1963). Sometimes there is the suggestion that operational definitions cannot provide logically necessary conditions for a quantity because that quantity may be assigned values beyond the range of values ascertainable by the operation (see Pap, p. 583). However, as already indicated, there is still an important sense in which an operational definition might be thought of as providing a logically necessary (or logically sufficient) condition for a quantity—within a certain range of values.

that they can, and generally do, supply conditions relevant for quantities and that some, at least, provide semantically relevant conditions. Sentences attributing operational conditions of the latter sort to a quantity may be used to express empirical statements, but they can also be used to express statements defensible solely by appeal to the use of terms.

11. CONCLUSIONS ON LIST C

Mathematical and operational conditions for quantities have been examined, and similar analyses are possible for definitions citing other facts about quantities (section 7). Some definitions of the latter sort might provide logically necessary and sufficient conditions (for example, "temperature" defined as degree of hotness); others might not, but might provide relevant conditions ("entropy" defined as a quantity measuring the loss of available energy in a system).

In general, I have tried to show how the concepts of logical necessity, logical sufficiency, and relevance, applicable to lists A and B, can be applied as well to list C. A definition for a quantity will cite conditions which in some cases will be logically necessary or sufficient and in others may be relevant without being either. However, appeal to these concepts will not completely determine which conditions will or should be cited in formulating a definition for a quantity. Not all conditions that are relevant, or even logically necessary and sufficient, are illuminating; some may be quite vague (for example, "mass" defined as quantity of matter). And one who formulates a definition must consider as well the interests and level of sophistication of his intended readers. My claim is only that appeal to these concepts will be relevant in deciding which conditions to select for a definition and also in understanding the nature of definitions proposed.

The theses defended in this chapter and the previous one are applicable to many topics under current discussion in philosophy of science. A number of these will be examined in the following chapter on the interpretation of terms.

CHAPTER THREE

THE INTERPRETATION OF TERMS

I propose to consider two powerful and influential philosophical theories about terms in science. The first, contemporary Logical Positivism, is concerned with the introduction and interpretation of terms. Its proponents use the expression "introduction of a term" to refer to whatever may be done, linguistically or otherwise, when a term is first employed. They use the word "interpretation" to refer to what I have called the semantical aspect of use. However, since they generally speak of the meaning of a term rather than of its use, this procedure will also be followed in the present chapter. By "interpretation of a term," then, what is being referred to is a meaning the term has or is given. The second philosophical theory, expounded by those with a special interest in the history of science, is concerned mainly with the meaning of scientific terms and the manner in which such meaning depends upon theories and can change when theories are altered or replaced. I shall argue that both of these philosophical views provide inadequate accounts of terms in science. Important parts of the critique to be offered here will depend upon the theory of definitions developed in the first two chapters. In the final section I shall make further use of this theory in offering positive proposals concerning the introduction and interpretation of terms in science.

1. THE CONTEMPORARY POSITIVIST ACCOUNT

Logical Positivism began as a movement in the 1920's. Its members, including Schlick, Carnap, Neurath, and others, were concerned with demonstrating the impossibility of speculative metaphysics, which discourses of realms beyond experience, and with providing a foundation for empirical science. This was done by invoking a Principle of Verification that declared metaphysics meaningless and science significant on the ground that the former, but not the latter, is composed of statements incapable of empirical verification. One of the main problems with this position, however, was how such a principle should be formulated. Each of various proposals led to difficulties and required modification.[1] The doctrine I will consider here is one that has emerged from these efforts and is regarded by contemporary Positivists as the most adequate expression of their position. It can be found in the recent writings of Carnap[2] and Hempel.[3] It is also expounded by others, such as Nagel[4] and Braithwaite,[5] who could not be classified as Positivists. However, I shall use the label "Positivist account" in referring to the doctrine. It must be understood that I am referring only to a contemporary Positivist view, one that is espoused by some non-Positivists as well, and one with a number of variations, only some of which will be considered.

The Positivist account offers a reconstruction of science: it purports to describe how, ideally speaking, terms in science should be introduced and interpreted so that the resulting scientific system will be most clearly understood. Its aim is to reconstruct a scientific system, making as clear as possible its logical structure and empirical content.

According to this account, terms a scientist will introduce in the course of proposing a theory, formulating a law, describing experiments, and so forth, will be classifiable either as *theoretical* or as *nontheoretical*. To the nontheoretical terms, meanings are assigned that can be readily understood by anyone studying the theory, law, or experiment. This class will include so-called *primitive* terms (those for which no necessary and sufficient conditions are given by using other terms in the

[1] See Carl G. Hempel, "Problems and Changes in the Empiricist Criterion of Meaning," *Revue Internationale de Philosophie,* 4 (1950), 41–63.

[2] Rudolf Carnap, "The Methodological Character of Theoretical Concepts," *Minnesota Studies in the Philosophy of Science,* ed. H. Feigl and M. Scriven (Minneapolis, 1956), I, 38–76. *The Philosophy of Rudolf Carnap,* ed. Paul Arthur Schilpp (LaSalle, Illinois, 1963), pp. 958–66.

[3] Carl G. Hempel, "The Theoretician's Dilemma," *Minnesota Studies in the Philosophy of Science,* ed. H. Feigl, M. Scriven, and G. Maxwell (Minneapolis, 1958), II, 37–98.

[4] Ernest Nagel, *The Structure of Science* (New York, 1961).

[5] R. B. Braithwaite, *Scientific Explanation* (Cambridge, England, 1953).

system);[6] it will also include *explicitly defined* terms (those for which necessary and sufficient conditions are given by employing primitive terms in the system). A meaning is assigned to a primitive term by a *semantical rule,* which relates that term to some item (object, property, relationship) that is familiar and understood. The semantical rule is expressed not in the language of the system itself, the object language, but in a so-called metalanguage which contains terms that are antecedently understood. An example of a semantical rule would be " 'R' means (or designates) the property *red,*" where "R" is a term in the scientific object language and "red" a term in the metalanguage. To terms in the second class, the theoretical terms, meanings are not assigned by semantical rules; nor are they explicitly defined by using terms of the first type.

How do we decide which terms are theoretical and which are nontheoretical? Here we appeal to the concept of observability. Terms like "blue," "hot," and "longer than," which purport to refer to observables, are nontheoretical. Terms like "electron," "field," and "kinetic energy," which purport to refer to unobservables, are theoretical. Now a realm of unobservables is suspect; indeed for Positivists, who demand empiricism and eschew speculative metaphysics, such a realm is unintelligible. So instead of assigning a semantical rule to a theoretical term, which would make it refer to something unobservable, the proposal is to refrain from assigning any such rule. How, then, can theoretical terms be used in science?

They can be used because, within a theory, connections are made between the theoretical and the nontheoretical terms that provide a "partial" and "indirect" interpretation for them. Statements expressing these connections are classified as *correspondence rules* (or postulates). They are what Carnap calls "mixed sentences": they contain at least one theoretical term and at least one nontheoretical one and will be part of the theory itself.[7]

What is a theory according to this account? It is a set of sentences consisting of axioms and of theorems that follow deductively from these.[8]

[6] Note, then, the difference between this sense of "primitive" and its use in the previous chapter for quantity-terms for which *mathematical* definitions are not given.

[7] *The Philosophy of Rudolf Carnap,* p. 959.

[8] This "hypothetico-deductive" characteristic attributed to theories will be examined in Chap. Four.

69

Axioms and theorems may be purely theoretical sentences (those in which only theoretical terms occur) or correspondence rules. However, some will be sentences in which only observational terms occur. It is these sentences that are tested and that provide a basis for confirming the theory. To make this more concrete, let us consider the kinetic theory of gases as an example. According to this theory, a gas contains an enormous number of tiny molecules in rapid motion; these are subject to the conservation laws of classical mechanics; their diameters are small compared to the mean-free path of the molecules; they collide elastically with each other and with the walls of the container; and the absolute temperature of the gas is a function of the mean kinetic energy of the molecules. From the set of principles of this theory, one can derive laws relating pressure, volume, and temperature of gases, laws about the specific heats of gases, laws about diffusion of one gas through another, and so forth.

A Positivist might reconstruct this theory as follows. He might claim that terms such as "gas," "pressure of a gas," "temperature of a gas," "volume of a gas," and "specific heat of a gas" refer to observables and so are to be treated as nontheoretical—either as primitive interpreted terms or as terms for which necessary and sufficient conditions can be given by using only primitive interpreted terms. He might also claim that the term "molecule" as well as expressions such as "mass of a molecule," "momentum of a molecule," and "pressure exerted by molecules" refer to unobservables and so are to be treated as theoretical terms. This means that although necessary and sufficient conditions may be given for such terms by reference to each other, no necessary and sufficient conditions will be given for them by reference to the non-theoretical terms; nor will semantical rules be assigned to them. (I do not here assume unanimity among Positivists regarding which terms are theoretical and which nontheoretical. I claim only that this is one way a Positivist might make the division in the kinetic theory.[9])

The kinetic theory will contain some purely theoretical sentences. In symbolic form one of these will be $p = \frac{1}{2}mn\overline{v^2}$, where p is the pressure of all the molecules on the walls of the container, m is the mass of a molecule, n is the number of molecules per unit volume, and $\overline{v^2}$ is the mean square velocity of the molecules. (Of course, all these are to be construed as mere symbols with no interpretations assigned.) The

[9] Problems associated with the theoretical-nontheoretical distinction will be treated in Chaps. Five and Six.

kinetic theory will also contain correspondence rules. One such will be the following: $\frac{1}{2}m\overline{v^2} = \text{const.} \times T$, where $\frac{1}{2}m\overline{v^2}$ is the mean kinetic energy of a molecule and T is absolute temperature. Another will be $p = P$, where p, as before, is the pressure of all molecules on the walls of the container and P is the pressure of the gas. From the set of axioms containing purely theoretical sentences and correspondence rules we can derive the ideal gas law, which uses only nontheoretical terms and can be expressed as $PV = \text{const.} \times T$, where V is the volume of the gas and T is its absolute temperature. The derivation of sentences with nontheoretical terms does not require that the theoretical terms in the axioms be assigned meanings or that they be explicitly definable using nontheoretical terms. The axioms will serve their explanatory and predictive roles even if the terms within them are uninterpreted.

On the Positivist account, then, there are three ways to introduce a term: (1) Use the term in axioms or theorems of a theory; (2) Give a semantical rule for the term (not within the language of the system itself) by relating it to something observable; (3) Give necessary and sufficient conditions for the term (within the language of the system itself) using terms for which semantical rules are given. For some terms (1) and (2) can be done; for some, (1) and (3); for some, only (1). On this account terms are said to be (completely) interpreted if either (2) or (3) is satisfied. That is, some terms are interpreted by indicating what observables they refer to; others, by being assigned necessary and sufficient conditions using only interpreted terms. Some terms are not interpreted in either of these ways but are simply related to the interpreted ones via sentences of a theory. If so, they are sometimes said to be "partially" interpreted.[10]

Should it be objected that the Positivist account does not reflect the actual procedure of scientists, the reply will be that it is meant to serve as an ideal standard for introducing and interpreting terms. By reconstructing a theory in the proposed manner, we can readily see which terms are (completely) interpreted and which not. For those that are, we can ascertain semantical rules in the metalanguage or necessary and sufficient conditions in the object language relating them to observables. For those that are not, we can ascertain how the theory relates them to what can be observed. In either case, we can reconstruct a scientific theory so that no term need be interpreted as designating any-

[10] This notion will be discussed in sec. 4.

thing unobservable. We can reconstruct a theory rendering it entirely empirical and can exhibit precisely the relationships, however complex and indirect, that hold between its terms and what is observable.

2. ON THE SIGNIFICANCE OF THEORETICAL TERMS

Positivists maintain that theoretical terms in science are significant, meaningful, capable of being understood, distinguishable from nonsense terms, and more particularly, distinguishable from terms used in speculative metaphysics. (These claims are somewhat different, although the authors in question do not distinguish them; nor, for the present purposes, do we need to do so. In my discussion I shall use the term "significant" where I mean to cover all of the other claims as well.) What is supposed to make such terms significant are correspondence rules that relate them to interpreted terms.

The first difficulty with this account is that it is much too liberal. It admits as significant any theoretical term in any theory whatever, including the terms of the speculative metaphysician. To see this, let us formulate a principle of significance that seems implicit in many Positivist writings:

(I) A theoretical term M, which occurs in a theory T, is significant (meaningful, and so on) if and only if there is within the theory a correspondence rule for M.

This is unacceptable, for it implies that any theoretical term in any theory is significant, whether or not correspondence rules have been explicitly stated for that term.

To understand why, consider any theory whatever and from it choose any axiom or theorem T that contains a theoretical term M. T logically implies $O \supset T$, where O is any sentence all of whose terms are nontheoretical, and $\supset$ signifies the truth-functional conditional, roughly: "if . . . , then _____." (By definition, $O \supset T$ is false when O is true and T false, and true otherwise.) But $O \supset T$ is a correspondence rule for M, since it is a "mixed sentence" containing both M and nontheoretical terms. Hence, according to (I), the term M is significant. Since every theoretical term in a theory occurs in at least one axiom or theorem of the theory, the above argument can be repeated for each such term. Consequently, the theory contains a correspondence rule for every theoretical term. It follows that no matter what theoretical terms are employed in a theory, and no matter what the axioms or theorems of the theory might be, every theoretical term necessarily is significant.

Such a criterion confers significance upon terms in speculative metaphysics also, for we have only to think of a metaphysical theory as a set of sentences containing theoretical (metaphysical) terms. In accordance with (I), any term that occurs in any metaphysical axiom T is significant, since T implies the correspondence rule $O \supset T$, where O is any nontheoretical sentence you please. It might be replied that a metaphysical theory so construed is quite different from the original one and not what the metaphysician intended. But in what way will it be different? It will contain the same terms and definitions as the original theory. Of course there will not be semantical rules or logically necessary and sufficient conditions for the theoretical terms relating them to observables. But presumably there were no such rules or conditions in the original theory either. Moreover, it will contain all the postulates of the original theory, that is, all the sentences treated as such in that theory.

At this point two possibilities seem open to the Positivist. He might either modify the notion of a correspondence rule or propose additional requirements for a theoretical term to satisfy.

One way to modify the notion of a correspondence rule would be to disallow truth-functional connectives. This would prevent sentences like $O \supset T$, deducible from any sentence T, from counting as correspondence rules. But such a proposal would violate both the spirit and the letter of the Positivist position. This position requires the "language of science" to be an extensional one and to contain "only truth-functional connectives, no terms for logical or causal modalities (necessity, possibility, etc.)." [11] Even if stronger connectives were admitted, truth-functional ones would not be precluded.[12]

Another way to modify the notion of a correspondence rule would be to require stronger relationships between theoretical and nontheoretical terms. We might require that *terms* and not sentences be related truth-functionally; for example, that correspondence rules have the logical form $(x)(M_1x \supset M_2x)$, which means "Anything is such that if it is an M_1 it is an M_2."

This would not do since Positivists explicitly allow correspondence

[11] Carnap, "The Methodological Character of Theoretical Concepts," p. 41.
[12] *Ibid.*, p. 42.

rules to relate sentences containing theoretical terms, *as wholes,* to sentences containing only nontheoretical terms.[13] Moreover, the previous difficulty would still arise. For consider the axiom or theorem $(x)(M_1x \supset M_2x)$, which contains only the theoretical terms M_1 and M_2. This implies $(x)[Ox \supset (M_1x \supset M_2x)]$, where O is any nontheoretical term you please. But the latter is a correspondence rule even by the stricter criterion just mentioned and thus confers significance upon M_1 and M_2. Correspondence rules can similarly be generated for all theoretical terms in the theory. For these reasons the most advisable course for the Positivist is to formulate additional requirements a theoretical term must satisfy to be significant.

The previous difficulties arise, it might be argued, because the correspondence rules cited are trivial ones: If T is the conjunction of axioms of the theory, then $O \supset T$ follows, but so does $\sim O \supset T$ ($\sim O$ means not $= O$). Correspondence rules that confer significance upon theoretical terms need to be axioms of the theory and not simply theorems of it. Thus:

(II) A theoretical term M, which occurs in a theory T, is significant if and only if the conjunction of axioms for the theory contains or itself constitutes a correspondence rule for M.

In one respect such a criterion would be too stringent, for some explicitly defined theoretical terms might appear only in theorems of the theory, not in its axioms. In another respect it is much too broad, since it fails to eliminate the sort of problem besetting (I). Consider the conjunction T of any axioms of any theory. Instead of formulating such a theory as T, one can formulate it as a conjunction of two axioms: $O \supset T$ and $\sim O \supset T$. This conjunction is logically equivalent to T and constitutes a correspondence rule for each of the theoretical terms in T. In this logically equivalent reformation of the original theory every theoretical term is significant, according to (II).

In view of these difficulties we might adopt the following modification of (II), where the axioms of the theory are assumed to be stated using primitive terms only:

(III) A primitive theoretical term M, which occurs in a theory T, is significant if and only if (*a*) the conjunction of axioms of T contains or

[13] See Hempel, "The Theoretician's Dilemma," p. 72; Nagel, *The Structure of Science*, pp. 97–105.

itself constitutes a correspondence rule for M, and (b) the conjunction of axioms of any logically equivalent reformulation of T contains or itself constitutes a correspondence rule for M. Nonprimitive theoretical terms will be significant if and only if they are explicitly definable using significant primitive theoretical terms.

Here the previous difficulties are avoided. Yet a serious problem remains which besets this as well as earlier formulations.

By modifying a theory in an essentially trivial way, every theoretical term in that theory can be shown to be significant; yet it would be unreasonable to claim that the theoretical terms in question gain significance from the procedure I am about to describe. Consider any set of nontheoretical statements O_1, O_2, . . ., O_n, all of which are known to be true. Such a set might include established empirical generalizations such as "ravens are black," and "the sea is salty," and in addition simple existential truths such as "something is green," and "something is warm." Consider now a speculative metaphysician who, although not especially concerned with statements of this sort, will doubtless be willing to admit their truth. Let us choose as our example of a true nontheoretical statement "The sea is salty," to be designated O_1. One of the axioms of the metaphysician's theory is the following, to be designated T_1: "The Absolute is each appearance, and is all, but it is not any one as such." [14]

If the metaphysician grants the truth of each of the sentences T_1 and O_1, then he must admit the truth of the sentence $T_1 . O_1$, which expresses their (truth-functional) conjunction. Let us then reconstruct the metaphysician's theory so that $T_1 . O_1$ is one of his axioms, where "the Absolute" is one of his primitive terms. We proceed in a similar manner for every axiom containing a primitive metaphysical term. Each $T . O$ is a correspondence rule for the metaphysical terms in T; and their conjunction is a correspondence rule for all the primitive metaphysical terms in the theory. The axioms of any logically equivalent reformulation of such a theory will also be a correspondence rule for the metaphysical terms. So, according to (III), as well as (I) and (II), reformulating the original theory using the above correspondence rules as axioms will guarantee significance for the metaphysical terms. Modifying his theory in this way should not be objectionable to the metaphysician, whose interest, after all, lies in developing the purely meta-

[14] F. H. Bradley, *Appearance and Reality* (Oxford, 1897), p. 431.

physical part of his theory and not in generating consequences of the sort made possible by the type of correspondence rules in question. Furthermore, since all nontheoretical consequences afforded by the correspondence rules are true, the world of experience will have no more effect than it previously did upon the truth of the purely metaphysical postulates.

Is it reasonable to maintain that such a procedure, if adopted by a metaphysician, would guarantee that his terms are significant (meaningful, capable of being understood, and so forth)? According to theses (I), (II), and (III), it is possible for sentences such as the following to confer significance upon the metaphysical terms they contain:

> The Absolute is each appearance, and is all, but it is not any one as such, and the sea is salty.
> The Absolute is . . . , and the sky is blue.
> The Absolute is . . . , and grass is green.

However, sentences of this sort fail to shed any light on the nature of the Absolute. If we were attempting to formulate a definition for the term "the Absolute," we would find no help whatever in the fact that we can, in such a way, relate a sentence with this term to these empirical truths. This suggests that if a sentence that contains only theoretical terms is connected simply by means of conjunction to another sentence all of whose terms are nontheoretical, the terms in the former sentence gain no significance from such a procedure. That is:

PRINCIPLE A: If a sentence S (in a theory T) is a conjunction of two sentences S_1 and S_2, and if all the terms in S_1 are theoretical and all the terms in S_2 are nontheoretical, then the occurrence of S (in T) does not suffice to guarantee that the theoretical terms in S_1 (and therefore in S) are significant.

In accordance with this principle the theoretical term "the Absolute" cannot be shown to have significance merely by citing a conjunction of sentences, one of which contains only theoretical terms (including "the Absolute") and the other, only nontheoretical terms.[15]

---

[15] A number of Positivists have themselves maintained this principle. See Hempel, "The Concept of Cognitive Significance: A Reconsideration," *Proceedings of the American Academy of Arts and Sciences,* 80 (1951), 62; Carnap, "The Methodological Character of Theoretical Concepts," p. 58.

Each of the previous formulations of significance violates **Principle A**. Suppose a theory consists of an axiom or conjunction of axioms T, which contains only primitive theoretical terms, and an axiom or conjunction of axioms O, which contains only nontheoretical terms. According to the previous criteria, the terms in T are significant, for $T . O$ is a correspondence rule for the terms in T, and any logically equivalent reformation of $T . O$ will contain correspondence rules for such terms. Hence, $T . O$ guarantees significance for the terms in T. However, according to Principle A, the terms in T cannot be shown to be significant by citing their occurrence in the conjunction $T . O$.

For these reasons the preceding formulations of significance are objectionable. First, by supplementing a metaphysical theory (or any set of sentences regarded as lacking in meaning) with a set of innocuous propositions that provide no information about the metaphysical terms, the metaphysician can nevertheless claim significance for all his primitive terms. Second, the previous formulations are incompatible with a principle of significance that seems reasonable (and is accepted by some of the strongest advocates of the Positivist account).

At this point it might be suggested that an important aspect of significance has been neglected. The essential matter is that a term be such that nontheoretical consequences can be deduced from an axiom of the theory in which it occurs, together with other axioms of the theory. It is their "cash value," measured by means of the conclusions they afford, that assures significance for the theoretical terms in a theory. In this pragmatic spirit, the thesis of significance might be reformulated as follows:

(IV) A primitive theoretical term M, which occurs in a theory T, is significant if and only if there is in the theory an axiom in which M occurs essentially, and there is a nontheoretical sentence that can be deduced from the axiom together with other axioms of the theory (including correspondence rules), but cannot be deduced from these other axioms alone. Nonprimitive theoretical terms are significant if and only if they are explicitly definable using significant primitive ones.

Proponents of this formulation might argue that it renders the Positivist account perfectly compatible with Principle A. For if an axiom T, which contains only primitive theoretical terms, is connected by means of conjunction to an axiom O, which contains only nontheoretical terms, then, even though O will be a consequence of this enlarged theory, T

will be irrelevant for its derivation. Hence, according to (IV), it will not be possible to show that the terms in T are significant by citing the conjunction $T . O$.

This does not suffice to make (IV) acceptable. Although it does not violate Principle A taken by itself, (IV) is incompatible with the conjunction of A with the following principle, which seems unexceptionable and indeed has been assumed in previous discussion:

PRINCIPLE B: If a sentence (or conjunction of sentences) S is such that the occurrence of a term M in S suffices to guarantee that M is significant, then the occurrence of M in any sentence logically equivalent to S also suffices to guarantee that M is significant. And if S is such that the occurrence of M in S does not suffice to guarantee that M is significant, then the occurrence of M in any sentence logically equivalent to S also does not suffice to guarantee that M is significant.

To show that (IV) is incompatible with Principles A and B, consider once more the sentences "The Absolute is each appearance, and is all, but it is not any one as such" and "The sea is salty," designated T_1 and O_1, respectively. The conjunction of these sentences $T_1 . O_1$ is logically equivalent to the sentence $T_1 . T_1 \supset O_1$. But the latter constitutes in effect a theory whose theoretical postulate is T_1 and whose correspondence rule is $T_1 \supset O_1$. This theory has O_1 as a consequence, and, stated in such a way that T_1 and $T_1 \supset O_1$ are axioms of the theory, T_1 is required in order that O_1 be generated as a consequence. Hence, in accordance with (IV), the theory $T_1 . T_1 \supset O_1$ guarantees significance for the terms in T_1. But since the theory $T_1 . T_1 \supset O_1$ is logically equivalent to $T_1 . O_1$, which according to Principle A fails to guarantee significance for the terms in T_1, it follows from Principle B that the theory $T_1 . T_1 \supset O_1$ also does not suffice to guarantee significance for the terms in T_1. Thus (IV) cannot satisfy A and B together.

Furthermore, (IV) violates B by itself, irrespective of A: according to (IV), in a theory whose axioms are just T and O, where T contains only primitive theoretical terms and O only nontheoretical terms, the terms in T have no significance; whereas in the theory whose axioms are T and $T \supset O$, the terms in T do have significance. Since these theories are logically equivalent, B is violated.

For these reasons, if we wish to incorporate the notion of "cash value" into the thesis of significance, a more felicitous formulation is required. With this in mind let us turn to a proposal of Carnap's.[16]

Although in a number of passages Carnap suggests that the existence of a correspondence rule for a theoretical term suffices to confer significance upon it [that is, thesis (I)], he does wish to propose a more rigorous criterion than this. According to Carnap, a theoretical term M has significance if, roughly speaking, an assumption using M that is added to the theory makes a difference for the prediction of an observable event. His criterion may be expressed as follows:

(V) A theoretical term M, which occurs in a theory T, is significant if and only if the following conditions are satisfied:
   There is a sentence S_M that has M as its only descriptive predicate.
   There is a sentence S_K all of whose descriptive terms are significant.
   The conjunction $S_M . S_K . T . C$ is logically consistent, where C is the set of correspondence rules of the theory.
   There is a sentence S_O, containing only nontheoretical terms, that is logically implied by the conjunction $S_M . S_K . T . C$ but not by the conjunction $S_K . T . C$.

This formulation, however, is not immune to difficulties which beset thesis (IV). Consider any theory T containing only theoretical terms. Let S_M be any sentence which is compatible with, but not deducible from, T, and whose only descriptive predicate is the theoretical term M. Let us add to theory T the correspondence rule $S_M \supset S_O$, where S_O is any nonanalytic statement all of whose descriptive terms are nontheoretical. It follows from Carnap's criterion that M is significant, since the conjunction of S_M with T and the correspondence rule $S_M \supset S_O$ implies the nontheoretical statement S_O, and S_O is not implied by the conjunction of T and the correspondence rule alone. That is, in accordance with thesis (V), the occurrence of M in the sentence $S_M . T . S_M \supset S_O$ guarantees significance for M. Note, however, that $S_M . T . S_M \supset S_O$ is logically equivalent to the conjunction $S_M . T . S_O$. But in accordance with Principle A, since all terms in S_M and T are by hypothesis theoretical, such terms cannot be shown to be significant by citing their occurrence in the conjunction $S_M . T . S_O$; and in particular the theoretical term M cannot be shown to be significant by invoking this conjunction. Since the conjunction $S_M . T . S_O$ is logically equivalent

---

[16] "The Methodological Character of Theoretical Concepts," p. 51.

to $S_M . T . S_M \supset S_0$, it follows from Principle B that the occurrence of M in the latter conjunction also does not suffice to guarantee significance for M; and this violates Carnap's thesis (V).[17]

Moreover, (V) is incompatible with B taken by itself. Consider a theory containing the axioms T and $S_M \supset S_0$, where T contains only theoretical terms, where S_M contains the theoretical term M and is compatible with, but does not follow from, T, and where S_0 is any non-analytic nontheoretical statement whatever. According to (V), by adding the assumption S_M to this theory we show that the term M is significant, since from this assumption, together with the theory, the nontheoretical sentence S_0 follows, whereas it does not follow from the theory by itself. In other words, the occurrence of M in the conjunction $S_M . T . S_M \supset S_0$ suffices to guarantee that M has empirical meaning. Consider now the theory whose axioms are merely T and S_0. According to (V), by adding the assumption S_M to this theory (thus yielding $S_M . T . S_0$) the term M cannot thereby be shown to be significant, since the sentence S_0, the only nontheoretical consequence of this enlarged theory, does not depend for its derivation upon the assumption S_M. Thus, in accordance with (V), the occurrence of M in the conjunction $S_M . T . S_0$ does not suffice to guarantee significance for M. But the conjunctions $S_M . T . S_M \supset S_0$ and $S_M . T . S_0$ are logically equivalent. Therefore, according to Principle B, if the term M can be shown to be significant by citing its occurrence

---

[17] Grover Maxwell ("Criteria of Meaning and of Demarcation," *Mind, Matter, and Method,* ed. P. Feyerabend and G. Maxwell [Minneapolis, 1966], p. 322) has objected that my argument against Carnap is not sound since Carnap requires correspondence rules to be universal postulates, or at least statistical laws; and the correspondence rules of the sort I have invoked are not of this type.

Two points can be made in reply. First, in the paper to which Maxwell refers ("The Methodological Character of Theoretical Concepts") Carnap says (p. 49) that he uses correspondence rules of universal form only as examples. Earlier, in characterizing the notion of a correspondence rule, he says simply that "they connect sentences of L_0 [the observation language] with certain sentences of L_T [the theoretical language]" (p. 47), without indicating anything about whether or not they are universal postulates. And in other writings he defines correspondence rules simply as "*mixed sentences,* i.e., those in which at least one V_0–term and at least one V_T–term occur" (*The Philosophy of Rudolf Carnap,* p. 959). Second, even if Carnap did require correspondence rules to be universal in form, my argument would still be valid: we have only to pick an S_M that begins with an existential quantifier ("there exists some x such that. . . .") or an S_0 that begins with a universal quantifier ("for all x, ..."), and then take what logicians call the "prenex normal form" of $S_M \supset S_0$ (where all quantifiers govern the entire sentence). In the present case we obtain a sentence universal in form, and it will be logically equivalent to $S_M \supset S_0$.

in the first conjunction, it must also be possible to demonstrate its significance by citing its occurrence in the second conjunction—thus violating Carnap's thesis (V).

3. ON THEORY CONSTRUCTION

So far I have considered difficulties in the Positivist account pertaining to the significance of theoretical terms. My second criticism is that this account, together with the concept of a theory it presupposes, renders the task of theory construction trivial.

Suppose we seek to provide a theory which will explain why gases behave in accordance with a set of well-confirmed laws L. These laws are to be construed as expressed by sentences containing only nontheoretical terms. To furnish the desired theory in a completely trivial manner, it suffices to construct any set of sentences T using only theoretical terms and to add $T \supset L$ as a correspondence rule. According to previous criteria, the terms in T have significance within this theory.[18] And since the empirical laws in question follow deductively from the theory, they can be said to be explained by the theory, on the deductive model of explanation usually accepted by contemporary Positivists.[19] This reduces scientific theory construction to a trivial task that can be accomplished by anyone with a modicum of logic.

Hempel has recognized this as a possible objection to the Positivist account, and suggests a reply.[20] First, says Hempel, a theory constructed in the trivial manner indicated would not be a "potentially interesting theory" and hence presumably would not be a serious contender for an explanatory role. This claim is puzzling, for according to the analysis of explanation proposed by Hempel himself, either an *explanans* explains

---

[18] Carnap's thesis (V) is an exception, but the identical effect can be achieved for (V) as follows. Construct the same theory $T \cdot T \supset L$ as above. Construct a sentence S_M that contains M as its only theoretical term and that is compatible with, but does not follow from, T. Add to the theory the postulate $S_M \supset S_o$, where S_o is any true nontheoretical sentence you please that does not follow from the theory. Do this for each theoretical term in T, where S_o may be different in each case. By adding such postulates we are guaranteed that each theoretical term in the theory is significant.

[19] For an account of this model see Carl G. Hempel and Paul Oppenheim, "Studies in the Logic of Explanation," *Philosophy of Science,* 15 (1948), 135–75.

[20] "The Theoretician's Dilemma," p. 84.

an *explanandum* or it does not.[21] In his analysis no reference is made to any notion of how interesting the explanans might be.

Hempel does say that the possibility of constructing theories along the lines indicated reminds us that in addition to having significance a scientific theory must satisfy other requirements as well: its nontheoretical consequences must be well-confirmed, it must meet some criterion of logical simplicity, and it must suggest further laws.

The additional criteria Hempel suggests pose no obstacle to trivial theory construction. First, the requirement that nontheoretical consequences be well-confirmed is automatically satisfied, since the only nontheoretical consequences of the type of theory constructed are the laws to be explained, and these, by hypothesis, are well-confirmed. Second, if we consider some standard criteria of simplicity, such as paucity of assumptions, economy of postulated entities, or lack of complexity in mathematical equations, the task of theory construction remains trivial. To meet such requirements of simplicity it is necessary merely to construct sentences in T that are few in number, or that utilize few theoretical terms, or whose mathematical expressions exhibit simplicity of form. Third, if additional laws must be "suggested" by the theory, in the sense of being implied by it, we have only to append any laws desired to the consequent of the correspondence rule $T \supset L$. By adding laws from various sciences the theory we construct becomes quite powerful in scope, since one set of postulates will then suffice to explain laws in a wide variety of areas. And if we require these additional laws to be ones not already well-confirmed, we can take some other theory T' (satisfying the other criteria), not all of whose consequences have been tested (or drawn), and construct the following grand theory: $T . T \supset T'$. $T \supset L$. This will yield laws not yet tested and will also provide a more comprehensive theory into which to incorporate T'. In short, Hempel's additional requirements in no way preclude the type of trivial theory construction which the Positivist account makes possible.

To meet the present difficulty as well as those concerning the significance of theoretical terms, two proposals might be considered. According to the first, that of N. R. Campbell, although the methods outlined above will yield a theory, it will be a worthless one, since it will lack one essential feature of significant theories—what he calls an "analogy" or "similarity in form" to known laws.[22] Campbell claims, for

---

[21] See footnote 19.

[22] N. R. Campbell, *Physics: The Elements* (Cambridge, England, 1920), pp. 128ff.

example, that one of the reasons why the kinetic theory of gases is a significant one is because its principles are similar in form to mechanical laws governing small elastic bodies. He further notes: "It is never difficult to find a theory which will explain the laws logically. What is difficult is to find one which will expain them logically and at the same time display the requisite analogy." [23]

Campbell's solution is not successful, for using theoretical terms we may construct any set of postulates T we like, making them similar in form to any known laws we wish. By taking as a correspondence rule the sentence $T \supset L$, where L is the set of laws to be explained, theory construction remains as trivial a procedure as before.

The second proposal derives from a suggestion made by F. P. Ramsey in 1929.[24] It is more radical since it involves some fundamental changes in the Positivist account as formulated above. Ramsey showed how any theory containing theoretical terms can be replaced by another theory whose terms are all nontheoretical; and the new theory, though not logically equivalent to the original, will have as consequences the same nontheoretical sentences as the original. To construct this replacement, form a conjunction S of all the sentences in the original theory; take the theoretical terms in S and replace them by variables; then place existential quantifiers at the beginning of this conjunction to govern these variables. The resulting sentence ^RS is called the "Ramsey-sentence for S." ^RS has as theorems all those theorems of S containing nontheoretical terms.

For example, let S be the sentence "Electrons leave tracks in cloud chambers and produce scintillations on a zinc sulfide screen," where "electron" is a theoretical term. The Ramsey-sentence for S is "There is a property such that anything with that property leaves a track in a cloud chamber and produces a scintillation on a zinc sulfide screen"; or symbolically: $(\exists P)(x)(Px \supset . Lx . Sx)$, where L means "leaves a track in a cloud chamber," and S means "produces a scintillation on a zinc sulfide screen."

The suggestion is to replace the original theory by its Ramsey-sentence. Using the Ramsey-sentence for a theory will eliminate all the theoretical terms in favor of variables. Instead of talking about electrons, fields, and so forth, we talk about various properties and relationships unspecified except for their connections with observables. Since new

[23] *Ibid.*, p. 130.

[24] F. P. Ramsey, "Theories," *The Foundations of Mathematics and Other Logical Essays,* ed. R. B. Braithwaite (London, 1931).

variables but not new terms are introduced by the Ramsey-sentence, the question of the significance of terms does not arise. Hence, it might be concluded, the previous difficulty concerning significance, as well as that concerning theory construction (based on criteria of significance), is avoided.

Such is not the case, for this approach can be adopted by anyone regarded as producing nonsignificant discourse, as well as by the theoretical physicist. Thus, if you disapprove of the metaphysician's talk about the Absolute, about the transcendent ego, and so forth, he can simply replace such terms by variables and put existential quantifiers at the beginning of the conjunction of all those sentences constituting his theory. And if observational conclusions are required of his theory, before he replaces it with its Ramsey-sentence he can append to his theoretical postulates, in ways earlier indicated, observational truths that will satisfy this requirement and will have no effect on his metaphysics. In short, the Ramsey-sentence cannot be used to distinguish discourse regarded as nonsignificant from allegedly significant empirical science.

Moreover, contrary to what might be supposed, theory construction remains trivial with the Ramsey-sentence approach. To generate a theory which has laws L as a consequence, simply construct any set of postulates T and conjoin this with $T \supset L$; then, replacing any theoretical terms in T by variables, construct the Ramsey-sentence for the conjunction $T . T \supset L$. The laws L can be deduced from this Ramsey-sentence.

Furthermore, some theories will turn out to have trivially true Ramsey-sentences even though these theories are not themselves trivially true. Consider an example of a theory about magnetism (used in another context by Hempel[25]). It has two principles:

a) The parts obtained by breaking a magnetic rod-shaped object in two are themselves magnetic. In symbols, $(x)(y)(z)[(Bxyz . Mz . Rz) \supset (Mx . My)]$, where $Bxyz$ means "z is broken into x and y," Mz means "z is magnetic," and Rz means "z is rod-shaped."

b) If an object is magnetic, then whenever a small piece of iron filing is brought into contact with it, it clings to it. In symbols, $(x)[Mx \supset (y)(Fxy \supset Cxy)]$, where Mx means "x is magnetic," Fxy means

[25] "Implications of Carnap's Work for the Philosophy of Science," *The Philosophy of Rudolf Carnap*, p. 700.

84

"y is a small piece of iron filing brought into contact with x" and Cxy means "y clings to x."

Suppose we consider "magnetic" to be our theoretical term. The Ramsey-sentence for this theory, that is, the Ramsey-sentence for the conjunction of (a) and (b), can be constructed, and it is equivalent to the following:

c) $(\exists V)(z)([Vz \supset (x)(y)(Bxyz . Rz . \supset . Vx . Vy)][Vz \supset (v)(Fzv \supset Czv)])$

But (c) is trivially true. It asserts the existence of at least one property V satisfying certain conditions that happen to be satisfied by any property that nothing has; and there are many such properties, for example, being a perpetual motion machine or being a solid at ten billion degrees centigrade. The original theory [(a) and (b)] is not trivial in this way. It cannot be established as true by citing the existence of any property that nothing has.[26] In short, the Ramsey-sentence approach not only fails to avoid the previous difficulties of the Positivist account but also introduces a stumbling block of its own.

4. ON PARTIAL AND INDIRECT INTERPRETATION

According to the Positivists, theoretical terms will receive no semantical rules—that is, no rules saying what they mean, designate, or refer to. Nor will they be explicitly defined using terms for which there are semantical rules. Still, various proponents of this account claim that such terms are *partially* as well as *indirectly* interpreted by the correspondence rules. How might those claims be construed? [27]

1) To speak of a term "X" as partially interpreted might be to say that although the term has a meaning, in the sense of a semantical rule

---

[26] For an excellent discussion of Ramsey-sentences see Israel Scheffler, *The Anatomy of Inquiry* (New York, 1963), pp. 203–22. Scheffler (p. 218) also notes the possibility of nontrivial theories having trivially true Ramsey-sentences.

[27] A discussion of what "partial interpretation" might mean as applied to theories, terms, and languages is contained in Hilary Putnam, "What Theories Are Not," *Logic, Methodology, and Philosophy of Science,* ed. E. Nagel, P. Suppes, and A. Tarski (Stanford, 1962). In what follows I am concerned only with *terms,* since it is primarily with respect to these that Positivists introduce the notion of partial interpretation.

or explicit observational definition, only part of that meaning has been given. I might be said to give a partial interpretation for the term "bachelor" (you will know part of its meaning) when I tell you that a bachelor is a man with a certain marital status. However, this sense of partial interpretation would not be consistent with the Positivist account, for it presupposes that the term in question has a meaning (that there is either a semantical rule or explicit observational definition for the term). And for theoretical terms this is denied.

2) To speak of a term "X" as partially interpreted might be to say that there are no observational conditions all of which are logically necessary for X and whose conjunction is logically sufficient, although there are observational conditions that are either logically necessary or else logically sufficient; or at least there are other sorts of analytic statements relating "X" to observational terms. For example, I might introduce a term "X" by saying that being red is logically necessary though not logically sufficient for being X; and I might say that no other conditions are logically sufficient for X. If so, "X" might be called partially interpreted.

This, or some modification of it, is a possible sense of "partial interpretation" for the Positivists. However, in accordance with this sense, semantical rules could be given for theoretical terms, though admittedly rather peculiar ones. For example: "X designates a property for which a logically necessary condition is being red and for which there is no logically sufficient condition." All the descriptive terms in this semantical rule are observational. Moreover, on the present construal, if sentence S partially interprets a term "X," then S expresses an analytic statement. So if correspondence rules partially interpret theoretical terms, they are analytic. This would render the entire theory analytic, since the latter is the conjunction of theoretical postulates T with the correspondence rules C, and this conjunction is itself a correspondence rule. But analyticity for the entire theory, or even for the set of its correspondence rules, is something no Positivist wants to grant.

Some, following Nagel, claim that certain correspondence rules are analytic whereas others are not.[28] For them (2) is a possible sense for "partial interpretation." However, if this is the sense they intend, then they cannot claim, as they do, that the set of correspondence rules provides a partial interpretation for the theoretical terms in them. They shall have to claim that some correspondence rules in this set provide

[28] *Structure of Science,* Chap. 11.

a partial interpretation for the theoretical terms, whereas some do not. Nor can they claim that semantical rules cannot be given for theoretical terms. They shall have to say that a semantical rule of a certain type cannot be given: one that says that "X" designates a property for which a logically necessary and sufficient condition is _____ (where the _____ contains only observational terms). They can then say that any term that has this sort of semantical rule, or can be explicitly defined using terms with this sort of semantical rule, is *completely* interpreted.

Other philosophers, following Carnap, assert that *no* correspondence rules in a theory are analytic.[29] On this view, sense (2) of partial interpretation would be excluded. Still other philosophers, following Hempel,[30] reject the analytic-synthetic distinction altogether for sentences with theoretical terms. For them also (2) is precluded.

3) To speak of a term "X" as partially interpreted might be to say that among the sentences in which "X" appears in the theory there is none of the form "$Xa \equiv$ _____," which means "a is X if and only if _____," where the "_____" contains only interpreted (observational) terms, and where the "if and only if" is not construed as *logical* necessity and sufficiency or as generating any other form of analytic statement. (This seems to be the sense adopted by Carnap and Hempel.) Even if there were such sentences in the theory, "X" would not be interpreted in the sense of being given a semantical rule or what I have called a linguistic description. This sense of partial interpretation is different from giving meanings to terms (a sense assigned to "interpretation" in Carnap's earlier writings on semantics[31]). Accordingly, it would seem much less misleading to avoid talk of partial interpretation. Given this version of the Positivist account we might say instead that a theoretical term "X" is completely uninterpreted even though it is related to interpreted terms by means other than biconditionals of the form "$Xa \equiv$ _____."

Corresponding to the three senses of partial interpretation are three senses of indirect interpretation.

a) I might be said to interpret a term indirectly by providing in-

[29] *The Philosophy of Rudolf Carnap,* p. 965. The only exception for Carnap is the conditional $^RTC \supset TC$ whose antecedent is the Ramsey-sentence of the conjunction of theoretical postulates T and correspondence rules C and whose consequent is simply the conjunction of T and C. But Carnap's proposal leaves all those sentences I am classifying as correspondence rules, that is, C, as nonanalytic.

[30] "Implications of Carnap's Work for the Philosophy of Science," pp. 704ff.

[31] See, for example, *Introduction to Semantics* (Cambridge, Mass., 1942).

direct clues to its meaning. Suppose I say, "Funches are green." Grammatical clues alone suggest that "funch" refers to a type of thing, not to a stuff or property, and the context may suggest that being green is logically necessary for being a funch. This sense of indirect interpretation is not possible for the Positivist, since it assumes that theoretical terms have meanings.

b) I might be said to interpret a term indirectly by providing indirect clues to its partial interpretation, in sense (2) above. But here it is not clear how the correspondence rules, which allegedly provide a partial interpretation for the theoretical terms, provide an *indirect* rather than a *direct* interpretation. Indeed, since they are explicitly stated in the theory, and since (on this view) it is indicated which are analytic and which not, the analytic correspondence rules would seem to provide a direct interpretation for the theoretical terms involved.

c) I might be said to interpret a term indirectly simply by relating it to observational terms via nonanalytic statements of a theory. This seems to be all that most Positivists mean by indirect interpretation. Since this is to be distinguished from indirectly giving meanings (semantical rules, logically necessary and sufficient conditions, or other linguistic descriptions) for terms, it seems much less misleading to avoid talk of indirect interpretation. On this version, let us say instead that theoretical terms are to be construed as uninterpreted—they are not to be directly or indirectly interpreted—although they are related to interpreted terms by means of a theory.

What, then, is the Positivist position on interpretation? Two views are possible. One (perhaps the most likely) is that theoretical terms receive no interpretations (no observational logically necessary and sufficient conditions are given for them, nor are other analytic statements provided that relate them to observables); however, their legitimacy is assured because they are related to terms that do receive such interpretations. The other is that theoretical terms receive only partial interpretations [in sense (2)] by being related via analytic statements to terms that receive complete interpretations. On both views, to interpret a term *completely* is to supply a semantical rule (in a suitable metalanguage) that provides an observational logically necessary and sufficient condition or to define the term explicitly (in the object language of the scientific system) using other terms for which there are such semantical rules.

I now want to ask what arguments might be given in favor of either of these positions on the interpretation of terms. It might be said that one of them, at least, reflects what actually happens in the sciences; that the concept of meaning ("interpretation") in the sciences is such that to provide a meaning for a term is to provide observational logically necessary and sufficient conditions for it either in the object language or in the metalanguage; and that in the sciences some terms have a meaning, whereas others (on one view) have no meaning whatever or (on the other view) have a partial meaning, although (on both views) the latter terms are significant because of relationships they bear to terms with complete meanings. Later in this chapter I shall try to show how the concept of meaning actually employed in the sciences is different from that proposed by this view in either of its versions. But Positivists seem not to be claiming that their concept of meaning is the same as one actually employed in the sciences. Their position should be understood in connection with the doctrine of philosophical *explication* expounded by Carnap.

"By an explication," Carnap writes, "I understand the replacement of a pre-scientific inexact concept (which I call 'explicandum') by an exact concept ('explicatum'), which frequently belongs to the scientific language. . . . Although explications are often given also by scientists, it seems to me particularly characteristic of philosophical work that a great part of it is devoted to proposing and discussing explications of certain basic, general concepts." [32] According to Carnap, many of the concepts philosophers have discussed, for example, meaning, truth, entailment, number, physical object, theory, and probability, are unclear in the following sense: although in most everyday contexts ordinary use of these concepts creates no difficulties, there are certain "critical contexts" in which ordinary usage "involves confusions or even inconsistencies" and leads to unanswerable questions and paradoxes.[33] Accordingly, like tools too inefficient for the job, they must be replaced, just as in science the more or less intuitive and unclear concept of *warmth* is replaced by the exact concept of *temperature*. In philosophy as in science the requirements are that the new concept be more exact than the old one, that it be fruitful, simple, and bear *some* similarity to the old concept, although "close similarity is not required and considerable differences are permitted." [34]

---

[32] *The Philosophy of Rudolf Carnap,* p. 933.

[33] *Ibid.,* p. 935.

[34] *Logical Foundations of Probability,* 2nd ed. (Chicago, 1962), p. 7. For a critical discussion of explication, see my "Rudolf Carnap," *Review of Metaphysics,* 14 (1966), 517–49, 758–79.

What Positivists are doing is constructing a new concept of meaning to replace the one presently employed in the sciences. If we use the present concept, we shall interpret certain terms as designating unobservables. If we employ the new explicated one, we shall treat such terms as completely uninterpreted or else as partially interpreted by reference to observables; in no case shall they be interpreted either in whole or in part as designating unobservables.

If Positivists are proposing a new concept to replace the present one, they must (in accordance with the doctrine of explication) defend their new concept by showing what is wrong with the present concept, how the new concept avoids the difficulties, and in what ways it is more exact and more fruitful.

Concerning the weakness in the present concept, their reasoning seems to be this. If a term is interpreted as referring to what is unobservable, then the concept it expresses is unintelligible or scientifically meaningless. Accordingly, terms that scientists might be tempted to use to refer to unobservables should not be used in this way. They should be treated as uninterpreted terms and hence as not referring to anything, observable or unobservable; or else they should be treated as partially interpreted ones whose interpreted part refers only to observables. This argument depends on two assumptions. One is that items proponents of this view classify as theoretical (electrons, fields, kinetic energy) are unobservable. The other is that if a term is interpreted as referring to something unobservable, it expresses a concept that is unintelligible or scientifically meaningless. Both of these assumptions I regard as dubious. However, an examination of them will be postponed until later.[35]

With respect to advantages of the new concept, the claims are these. The explicated concept of meaning allows us to avoid the problem of unintelligibility that arises when terms are interpreted as referring to unobservables. It allows us to avoid this problem by treating such terms either as uninterpreted and thus as not referring at all, or else as partially interpreted and thus as referring (where they do) only to observables. Moreover, it allows us to distinguish the intelligible terms of science, which purport to refer to unobservables, from the (allegedly) unintelligible terms of speculative metaphysics, which also purport to refer to unobservables. This is done, in effect, by showing that when used in appropriate theories the former, but not the latter, are related in certain

[35] The first will be considered in Chap. Five and the second in sec. 7 of the present chapter.

ways to observational terms. Finally, the new concept allows us to re-construct a scientific theory in a more perspicuous way so that its ob-servational content becomes immediately apparent.

Such claims are unjustified. The alleged problem of meaning is spurious because it is based on the unwarranted assumption—to be ex-amined subsequently—that terms interpreted as referring to unobserva-bles are unintelligible. Nor have proponents of the Positivist account shown that their new concept allows them to distinguish legitimate sci-ence from illegitimate metaphysics. Quite the contrary, since given the explicated concept of meaning and the criterion or criteria they propose, we have seen that almost any term in any theory becomes meaningful. Finally, the explicated concept of meaning does not allow a more ade-quate reconstruction of theories, since it renders the task of theory con-struction a trivial one.

5. A DOCTRINE ABOUT MEANING-DEPENDENCE

The doctrine I will now consider has emerged in recent years as a major alternative to Logical Positivism. Its proponents are influenced by a study of the history of science. They object to the abstractness of the Positivist account, to the intellectual strait jacket they say it im-poses on science by the use of symbolic logic, and to what they regard as its lack of concern with actual scientific procedures. In particular, they emphasize, attention to the history of science will show that the terms employed are "burdened" or "laden" with the scientific theory in which they are used. Accordingly, to understand what such terms mean, one must learn that theory; and the meaning of the terms will change if the theory is modified or replaced by another. To say this is to reject a fundamental assumption of Positivism—namely, that there are, and in-deed must be, terms in a theory (the nontheoretical terms) whose mean-ings can be given independently of the theory and can remain constant from theory to theory. The doctrine I want to consider, then, contains the following theses:

1) The meaning of a term that occurs in a scientific theory is de-pendent upon principles of that theory, so that to know what the term means requires a knowledge of that theory.

2) The meaning of a term that occurs in a scientific theory changes when the theory is modified or replaced by another theory in which that term also occurs.

Many have been willing to defend some form of this view for at least some terms. I shall consider this doctrine in a form held by Feyerabend.[36] In this form the doctrine is supposed to apply to *all* terms utilized in a theory, including all those used for describing observations which support the theory. The meanings of the terms in the theory are supposed to be entirely dependent upon the theory; there are no theory-neutral or partly theory-neutral terms in a theory. Indeed, Feyerabend claims, "the description of every single fact [is] dependent on *some* theory. . . . The meaning of every term we use depends upon the theoretical context in which it occurs. Words do not 'mean' something in isolation; they attain their meanings by being part of a theoretical system." [37] Moreover, when a new theory emerges to replace the old one, the terms involved will change in such a way that there will be an "elimination of the old meanings," and the same term, although employed in both cases, will express two different and "incommensurable" concepts. "Introducing a new theory," Feyerabend writes, "involves changes of outlook both with respect to the observable and with respect to the unobservable features of the world, and corresponding changes in the meanings of even the most 'fundamental' terms of the language employed." [38]

There are, I think, important insights here, but, stated in the manner proposed by Feyerabend, the doctrine has several unacceptable consequences. First, if it were true, no theory could contradict another. Consider the Bohr theory of the atom, which assumes that electrons revolve about the nucleus of an atom in such a way that their orbital angular momentum is quantized (it is a whole multiple of $\frac{h}{2\pi}$, where h is Planck's constant); it also assumes that energy is radiated or absorbed by the atom only when an electron jumps from one stable orbit to another and that this energy is also quantized. When the Bohr theory

[36] P. K. Feyerabend, "Explanation, Reduction, and Empiricism," *Minnesota Studies in the Philosophy of Science,* ed. H. Feigl and G. Maxwell (Minneapolis, 1962), III, 28–97. See also "Problems of Empiricism," *Beyond the Edge of Certainty,* ed. R. G. Colodny (Englewood Cliffs, N.J., 1965), pp. 145–260. Cf. Thomas S. Kuhn, *The Structure of Scientific Revolutions* (Chicago, 1962).

[37] "Problems of Empiricism," pp. 175, 180.

[38] "Explanation, Reduction, and Empiricism," p. 29.

claims that angular momentum and radiant energy of electrons cannot have continuous values but must be quantized, it *denies* the assumption of classical electrodynamics that angular momentum and radiant energy of electrons can have continuous values. Bohr himself writes as follows:

> Now the essential point in Planck's theory of radiation is that the energy radiation from an atomic system does not take place in the continuous way assumed in the ordinary electrodynamics, but that it, on the contrary, takes place in distinctly separated emissions. . . .[39]

All such denials are mere illusions, on the present account, for the terms in the Bohr theory have different meanings from those in classical electrodynamics. They express "incommensurable" concepts. When Bohr asserts that "the energy radiation from an atomic system does not take place in [a] continuous way" and when a classical theorist asserts that "energy radiation from an atomic system takes place in a continuous way," they are using words with different meanings and so cannot be contradicting each other. Nor could other terms from the two theories be used to express their disagreement, since all pairs of terms from different theories express "incommensurable" concepts. This is an absurd consequence.

It eliminates or at least seriously weakens the concept of negation. When does the meaning of the terms used in asserting something become dependent upon what is asserted? Perhaps this is so for any assertion. If I say that an atomic system radiates energy continuously and you say that an atomic system does not radiate energy continuously, then by an atomic system I mean (among other things) something which radiates energy continuously and you mean something else. According to this approach, if I assert *p* and you assert *not-p*, we are not and cannot be disagreeing, because the terms in my assertion are *p-laden* and so mean one thing, whereas those in *not-p* are *not-p-laden* and so mean another. *Not-p*, then, is not the negation of *p*. In short, negation is impossible! On the other hand, if every assertion does not burden its terms with what is asserted, then which ones do and why? The answers are not forthcoming.

Feyerabend does claim that disagreement between two theories can be established without appealing to the meanings of terms and hence without assuming identity in meanings. His proposal, although vaguely

[39] Niels Bohr, "On the Constitution of Atoms and Molecules," *Philosophical Magazine,* 26 (1913), 4.

formulated, seems to be this: two theories are incompatible or in basic disagreement if (and possibly only if) a lack of isomorphism exists between them. Feyerabend seems to be speaking of isomorphism between the elements described by the theory, but he may also have in mind isomorphism with respect to the theoretical sentences themselves; and, he insists, lack of isomorphism can be established without appeal to meanings.[40]

Lack of isomorphism in either case is not a *sufficient* condition for what would normally be regarded as a disagreement between theories. Keynesian theory and quantum theory are lacking in isomorphism with respect to the elements they describe and also with respect to the formal properties of the sentences used in describing them. They are not, however, in disagreement, or agreement either. (They are genuinely incommensurable.) Nor is lack of isomorphism a *necessary* condition for what would normally be regarded as a disagreement between theories. This can be seen in a simple way if we consider the following sets of propositions that, by normal standards, would be considered incompatible:

Theory 1	Theory 2
All planets in our solar system attract each other	All planets in our solar system repel each other
There exist nine planets in our solar system	There exist nine planets in our solar system
No planets that attract each other repel each other	No planets that attract each other repel each other

These sets of propositions, although incompatible, are formally speaking isomorphic, and there is an isomorphism between the postulated elements (the planets and the relationship of attracting and repelling).

In reply to an earlier criticism of mine,[41] Feyerabend claims that in certain cases two theories may disagree and yet have terms with common meanings; but these he seems to regard as trivial and uninteresting cases, for example, classical mechanics and a theory imagined to be just like it except for a slight change in the strength of the gravitational potential.[42] He then explains how differences in meaning can be ascertained.

[40] "Reply to Criticism," *Boston Studies in the Philosophy of Science,* ed. R. Cohen and M. Wartofsky (New York, 1965), II, 232–3.

[41] Peter Achinstein, "On the Meaning of Scientific Terms," *Journal of Philosophy,* 61 (1964), 497–509.

[42] Feyerabend, "On the 'Meaning' of Scientific Terms," *Journal of Philosophy,* 62 (1965), 266–74.

A theory T will provide "rules according to which objects or events are collected into classes. We may say that such rules determine concepts or kinds of objects." [43] If a new theory T' simply produces changes within the extension of these classes, as happens presumably in celestial mechanics when a slight change is made in the strength of the gravitational potential, there is no change in meaning. However, if the new theory "entails that all the concepts of the preceding theory have extension zero or if it introduces rules which cannot be interpreted as attributing specific properties to objects within already existing classes, but which change the system of classes itself," then terms in the two theories have different meanings.[44]

I find this proposal unworkable, for how can the new theory entail that the concepts of the preceding theory have extension zero unless there are terms in the two theories with common meanings? If we rely on the second part of the alternation to ascertain differences in meaning, difficulties also emerge. As Dudley Shapere has pointed out in discussing Feyerabend's present proposal, given the principles of a theory, in general there will be a number of ways we might collect the items described by these principles into classes, depending on our purposes.[45] If we make our class-descriptions sufficiently general (for example, "physical processes," "physical objects"), then any two theories, no matter how much in disagreement, will involve the same "system of classes" and will simply be attributing different "specific properties to objects within already existing classes." If we make our class-descriptions sufficiently specific, then two theories that disagree, even in trivial ways, would involve different systems of classes. For example, celestial mechanics and a theory indistinguishable from it, except for a difference in the strength of the gravitational potential, can be construed as generating different classes (different "kinds of objects"): the former postulates a class of bodies subject to one force law; the latter, a class of bodies subject to a different one. In short, Feyerabend's present suggestion does not yield the sort of method he desires for determining meaning-changes; nor does it even allow him to distinguish trivial cases where meanings are constant from interesting ones where they are not.

The second unacceptable consequence of Feyerabend's general doc-

[43] *Ibid.*, p. 268.
[44] *Ibid.*
[45] Dudley Shapere, "Meaning and Scientific Change," *Mind and Cosmos,* ed. R. Colodny (Pittsburgh, 1966), pp. 41–85.

trine is related to the first and can be stated briefly. Not only is any disagreement impossible for proponents of two different theories but, for the same reason, so is any agreement. It will be impossible for theorists to agree even on a description of the data to be explained by their respective theories, for in such a description all the terms employed will depend for their meanings upon the given theory. But if there can be no agreement and no disagreement either, in what sense can two different theories be about the same thing? In what sense can two different theories be (as Feyerabend calls them) *alternatives*?

There is a third untoward consequence of this doctrine. When it is claimed that the meaning of a term in a theory depends entirely on principles of that theory, the suggestion is that these principles in effect say what the term means. If so, then such principles would always be construable as analytic, that is, as defensible solely by appeal to the meanings of their constituent terms. The claim of the Bohr theory that the electron's angular momentum is quantized could be defended by appeal solely to the fact that "electron" and "angular momentum" mean just those sorts of things such that the angular momentum of the electron is quantized.

To this it might be replied that although most of the principles of the theory will turn out to be analytic its existence claims will not. For example, the claim that there exist atoms satisfying the principles of the Bohr theory will be empirical. On this construal, the postulates of the theory are analytic, and the question whether anything satisfies these postulates is empirical.

One might object to this extreme manner of reconstructing a theory so that many sentences one would normally take to be expressing only empirical propositions, sentences scientists treat as such, now express statements defensible simply by appeal to the meanings of their terms. But there is a more serious problem. If all terms employed by the theory are theory-laden, including the terms employed in describing observations made in connection with the theory, then a description of any such observations will presuppose the theory. No observed item could be described as failing to satisfy the postulates of the theory. Nor could any other theory T' be used to show that items exist that do not satisfy the theory T; since the concepts of any such T' are incommensurable with those of T, T' cannot be used to show that items exist which satisfy the negation of T. This would make the existence claims of a theory irrefutable by any observations that could be described or by other theories based on such observations. In what sense, then, could such claims be called empirical? Even independently of language, observations could not be made that would refute existence claims of a theory, since, for Feyerabend, observations themselves must always presuppose a theory; they are theory-dependent. If they are made presupposing T, then T could not be refuted; nor could it be refuted if T' were presupposed, since T' and T cannot be conflicting theories.

The fourth consequence I find unacceptable is that if the doctrine were true, a person could not learn a theory by having it explained to him using any words whose meanings he understands before he learns the theory. Consider the terms "electron," "electron orbit," "angular momentum," and "radiant energy," which appear in the Bohr theory. According to thesis 1 (page 91), in order to know what these terms mean, I must know what the Bohr theory asserts. One of the central principles in this theory can be expressed like this:

> Of all the electron orbits only those orbits are permissible for which the angular momentum of the electron is a whole multiple of h/2π, and there is no radiant energy while the electron remains in any one of these permissible orbits.

But how can I know what is asserted here unless I know what the terms "electron," "electron orbit," "angular momentum," and "radiant energy" mean? It is useless to appeal to what they mean *in other theories;* for, on this doctrine, what they mean in two theories is different and "incommensurable." Nor can I explain what they mean by using words whose meanings are independent of any theory, since there are supposed to be no theory-neutral terms. Therefore, I cannot use any words whose meanings I understand in order to learn the meanings of the terms in the theory. The only thing I can do is try to learn the meanings *extralinguistically*. I must watch what those who use the theory do in their laboratories, the sorts of items to which they apply their terms, and so forth. I must learn each new theory like a child first learning language (rather than like someone learning more of his own language or a second language after learning a first one). Perhaps it would be possible (though, I suspect, exceedingly difficult) to learn scientific theories this way. What I find unacceptable is the consequence that they *must* be learned this way. In actual practice at least some if not most terms in a new theory are explained to those learning the theory by using words whose meanings the learners already know. Those who learn the Bohr theory do not do so only by observing the behavior of those who already know it and the phenomena such people may point out.

6. CRITERIA FOR MEANING-DEPENDENCE AND FOR CHANGE IN MEANING

The four consequences I have noted all stem from the same source, dubious assumptions about *meaning*. Feyerabend fails to propose any theory of meaning, or at least any adequate one, that will support his claim that the meaning of a term in a theory depends upon principles of that theory and will change when the theory is altered or replaced. He does, of course, cite examples in propounding this thesis.[46] Some of these are convincing on intuitive grounds, but others are not. Still further examples that could be cited seem, intuitively, to violate this thesis.

On intuitive grounds, at least, it seems absurd to claim that one cannot understand what meaning is associated with terms such as "angular momentum," "radiant energy," and "electron" unless one knows the Bohr theory, since all these terms were in use prior to this theory and Bohr simply appropriated them for his theory. On intuitive grounds, it also seems absurd to say that the terms "angular momentum" and "radiant energy" suffered a complete change in meaning when Bohr postulated that the quantities they designate cannot have continuous values but must be quantized. I shall say something about these intuitive grounds and afterward show how the position developed in the chapters on definition can be used to explain and defend these intuitions.

One set of considerations relevant for deciding whether a term means the same in two theories and also whether its meaning depends upon a theory are "behavioral." Suppose a term used in a well-known theory T comes to be used also in a different theory T'. And suppose T' is presented in such a way that an explanation of the semantical aspect of the use of this term is not given, nor are contexts supplied that would indicate very much if anything about this. Do those studying such a presentation of T', knowing the theory T, request an explanation for the meaning of this term, and if not, do they seem to misunderstand what T' is supposed to assert? Are there the usual signs of a lack of communica-

[46] See "Explanation, Reduction, and Empiricism," and "On the 'Meaning' of Scientific Terms."

tion and understanding when explanations or appropriate contexts are not supplied? If not, this provides at least some ground for saying that the meaning of the term can be understood without learning T' and that it means the same in both theories.

These considerations lend weight to the claim that the meaning of a term such as "angular momentum" could be learned independently of the Bohr theory and is the same in that theory as in classical mechanics. Bohr, who used this term, felt no need to define or redefine it or to present contexts that would make the semantical aspect of its use apparent; nor do texts on atomic physics, which propound and explain this theory for students already acquainted with classical mechanics.

Another consideration concerns the manner in which claims involving the term are held to be settleable. Suppose that one theory appears to be asserting, and another to be denying, that X's have P. If the terms "X" and "P" have the same meaning in each theory, then there should be facts that are or could be relevant in settling whether X's do have P, as "X" and "P" are used in each theory. If proponents of these two theories cannot agree in principle on how to settle, or on what might be relevant for settling, whether X's have P, this suggests that they are using the term "X" or the term "P" (or both) in different ways.

There are a number of facts that were taken to provide at least some support for the Bohr theory against that of classical electrodynamics. One is that spectra of the elements are not continuous but discontinuous: if, for example, an element (such as hydrogen) is suitably excited by having a current passed through it, it gives off light which, when analyzed with a spectroscope, is found to consist of a series of discrete lines of certain wavelengths. The fact that Bohr could deduce from this theory the exact wavelengths of these lines, whereas classical electrodynamics could not even explain their existence, was taken as some support for Bohr's assumptions regarding angular momentum and radiant energy against those of the classical theory. Another fact concerns resonance potential experiments. Through a tube containing hydrogen at low pressure a current is passed from a filament to a plate. As the voltage is increased, the current is increased to a certain point after which it drops off (where this is repeated for higher voltages). The drop in current is taken as indicating that the energy of electrons is just the right amount (the "quantum" or multiple of it) to raise the hydrogen atoms from a normal state to an excited state. This was also claimed to provide some support for Bohr's assumption (against that of classical theory) regarding quantization of energy within the atom.[47]

A third consideration for deciding whether a term means the same in two theories and whether its meaning depends on a certain theory is suggested by Putnam.[48] Suppose I know or am told how the term "X" is now used in a set of circumstances C (or in connection with a set of assumptions C). That is, suppose I know the sorts of items, actual and hypothetical, to which the term is applicable and also in virtue of what it is applicable. If, from this knowledge alone, it is possible for me to predict how the term "X" would be used in circumstances C' (or in connection with a different set of assumptions C'), this counts against speaking of a different meaning in these circumstances. To the degree that its use in circumstances C' is unpredictable from its use in present circumstances C, we can speak of a different meaning. For example, if in the future our scientific theories remain the same but the term "solid" comes to be used in such a way that items in gaseous form, and only these, are regarded as standard examples of solids, this would be a radically different meaning, since this use of "solid" would be wholly unpredictable on the basis of the present one. Furthermore, if, on the basis of the present use of "X" in principles constituting a theory T (that is, if knowing the sorts of items to which it is applicable and in virtue of what it is applicable), I could predict how it would be used in principles constituting a theory T', then this provides some grounds for saying that the meaning of the term "X" can be known independently of T'. Of course to know *that* "X" is being used in the same way in T' and T, I may have to learn T'. But it does not follow that to know *what* "X" means, I will have to learn T' (or T for that matter).

These considerations also suggest that the meanings of certain terms in the Bohr theory are the same as in classical electrodynamics and can be learned independently of the Bohr theory. We begin with the term "angular momentum" used in a theory that assumed that all atomic states are subject to principles of classical mechanics and that angular momentum in the case of electrons can have continuous values. From this it was certainly predictable how the term would be used (that is, how it would be defined, how its values could be determined) in a theory asserting that only stationary states of the atom are subject to principles of classical mechanics and that the angular momentum of electrons

---

[47] Other confirmation for Bohr's theory will be discussed in Chap. Four.
[48] "Dreaming and 'Depth Grammar,'" p. 223.

can have only discrete values proportional to $\dfrac{h}{2\pi}$ One could reasonably have supposed, for example, that the angular momentum of the electron in the latter case (assuming a circular orbit of radius r) would be given by the expression mvr, where m is its mass and v its velocity.

All three considerations mentioned allow for the possibility that terms in two theories can have the same meaning and that the meaning of a term used in a theory can be known without knowing the theory. Now I want to defend this by appeal to the position developed in the chapters on definition. According to this position, some properties attributed to an item X (or some conditions satisfied by X) are logically necessary or sufficient for X; others may be relevant. Among the latter I distinguished the semantically relevant from the nonsemantically relevant, while recognizing that some are not happily classifiable in either way. Properties semantically relevant for X (which include those that are logically necessary or sufficient) have a particularly intimate connection with the meaning of the term "X" (with the semantical aspect of use) as other properties do not.

Consider a term "X" and the properties or conditions semantically relevant for X. It is perfectly possible that there be two different theories in which the term "X" is used, where the same set of semantically relevant properties of X (or conditions for X) are presupposed in each theory (even though other properties attributed to X by these theories, properties not semantically relevant for X, might be different). If so, the term "X" would not mean something different in each theory.

Suppose $P_1, \ldots, P_n$ represent all the semantically relevant properties of X. Suppose that T is a theory that says that X's have $Q_1, \ldots, Q_m$, where each of these is semantically independent of (has no semantical relevance for) $P_1, \ldots, P_n$. Suppose that T' is a theory that says that X's have $Q'_1, \ldots, Q'_m$, where each of these is semantically independent of each of $P_1, \ldots, P_n$, but where some or all of the Q''s are logically incompatible with the corresponding Q's. If so, theories T and T' would be incompatible. But if $P_1, \ldots, P_n$ represent all the semantically relevant properties of X, as "X" is used in both theories, then "X" would mean the same in T' as in T, and its meaning could be learned independently of T' (and of T). There is no a priori reason why this cannot happen. Although this is an oversimplified schematization, I would claim that the semantically relevant properties of certain items designated by terms in theories can be known without learning those theories and are the same in other theories in which the terms appear.

This is so for "position" and "time" in the Bohr theory and in classical mechanics. Both theories use the same set of spatial and temporal concepts. Whatever conditions are semantically relevant for a particle having a position at a given time are the same for the Bohr theory as for classical mechanics. And the definitions of the terms "velocity" as "time rate of change of position" and "acceleration" as "time rate of change of velocity" provide logically necessary and sufficient conditions each of which is exactly the same in the two theories. Indeed, if the concepts I mention were not the same in both theories, Bohr could not have used principles of classical mechanics with these concepts in order to derive his expression for the total energy of the electron in the hydrogen atom. One of the things Bohr did was use Newton's second law of motion, $F = ma = \dfrac{mv^2}{r}$, where F is the force of attraction on the electron by the nucleus, a is its centripetal acceleration, and v its velocity.[49] From this, together with Coulomb's law of attraction, the kinetic energy formula in classical mechanics, and Bohr's assumptions regarding quantization of angular momentum and energy, it was possible to arrive at a formula relating the total energy of the electron to its mass, charge, the number of its orbit, and Planck's constant.

Not only can two theories use a term with the same set of semantically relevant properties or conditions, but, as with terms such as "velocity," "acceleration," and "angular momentum" in the Bohr theory, it is also possible for one to learn what these properties or conditions are without learning the theory. In short, some terms employed by a theory T will be such that none of the semantically relevant properties attributed to the items they designate will be attributed to them by theory T itself or only by T (but perhaps by other theories or even independently of any theory). Moreover, some terms may be employed in two theories in such a way that the set of semantically relevant properties associated with items they designate are the same in each theory. In the first case, it is proper to speak of learning what the term means (learning the semantical aspect of its use) independently of the theory in question; in the second, it is proper to speak of the term as meaning the same in both theories (in both theories the semantical aspect of use is the same). It is proper to speak in these ways even though a knowledge of X's prop-

[49] Niels Bohr, "On the Constitution of Atoms and Molecules," p. 478.

erties that are not semantically relevant may require learning a theory or theories, and even though two theories may attribute to X different (and even conflicting) properties that are not semantically relevant.

Let me relate this to the three intuitive considerations governing meaning-dependence and meaning-change noted earlier. These concerned behavior, settleability, and predictability. The reason why such considerations are relevant can be understood on the basis of the view I have been expounding. It is because of knowledge (or lack of it) of semantically relevant properties of X that those who learn the new theory exhibit none (or all or some) of the "behavioral" symptoms of understanding when meeting the term in a new theory. Moreover, if proponents of two theories cannot agree in principle on how to settle, or on what might be relevant in settling, whether X's have P, this suggests that they disagree on that in virtue of which something is classifiable as X, P, or both. In short, this suggests that they cannot agree on the semantically relevant properties of X, the semantically relevant conditions for P, or both. This is why lack of agreement on what might settle whether X is P is relevant to the question of whether the terms mean the same for both parties. Finally, one's prediction about the use of a term in a new context on the basis of its use in the present one derives from a knowledge of what properties or conditions are semantically relevant in the latter and whether the same or similar ones are apt to be semantically relevant in the new context as well.

I have argued that it is possible for there to be terms in a theory whose meanings can be learned without learning the theory and can be the same as those of terms in a different theory. But two other sorts of cases should be noted. There may be terms in a theory T that designate items some of whose semantically relevant properties will be attributed to them by T and only by T, whereas others will be attributed to them independently of T, perhaps by some theory T'. For such terms, neither of Feyerabend's labels "meaning-dependent (upon T)" or "meaning-independent (of T)" may be appropriate (where these are construed in his sense, requiring complete dependence or independence). It may be best to avoid these oversimplified classifications and indicate that certain semantical aspects of the use of these terms depend upon T, whereas others do not. Similarly, there may be terms used in two theories T and T' in such a way that although some of the semantically relevant properties attributed to the items they designate are the same in each theory, others are not. For such items, neither the label "same meaning" nor "different meaning" may be appropriate (where, again, these are understood as requiring complete sameness or difference).

The second type of case to be noted does fit Feyerabend's account: some terms utilized by a theory will be such that all or most of the properties or conditions semantically relevant for X will be attributed to X by that particular theory and only by that theory. Even though the same term may be used in another theory, the properties semantically relevant for X will be substantially different in each theory. Consider the term "entropy" in classical thermodynamics. Many if not most of the conditions satisfied by entropy and likely to be treated as semantically relevant would be conditions specified by, or consequences of, the principles of classical thermodynamics; for example, that the entropy of an isolated system increases in any process or remains constant in equilibrium, that entropy measures the loss of available energy, and so forth. Now statistical mechanics, which also uses the term "entropy," goes beyond the assumptions of classical thermodynamics by introducing postulates concerning the molecular microstructure of a thermodynamic system. A complete specification of the position and velocity (within certain limits) of each particular molecule defines a *microstate* of the system; and the specification of the number of molecules with each given set of dynamical properties defines a *macrostate*. According to the Boltzmann postulate, the entropy of a thermodynamic system (as defined in classical thermodynamics) is proportional to the logarithm of the number of microstates belonging to the given macrostate of the system. This postulate is expressed symbolically by $S = k \log W$. One way to construe this (adopted by Boltzmann) is to take S as classical entropy. If so, then statistical mechanics attributes certain new properties to entropy, while retaining many others from classical thermodynamics. However, another procedure (discussed by Fowler) is to treat $S = k \log W$ as providing a logically necessary and sufficient condition for entropy.[50] If this is adopted, then, I think, a "different meaning" label would be warranted, since the present condition is not logically necessary, logically sufficient, or otherwise semantically relevant for classical entropy.

Therefore, cases exist in which Feyerabend's labels "meaning-dependent (upon T)" and "different meaning (in T and T')" are appropriate. The merit of his position lies in reminding us that there are such cases, that terms *can* depend completely for their meanings upon a theory and suffer extensive meaning changes when theories are modified or

[50] R. H. Fowler, *Statistical Mechanics* (Cambridge, England, 1929).

replaced. However, there are also cases in which the labels "meaning-independent (of T)" and "same meaning (in T and T')" are warranted, and some where none of these labels fits. The view under discussion fails to recognize the latter sorts of cases. It fails in this because it treats *all* properties attributed to X by a theory as if they were semantically relevant for X.

The view also assumes that any term used by the proponent of a theory to describe *observations* made in connection with that theory will be a term whose semantically relevant conditions are supplied by the theory. In short, it assumes that any such term will depend completely for its meaning upon that theory. This position lies at the opposite pole from the Positivist view discussed earlier. According to the latter, to describe what is observed, a special "observational" vocabulary is required whose terms in no way depend upon a theory and, indeed, can be common to all theories. The position that should be taken, I suggest, lies somewhere between these extremes. To anticipate discussion in Chapter Five, there are numerous ways to describe one and the same set of observations. Some may employ terms that appear in the fundamental principles of a theory, others may not; but even if terms of the former sort are used, it does not necessarily follow that they will be entirely or even partially dependent upon the theory for their meaning.

In the previous section I noted four unacceptable consequences of Feyerabend's view. These were that if it were true, no theory could contradict another; any agreement between theories would be impossible; theories would be analytic; and it would be necessary to learn a theory completely extralinguistically. The position I have defended avoids these consequences. It is possible for two different theories to contradict each other since it is possible for them to be using terms with common meanings. For the same reason, some agreement between theories is possible, for example, agreement on at least some description of the data to be explained. Moreover, since not all properties attributed to X by a theory need be semantically relevant for X, it is not necessary that the principles of the theory be analytic. Finally, it is possible for a person to learn a theory by having it explained to him in words he understands before he learns the theory. For, at least in the case of some terms, since many, and perhaps all, of the semantically relevant properties of the items they designate may be attributed to them independently of the theory, it is possible to learn much about the semantical aspect of their use without presupposing the theory.

7. ON THE ACTUAL INTRODUCTION
AND INTERPRETATION OF TERMS

Earlier I considered a contemporary Positivist account which proposes a method of introducing and interpreting terms in science. This account assumes that terms interpreted as referring to unobservables are unintelligible, an assumption I claimed to be dubious. I also claimed that the Positivist account does not reflect how terms are actually introduced and interpreted in science. These claims remain to be justified. I shall do so in a series of points concerning the actual introduction and interpretation of terms.

1) Terms introduced into science are interpreted. By this I mean that linguistic descriptions can be given for them that will provide information about the semantical aspect of their use. Such descriptions can be given with varying degrees of complexity and completeness. A rather full one would not only indicate properties that are semantically relevant (including logically necessary or sufficient ones) but would also note differences in centrality, as well as whether there are unknown properties in some semantically relevant category (for example, some "inner structure" [51]). Less complete linguistic descriptions, such as D_1 and D_2 of Chapter Two (sections 5, 7), will not list every semantically relevant property or indicate differences in centrality, though this may be ascertainable by careful reflection on the use of the term. When a scientist first introduces a term he may not actually give a linguistic description, even a partial one. My claim is only that by careful attention to how he uses the term and also to what if anything he says about how he uses or proposes to use the term, linguistic descriptions can be formulated. This is not to say that all terms introduced into science have definite and precise uses. Some indefiniteness and imprecision can be reflected in linguistic descriptions themselves; for example, they may speak of items having many or most of a certain set of properties. And, of course, a scientist's use of a term may be so indefinite as to preclude any linguistic description. But, to the extent that it is definite, such descriptions can be formulated.

According to the Positivist, to interpret a term completely one must provide a set of observational conditions each of which is logically necessary and the conjunction of which is logically sufficient; this can be expressed either as a semantical rule in the metalanguage or

[51] Chap. One, sec. 6.

as an explicit definition in the object language. On one version of this view terms are interpreted completely (by being assigned logically necessary and sufficient conditions) or not at all. On the other version, certain terms may be *partially* interpreted by analytic correspondence rules. On both versions, terms which purport to designate observables are completely interpreted.[52]

I am suggesting that terms, as actually employed in science, need satisfy none of these requirements. To interpret a term completely, that is, to say what it means, one need not provide a set of logically necessary and sufficient conditions, for as the term is actually used, or to be used, there may be no such set. Depending upon the term, it may suffice to indicate which properties are semantically relevant and especially central, even though no one of them is logically necessary and even though the conjunction of those cited is not logically sufficient. Accordingly, one need not accept as exhaustive the following alternatives (suggested by one version): provide logically necessary and sufficient conditions or say nothing about meaning. Nor need one accept as exhaustive these alternatives (suggested by the other version): provide logically necessary and sufficient conditions, or indicate that certain correspondence rules containing the term are analytic, or say nothing about meaning. To cite properties semantically relevant for X without being logically necessary or sufficient and to indicate differences in centrality is to do none of these things. Yet it is to say what meaning the term has; it is to give the semantical aspect of its use.

2) There is no single way terms are *introduced* into science. This will depend upon the term and the particular context of introduction (for whom it is being introduced, the desired depth of explanation, and so forth). Sometimes a term will be introduced simply by being used in a sentence that, together with others, will suggest semantical aspects of its use. For example, Gilbert in his work *De Magnete* (1600) introduced the term "electrics" in the following passage:

> For it is not only amber and jet that attract small bodies when rubbed. The same is true of diamond, sapphire, carbuncle, iris gem. . . . Feeble power of attraction is also possessed under a suitable dry sky by rock salt, mica, rock alum. This one may observe when in midwinter the atmosphere is sharp and clear and rare—when the

[52] See sec. 4.

emanations from the earth hinder *electrics* less, and the electric bodies are harder. . . .[53]

Gilbert does not explicitly propose a definition for "electric," but this passage, together with others, suggests that he is treating the property "capable of attracting small bodies when rubbed" as semantically relevant (perhaps even logically necessary) for being an electric. In short, from observing how he uses the term in his writings, although he does not explicitly formulate a linguistic description, one can begin to construct at least part of such a description.

The introduction of a term may be somewhat more explicit. James Clerk Maxwell introduces several basic electrical concepts as follows:

> Let a piece of glass and a piece of resin, neither of which exhibits any electrical properties, be rubbed together and left with the rubbed surfaces in contact. They will still exhibit no electrical properties. Let them be separated. They will now attract each other.
>
> If a second piece of glass be rubbed with a second piece of resin, and if the pieces be then separated and suspended in the neighborhood of the former pieces of glass and resin, it may be observed—
>
> (1) That the two pieces of glass repel each other.
> (2) That each piece of glass attracts each piece of resin.
> (3) That the two pieces of resin repel each other.
>
> These phenomena of attraction and repulsion are called Electrical phenomena, and the bodies which exhibit them are said to be *electrified,* or to be *charged with electricity.*[54]

Here the expressions "are called" and "are said to be" suggest that the properties or conditions cited are semantically relevant for the phenomena or states designated by the terms "Electrical phenomena," "electrified," and "charged with electricity."

On other occasions the manner of introduction may be quite formal. Maxwell introduces the term "electric volume-density" in this way:

> *Definition.* The electric volume-density at a given point in space is the limiting ratio of the quantity of electricity within a sphere whose centre

---

[53] Quoted by Duane Roller and Duane H. D. Roller in "The Development of the Concept of Electric Charge," *Harvard Case Histories in Experimental Science,* ed. J. B. Conant (Cambridge, Mass., 1957), II, 548.

[54] *A Treatise on Electricity and Magnetism* (New York, 1954), I, 32.

is the given point to the volume of the sphere, when its radius is diminished without limit.[55]

Here he is proposing conditions that are logically necessary and sufficient for the quantity *electric volume-density*.

The passages in which a scientist introduces a term may, of course, be misleading. It may seem as if he is citing semantically relevant conditions or properties when he is not. One must consider, therefore, not only those few sentences that introduce the term but also the remainder of what he has to say, that is, how he uses the term in other contexts. By attending to this we can say something about which properties or conditions are semantically relevant and which are more central than others. The scientist himself may formulate what amounts to a dictionary entry, but even if he does not, this does not prevent the lexicographer from doing so. Nor does this prevent one concerned with a finer sort of analysis from attempting a more complex linguistic description.

My position, like the Positivist account, is a reconstruction of the scientist's procedures. It does not advocate that we simply describe what the scientist says about definitions and meaning. For this may be precious little, and even then, misleading. In providing linguistic descriptions one will often need to dig beneath the surface of what the scientist says. The difference between my view and the Positivists' is not over whether linguistic procedure in the sciences should be reconstructed. The difference arises from the fact that such a reconstruction, in my view, should reflect actual linguistic procedures, even if these are only implicit in what the scientist says and does. The Positivist maintains that such procedures, whether explicit or implicit, should be replaced by different ones.

3) Is there a standard sort of interpretation for terms? According to the Positivist, all interpretation is observational. For example, Carnap writes, "All the interpretation (in the strict sense of this term, i.e., observational interpretation) that can be given for L_T [the theoretical language] is given in the C-rules [correspondence rules]." [56] The only way to interpret a term (in Carnap's "strict sense") is by relating it to what can be observed.[57] Thus, if one were to ask nineteenth cen-

[55] *Ibid.*, p. 72.

[56] "The Methodological Character of Theoretical Concepts," p. 46.

[57] This could be construed as interpretation in either sense (2) or (3), pp. 86–87; Carnap would probably opt for (3).

tury physicists to interpret the term "molecule," all they could do, strictly speaking, is say that if this term (or rather the expression "contains molecules") is predicated of gases, and if various formulas containing this term are assumed, we can infer, among other things, that if the pressure of a gas is increased, keeping its volume constant, its temperature increases. Similarly, if one were to ask eighteenth century physicists to interpret the term "electricity," all they could do, strictly speaking, is say that if this term is attributed to items (that is, if we can say "these items are charged with electricity"), then we can infer, among other things, that they are capable of attracting light materials.

Certainly, information about what can be observed regarding pressure, volume, and temperature of gases may be relevant for being a gas molecule; just as information about the observable attraction of light materials may be relevant for being charged with electricity. However, in interpreting the terms "molecule" (or "gas molecule") and "electricity," there is much else one can do, and that physicists did. Here is what Maxwell had to say when he explained the concept of a molecule:

> A molecule of a substance is a small body such that if, on the one hand, a number of similar molecules were assembled together they would form a mass of that substance, while on the other hand, if any portion of this molecule were removed it would no longer be able, along with an assemblage of other molecules similarly treated, to make up a mass of the original substance. . . . The old atomic theory, as described by Lucretius and revived in modern times, asserts that the molecules of all bodies are in motion, even when the body itself appears to be at rest. . . . In liquids and gases . . . the molecules are not confined within any definite limits, but work their way through the whole mass, even when that mass is not disturbed by a visible motion. . . . These flying molecules must beat against whatever is placed among them, and the constant succession of these strokes is, according to our theory, the sole cause of what is called the pressure of air and other gases.[58]

Similarly, two historians of science have this to say about the use of the term "electricity" by certain eighteenth century physicists:

[58] *The Scientific Papers of James Clerk Maxwell*, ed. W. D. Niven (New York, 1965), II, 363ff.

Although Gray always wrote of transfer of the electric virtue, the mechanistically minded scientists of the 18th century were prone to consider the transfer of a *property* from one object to a second as being due to the transfer of a *substance*. Thus a bucket that gets heavier presumably has had something weighty put in it; an object that gets hotter has had heat added to it; and, by analogy, an object becomes electrified because some *electricity* is added to it. Thus soon after Gray's work the term "electricity" rather quickly comes to have the meaning of a substance within—or perhaps on the surface of—an electrified object. This substance is invisible, but postulation of its existence offers a reasonable explanation of electrification by contact: an object electrified by rubbing contains this invisible electricity, and when it touches an unelectrified object some of the electricity is transferred. The ease of transfer from one object, directly or through a string or other intermediary, to a second led to the view that this easily flowing electricity was a *fluid*, and it was often called the "electric fluid." [59]

As these passages indicate, in providing interpretations for the terms "molecule" and "electricity," eighteenth and nineteenth century physicists did more than simply note observations that could be made when these terms were used in theories. Maxwell indicated that molecules are small bodies, that they make up the mass of a substance, that in a gas they are in rapid motion and strike the walls of the container. Electricity was spoken of as a fluid within a substance or on its surface, as something that could flow from one substance to another. In short, molecules and electricity were characterized by invoking concepts already available and understood, such as that of a body in motion, a fluid, velocity, mass, and so forth. The only difference between the bodies and fluids postulated and the bodies and fluids more familiar to laymen is that the former could not be seen by those postulating them. It is this difference that impresses Positivists and leads them to the view that terms (such as "motion," "velocity," "mass") when applied to items not visible cannot mean what they do when used to refer to visible ones. This claim I shall discuss next. The point I have so far been trying to make is that in actual practice when introducing a new term, such as "molecule" or "electricity," that purports to refer to something unobservable, a scientist will not interpret it simply by relating it to what can be observed. He will characterize the item it

[59] Roller and Roller, "The Development of the Concept of Electric Charge," p. 589.

refers to using concepts he thinks can readily be understood, even though in his characterization he may refer to objects and properties he cannot observe.

4) I turn now to the claim that when terms normally used to refer to observable items are applied to ones held not to be observable they cannot mean the same. (The Positivist viewpoint is even stronger, for it holds that in the latter case the terms cannot be said to mean anything or can only have partial meanings.) Actually, those defending this position might want to argue as follows: when terms normally used for observables are applied to something claimed to be unobservable, either the terms are not being used in the same way (with the old meanings) or else what is said must be treated as one would a fairy tale for which the questions of truth and possible verification do not arise.

Even this thesis needs reformulation. I am not using the word "tomato" in a new way, nor am I telling a fairy tale, when I claim that the tomato in the box is not observable (because the box is closed). When terms normally used to refer to what is observable are applied to something unobservable there may be very good reasons why it is not observable: the view is obstructed by an opaque object, it is too far away, moving too fast, difficult to distinguish from its background, too small to be seen with the naked eye, and so forth. If conditions that (we claim) prevent the item from being observable are themselves not incompatible with the item's having properties attributed to it, there need be no reason to claim either that the words used in describing the item cannot mean what they do when observable objects are described or that the description is to be taken in the spirit of a fairy tale.

All this Positivists may grant. They may point out that they are speaking not of items unobservable in some contexts (or by some means) but observable in others (by other means). Some may want to say that they are speaking of items not *now* observable because of limited knowledge and limited methods of observation, though possibly someday they will be observed. Others may want to say that they are speaking of items claimed not to be observable *in principle*. By this they mean items that, according to some accepted theory, can never be observed (with or without instruments, no matter how complete our knowledge becomes).

For at least some items classified as unobservable (for example, molecules) there is no theory implying they cannot be observed; nor was there any such theory when they were postulated. Indeed, scientists postulating them may have believed that such items would someday be observed. Moreover, explanations were offered as to why they were not then observable; and what was claimed was in no way inconsistent with supposing that these items have certain properties normally attributed to observable objects. Maxwell, for example, spoke of the minimum visibility with microscopes of his day (1/4000 mm) and pointed out that a cube with sides of this length would contain from 60 to 100 million molecules of oxygen or nitrogen.[60] There is nothing here regarding, say, size of molecules or visibility with microscopes that would be incompatible with molecules having the mechanical properties attributed to them by the kinetic theory. Also, as I shall argue in Chapter Five, many of the items called theoretical by Positivists can be said to be observable, depending on the context and some intended contrast; so that if they are described using familiar and intelligible terms, presumably such terms would not have lost their original meanings.

Suppose, however, we consider only those contexts and special contrasts for which we may wish to classify certain objects as unobservable (meaning either "not yet observable" or "in principle unobservable"). And suppose that the terms P_1, P_2, and so forth, normally used with reference to observables, are used in connection with objects claimed to be unobservable. For P_1, P_2, and so forth, let us choose terms such as "sphere," "radius," "collide," "velocity," "mass"; and for the unobservable objects to which these are applicable let us choose molecules. Some of these terms, such as "velocity" and "mass," are used in classical mechanics with respect to items called *particles* supposed to have position but not extension; and such particles might be said to be unobservable. However, these terms are also used with respect to solid bodies that are observable, so let us consider their use in this latter case. The terms "sphere," "radius," and "collide," as well as "velocity," and "mass," are applied to observables. The question is, when applied to unobservables such as molecules, do they mean the same? Appealing to the considerations for meaning-change noted in section 6, the answer must be Yes.

Physicists such as Maxwell and Boltzmann, who presented the kinetic theory, found it unnecessary to provide explanations for the meanings of these terms or to use them in contexts that would make this apparent. Nor do those who study the kinetic theory, knowing only

[60] *Scientific Papers,* II, 460.

classical mechanics, require such explanations and contexts or otherwise display misunderstanding of what is said.

Moreover, claims attributing certain properties to molecules are considered establishable in ways identical with, similar to, or natural extensions of, ones that could, at least in principle, be used to establish corresponding claims about larger observable spheres with these properties. For example, the theoretical means Maxwell uses to establish his distribution law governing molecules (giving the number of molecules with a velocity between v and $v + dv$ as a function of v) would be exactly the same were molecules much larger and therefore visible. Maxwell needs to assume only that he is dealing with a large number of hard and perfectly elastic spheres acting on one another only during impact, where the radius of each sphere is small compared to its mean free path. He need not make, nor does he make, any assumptions about the absolute size of these spheres or about whether or not they are visible. Experimental methods for corroborating the Maxwell distribution law also involve principles that could be used for larger visible particles. In one experiment a beam of silver atoms is produced and aimed at a glass plate on which the silver is deposited in quantities sufficient to be visible. Rotating the source of the beam, the distribution of velocities of the molecules in the beam can be determined by measuring the density of the silver deposits at various distances from the source. This method would be the same if we were dealing with larger visible objects traveling in a beam and accumulating on a target.

Finally, from a knowledge of the use of terms in classical mechanics in connection with large visible solids (that is, knowing the sorts of items to which, and in virtue of what, they are applicable), it was certainly possible to predict how they would be used in connection with much smaller invisible ones satisfying the same principles. From the viewpoint of classical mechanics neither size nor visibility made any difference as far as the applicability of terms (or principles) was concerned.

Such considerations are relevant for deciding whether terms used to refer to unobservables are the same in meaning as those used to refer to observables because they provide important clues for answering the following decisive question: Are the conditions treated as semantically relevant for P_1, P_2, and so forth, when these are attributed to unobservable molecules also treated as semantically relevant when they are attributed to observable items?

Quantities such as diameter, velocity, pressure, kinetic energy, momentum, and density are attributed to molecules by the kinetic theory. In Chapter Two, I spoke of mathematical and operational definitions for a quantity as well as of definitions given by reference to other facts about it (including laws in which it functions). All of these can provide semantically relevant conditions for that quantity. Now the mathematical definitions of quantities such as velocity, pressure, kinetic energy, momentum, and density are exactly the same for molecules as for macroscopic objects. In both cases "velocity" is defined as time rate of change of position, "pressure" as force per unit area, and so forth. Definitions given by reference to facts about the quantity other than mathematical and operational ones are also the same. Kinetic energy, for molecules as well as for macroscopic objects, is the energy of a body due to its motion.

Are operational definitions the same? The actual operations necessary for measuring these quantities in the case of molecules cannot be the same as those that will suffice for larger objects. A tape measure can be used in determining the diameter of a baseball but not that of a molecule. However, recall that an operational definition cites conditions relevant only within certain ranges of values of the quantity.[61] The fact that there are different operations for a quantity Q does not mean that the term "Q" has a different semantical use with respect to each. "Q" refers to that quantity measurable by certain methods within a given range, perhaps by different ones within another range, and so forth. Within one range some methods may be more central than others. These will be ones whose use more decisively settles whether that quantity of such and such a magnitude is attributable to something. Within a given range some methods (often the less central ones) may be more indirect by contrast with others; and some method, indirect and noncentral within a given range, may be more central and direct for a different one.

For example, within a certain (macroscopic) range of values the most central and direct method for measuring the thickness of a film of oil would be to use a suitably calibrated measuring rod. A method less central and more indirect within this same range would involve determining the density of oil, the area over which it is spread, and the total mass of the oil involved, and then dividing the mass by the density multiplied by the area. When the range consists of much smaller values

[61] Chap. Two, sec. 10.

the latter method may be the most direct of the methods possible. Indeed this was the one used by Rayleigh in calculating the thickness (diameter) of unobservable oil molecules. Rayleigh assumed that the thickness of the thinnest continuous oil film is equal to the diameter of the oil molecule. He then calculated this diameter by measuring the mass of oil added to a pan of water of a certain area and then by dividing this mass by the product of the density of the oil and the area of the water.

Suppose, then, that a quantity Q is applied both to observable macroscopic objects and unobservable microscopic ones; and suppose that the operational conditions most central and direct in the case of macroscopic objects are different from those most central and direct for microscopic ones. This does not necessarily make the semantical aspect of the use of "Q" different in each case, for three reasons. (1) The operational conditions may be meant to be applicable only within certain ranges and not with respect to all possible values of the quantity; and those considered most central and direct for one range may be the same as, or natural extensions of, conditions applicable, though less central and direct, in a different range. (2) A mathematical definition of the quantity, which provides a semantically relevant condition, may be exactly the same in both cases. (3) Other semantically relevant facts about that quantity may be the same, for example, certain laws to which it is subject.

To the extent that (1), (2), and (3) are satisfied, the label "different in meaning," as between macroscopic and microscopic uses of quantity-terms, is unjustified. It is my claim that the operational conditions for quantities such as diameter, velocity, pressure, kinetic energy, momentum, and density are considered applicable only within limited ranges; and certain methods applicable at the microscopic level are the same as, or natural extensions of, methods applicable, though indirect, at the macroscopic level.[62] These quantities have the same mathematical conditions associated with them, whether they are applied to macroscopic objects or to invisible molecules in kinetic theory. And they are subject to the same laws and principles. In short, a "difference

[62] Of course, in kinetic theory certain quantities such as velocity and kinetic energy are not operationally defined for single molecules. What is operationally defined are the quantities "average number of molecules whose velocities lie between two limits," "root-mean-square velocity," "mean kinetic energy." I have shown above how operational conditions for the first of these are the same for molecules as for larger macroscopic bodies.

in meaning" label, as between macroscopic uses of terms for such quantities and microscopic uses in kinetic theory, is unwarranted.

Several considerations have been cited for determining whether a term normally used to apply to an observable and now used also to apply to an unobservable must be said to have changed its meaning. I have tried to show that there is no a priori reason why terms used in connection with observables and unobservables cannot mean the same, and I have tried to indicate that this is so with respect to certain terms in kinetic theory. This completes my argument against the claim, formulated at the beginning of point (4), that whenever a term normally used for observables is applied to unobservables it cannot mean the same. This does not imply that terms in such cases always mean the same. Some terms used in classical thermodynamics to refer to macroscopic systems and in (some formulations of) statistical mechanics to refer to systems of microscopic particles can plausibly be held to differ in meaning. An example noted earlier is "entropy." But there is a difference in meaning here not because the items to which this term applies in one case are unobservable whereas those in the other are observable, but because different semantically relevant conditions are satisfied by each.[63]

To interpret a term "X," I have claimed, is to do possibly several things; for example, to attribute to X semantically relevant properties or conditions; to indicate differences in centrality; and to indicate semantically relevant categories of unknown properties. It is to do this even if "X" is used to refer to what Positivists classify as unobservables. If "X" is so used, terms for properties attributed to X may be understandable because the properties are the *same* as certain ones attributable to observable items. This is the sort of situation I have been considering. But such terms may also be understandable because they refer to properties *similar* to certain ones attributed to observables without being identical with them; or because they refer to properties identical with or similar to properties attributed to other unobservables already introduced. In this connection, we might mention the importance of *analogies* in understanding the interpretation for terms.

When Maxwell introduced the concept of self-diffusion of molecules in a gas he invoked an analogy between the molecules and bees in a swarm:

---

[63] See sec. 6.

> If we wish to form a representation of what is going on among the molecules in calm air, we cannot do better than observe a swarm of bees, when every individual bee is flying furiously, first in one direction and then in another, while the swarm as a whole either remains at rest, or sails slowly through the air.[64]

Sometimes when a term is introduced an analogy is not explicitly drawn but only suggested. In electrostatics, to speak of a body as charged with electricity is not simply to refer to a capability to attract bits of light material. It is to suggest in addition the presence of some substance or mechanism that can explain the phenomenon of attraction, even though clues about how the substance or mechanism is to be observed are not provided. Yet an analogy is suggested between a body charged with electricity and other substances that are "charged" or "burdened" with other things in virtue of which they act in certain ways. The topic of analogies is sufficiently important to merit separate attention; this, as well as models, will be discussed in later chapters. Now let me present a number of conclusions reached in points (3) and (4) of the present section that are especially relevant for the Positivist account.

I have been attempting to refute the claim that the only way to interpret a term is by saying what observables it designates, or by explicitly defining it using only terms designating observables, or by formulating analytic statements that attribute to the items it designates properties that can be observed. My general argument has been this. In actual practice physicists (such as those of the eighteenth and nineteenth centuries) do interpret terms such as "molecule" and "electricity," and they do this by saying more than simply what observations can be made when these terms are used. They may provide such interpretations by ascribing to the items certain properties that can also be ascribed to observable ones—hence, by using terms many of which are already available and are used in connection with observables. Appealing to the semantical categories introduced in the chapters on definition, I have argued that such terms can have the same meanings in both cases; so if their meanings are intelligible in the one case, they are in the other as well. Physicists may also provide such interpretations by attributing to the unobservable items properties that are not identical with those attributed to observable ones but similar in possibly many respects; or by attributing to the unobservable items properties that are the same

[64] *Scientific Papers,* II, 368.

118

as or similar to those attributed to other sorts of unobservable items already introduced.

This constitutes my defense of the claim that terms interpreted as referring to items described as unobservable need not express unintelligible concepts. It is just this claim that Positivists have denied, and it is for just this reason that they express misgivings over any concept of meaning according to which terms can be interpreted as referring to what they classify as unobservable. If I am right, their misgivings are unjustified.

CHAPTER FOUR

THEORIES

One of the central aims of science is the construction of theories; and one of the central aims of the philosophy of science is the study of the concept "theory." Much use of this concept has already been made in the preceding discussion on definitions and the interpretation of terms; further appeals to it will occur later when we turn to the subject of theoretical terms and to analogies and models. The word "theory" has both a narrow and a broad use. The former is illustrated by expressions such as "the Bohr theory of the atom" and "the kinetic theory of gases"; the latter, by "physical theory" and "nuclear theory." Most of this chapter will concern the narrower use; the broader one will be examined briefly in the final section.

The first question to be raised is simply: What is a theory? I think the same considerations are relevant in answering this question whether we are dealing with theories inside or outside science. And I shall compare the view to be developed with several other conceptions of theories found in the philosophy of science. I shall then concentrate on theories in science, especially those in physics, and consider what elements can be distinguished in their presentations, the different types of presentations that are or might be given, and the advantages and disadvantages of each.

1. CRITERIA FOR THEORIES

Let me approach the question "What is a theory?" indirectly by first asking: What does it mean to say that someone has a theory?

Several conditions will be proposed as semantically relevant and quite central for this, although possibly only one (the fourth) is logically necessary. The nonsatisfaction of each of the other conditions would in and of itself tend to count, to some extent, against saying that someone has a theory without necessarily precluding it. I shall then show how the concept of a theory can be defined by reference to the conditions for having a theory. Let us consider, then, what is typically the case when someone, call him A, has a theory T.

1) A does not know that T is true, although he believes that T is true or that it is plausible to think it is. Moreover, he cannot immediately and readily come to know the truth of T, or could not at the inception of his belief in T. He may think he knows that T is true. But *we* say he has a theory T when we impute to A a lack of knowledge concerning the truth of T. Of course, A may later come to know that T is true. If so, it is no longer appropriate for us to say that he has a *theory* T (or that he has T as a theory) unless we doubt he knows the truth of T. This condition represents the conjectural or speculative element associated with theories.

Consider, for example, the kinetic theory of Daniel Bernoulli. One of the reasons we are willing to say Bernoulli had the theory that gases are composed of an enormous number of tiny particles in rapid motion is because he did not know, and could not immediately and readily come to know, that this was so. He did give certain arguments to support the theory. For example, he showed how it afforded a quantitative explanation of the relationship between pressure, temperature, and density of a gas.[1] However, such arguments could not be said to demonstrate the truth of the theory; Bernoulli could not be described as having known, or having been in a position to come to know immediately and readily, that gases contain particles of the sort he postulated. He might be so described if, for example, a super-microscope had always been available by means of which such particles could readily have been observed. But then there would be some hesitation in speaking of this as his *theory*. Thus, one reason why the proposition "My pen is filled with ink" is not a theory I have is because I know it to be true; and even if I did not, I could readily come to know it in a simple and direct way.

I have spoken here of truth, but this is a bit of an oversimplification, since truth is not always clearly ascribable to a theory as a whole. A theory may contain a large set of assertions some of which are true

---

[1] Daniel Bernoulli, "On the Properties and Motions of Elastic Fluids, Especially Air," *Kinetic Theory*, ed. S. G. Brush (Oxford, 1965), pp. 57–65.

and others of which are not, thus making the question of the truth of the entire set not clearly decidable. Moreover, there will be considerations of scope: how many sorts of items are subject to the principles of the theory? There will also be considerations of accuracy: within what limits does T describe what is actually the case? Usually the principles of the theory will be formulated without mention of scope, so that if items in a certain range are discovered that do not satisfy the theory, it may not be clear whether to say that the theory has been shown to be false or to be limited in scope. Certainly if very many such ranges are discovered, the former description might be given. Analogous remarks apply to accuracy.

Accordingly, when I speak here of knowing and believing that T is true, I mean to imply something complex, namely, knowing or believing either that T is true (where truth is clearly applicable to T) or that on the whole T says what is the case in a more or less accurate way and—where the question of scope is relevant—does so with respect to a reasonably extensive range of items.

2) A does not know, nor does he believe, that T is false. On the contrary, he believes that T is true or that it is plausible to think T is true. Moreover, he cannot immediately and readily come to know that T is false, or could not at the inception of his belief in T. Of course, A may later come to know or believe that T is false; but if so, we would no longer say that he has the theory T. For example, Kepler's first theory about the orbit of the planet Mars was that it was a perfect circle. However, this theory yielded consequences seriously at odds with what was observed, and he came to disbelieve it.[2] If anyone at that time had claimed that Kepler (still) had the "circular" theory, he would have been mistaken.

The same considerations regarding *truth* apply here as in the first condition. Accordingly, someone satisfies the present condition if he thinks it reasonable to suppose that T is more or less accurate for a fairly extensive range of items. (This is one feature that distinguishes a theory from what in Chapter Seven will be called a "theoretical model." As will be explained in that chapter, someone may propose a theoretical model knowing full well that it is applicable only within a very limited range and not very accurate even within that range.)

3) A believes that T provides, or will eventually provide, some (or a better) understanding of something and that this is or will be

[2] For an illuminating historical discussion, see N. R. Hanson, *Patterns of Discovery* (Cambridge, England, 1958), Chap. 4.

one of the main functions of T. By providing an understanding I mean something quite broad that can be done in a number of related ways, for example, by explaining, interpreting, removing a puzzle, showing why something is not surprising, indicating a cause or causes, supplying reasons, analyzing something into simpler, more familiar, or more integrated components. Also, what is to be understood may be of many different sorts. Some authors write as if a theory always provides an understanding of one thing, namely, some surprising phenomenon that has been observed. For example, Hanson suggests that whenever a theory is proposed the following inference is involved:

> Some surprising phenomenon P is observed.
> P would be explicable as a matter of course if H were true.
> Hence there is reason to think that H is true.[3]

No doubt very often when one has a theory he believes that it provides a better understanding of a surprising phenomenon that has been observed. But one may have a theory and believe that it provides a better understanding of something which could not be classified as surprising, or even as a phenomenon, and indeed may never have been observed. A may propose a particular theory about the atom because he believes that it provides a better understanding of its nature. Of course this may indirectly provide a better understanding of certain phenomena observed in cloud chambers, for example, but the latter need not be the only sort of thing for which A believes his theory provides understanding. Nor need it be the central thing as far as A is concerned. Indeed A could have proposed his theory without knowing of any observable phenomena for which his theory provides understanding.

I said that when A has a theory T he believes that one of T's main functions is to explain, interpret, remove puzzles, and so forth. Normally A will be able to indicate how his theory purports to do some of these things, but this is not absolutely required. A might be said to have a theory T even though he is unable to supply actual explanations, interpretations, puzzle-removers, and so forth. What will suffice, I think, is that he believes these are possible and central for the theory and that he be able to identify at least some of the sorts of items for which his theory might be able to provide understanding.

[3] *Ibid.,* p. 86.

In short, A believes that T is at least, and importantly, a *potential* explainer, interpreter, remover of puzzles, analyzer, and so forth. The less central these potential roles are for A, the less willing are we to speak of what A has as a theory.

There are cases in which the term "theory" is used where such roles may seem minimal or even nonexistent, as when someone is said to have the theory that Senator Claghorn will not be running in the next election. We might characterize such a use as stretched or even careless and say that, strictly speaking, this is not a theory but a conjecture, speculation, or guess. There is another possibility. In such a case, when we call this a theory we may be thinking of it in connection with a larger set of assertions that does more properly constitute a theory, for example, that the Republicans believe that they will be meeting stiff competition in the next election and so will want to nominate a more colorful, dynamic, and youthful personality. One of the important functions of the latter may indeed be to explain, analyze, provide reasons, and so forth.

4) T consists of propositions purporting to assert what is the case. For A to have a theory he need not actually have formulated such propositions in a language. And if he does formulate them, he may do so in several different ways, that is, use different sentences to express them. Moreover, contrary to what some instrumentalist philosophers suggest, T is not a set of *rules,* literally speaking, although it may contain rules expressed propositionally. For example, it may contain the proposition that if an electric current flows through a straight portion of wire and if we place the thumb of our right hand along the wire pointing in the direction of the current, the other fingers will point in the direction of the magnetic field (the so-called right-hand rule).

Which propositions *are* the theory? Normally when one speaks of a theory what is being referred to is a set containing at least its central and distinctive assumptions. By *assumptions* I mean those propositions of the theory that are not treated as being derived from others in the theory. By *central* I mean those regarded as expressing the most important ideas of the theory. By *distinctive* I mean those that more than others serve to identify it as that particular theory and distinguish it from others. Typically the central assumptions will be the distinctive ones, and vice versa.

A theory may have associated with it (use, presuppose, have as consequences) many propositions not in the set of central and distinctive assumptions. In referring to the Bohr theory of the atom one may be referring to assumptions concerning the quantization of angular momentum of the electron in the atom and the quantization of energy radiated or absorbed by the atom. Yet, in addition, the theory uses Coulomb's law, Newton's second law of motion, and the principle of conservation of mechanical energy in order to derive the desired consequences. These additional laws and principles might be spoken of as part of the theory *in the sense that* they must be used to derive the desired consequences. Similarly, when one refers to Newton's theory of mechanics one may be referring to his three laws of motion and the law of gravitation. Yet there are principles that are derivable from these laws together with special assumptions about specific systems, for example, principles governing unsupported bodies, oscillator motion, and accelerated reference systems. Such derived principles might be spoken of as part of the theory *in the sense that* they are derivable from its central and distinctive assumptions when further assumptions are made about systems of particular sorts.

With respect to the question "Which propositions are the theory?" two extreme answers might be given. One is that only the central and distinctive assumptions are the theory (only Bohr's two assumptions, only Newton's four laws). The other is that everything associated with the theory (including additional assumptions and consequences) is the theory. Both answers are somewhat arbitrary. I think the best procedure is simply to distinguish the central and distinctive assumptions of a theory from the additional principles (possibly from other theories) it may use or presuppose, and these in turn from consequences of the theory. These are all "associated with" the theory, but in different ways. In short, there is no simple and nonarbitrary answer to the question "Which propositions are the theory?"

Finally, there is a sense in which items other than propositions, for example, concepts and definitions, may be said to belong to a theory; but to speak of *A*'s theory, in the sense I am now considering, is to speak of such items primarily in connection with propositions; as being part of them, in the case of concepts, as presupposed by them, in the case of definitions. Concepts and definitions may be cited and explained in a presentation of *A*'s theory, though the theory proper is a set of propositions with which they are associated.

5) *A* does not know of any more fundamental (theory) *T'* from

which he knows that the set of central and distinctive assumptions of T can be simply and directly derived, where A satisfies all the other conditions with respect to T'. Newton, for example, in Book I of the *Principia,* formulated the principle of conservation of momentum (Corollary III) and the principle of inertia for the center of mass of a system of bodies (Corollary IV). Yet in doing so he did not formulate a theory that he had, but only certain propositions that follow, and that he knew to follow (simply and directly), from such a theory. Of course a scientist may have a theory that he applies to some relatively specific system S; and what he says about S may also be described as a theory that he has. For example, in Book III of the *Principia,* Newton applied his theory of mechanics to the tides on the earth, and what he said might be described as his theory of tides. But to obtain this theory he needed to go beyond the laws of dynamics and gravitation and introduce special assumptions and observations about the character of the earth. Moreover, the derivations are neither simple nor direct.

In short, A may know that some of the principles of a theory that he has are (or are simply and directly derivable from) principles of some more fundamental theory that he also has. However, he does not know this about the entire set of his central and distinctive assumptions.

6) A believes that each of the assumptions in the set regarded as distinctive and central will be helpful, together with others associated with the theory, in providing an understanding of those items for which A believes the theory may provide an understanding. He need not believe that each such assumption is required for this purpose; he may, indeed, believe that some are redundant. Nor must he believe that each such assumption will help provide an understanding of *every* item for which the theory provides some understanding, though he should believe that there will be items that all or most of these assumptions will help to illuminate; that is, he should believe in a *joint* effort on the part of his central and distinctive assumptions.

This condition is intended to capture what I regard as a weak "working together" requirement on theories. It precludes conjoining the central and distinctive assumptions of what are viewed as wholly unrelated theories and calling the result a theory. It also precludes stringing together wholly unrelated propositions, where each is intended to illuminate something different, and calling the result a theory. Even if someone were committed to Malthus' theory of population and to Bohr's theory of the atom, he would not have a theory consisting of the conjunction of these; nor would he have one consisting of a conjunction formed by taking one principle from Malthus' theory, one from Bohr's, one from Newton's, and so on.

I have cited six conditions for having a theory. Can these be used in saying what it is to be a theory? [4] One might be tempted to define a theory as follows: Where T is a set of propositions, T is a theory if and only if there is some person A who, with respect to T, satisfies the six conditions specified above. But this would be too stringent, for in some situations we might want to count T as a theory even if no one now satisfies these conditions, that is, even if no one now has T. Let us try a weaker definition: T is a theory if and only if there is some person A who, with respect to T, now satisfies these conditions or did so at some previous time. However, this would preclude counting as a theory some T that no one ever had, has now, or even will have—but that it might be plausible to imagine someone as having (had). In some situations a T of the latter sort will count as a theory; for example, we are considering various possible structures that might be imputed to the atomic nucleus. In other situations such a T will not be counted as a theory; for example, we are considering only theories of the atomic nucleus that someone has actually had, or only theories that someone has actually had and are at present live options in physics: in such situations if a T was mentioned that no one ever had, the reply might be that there is no such theory, or that it does not count as a theory for present purposes. This reply would be inappropriate in a situation of the former sort.

What is classifiable as a theory, then, depends in part on the context of classification: this can vary so that in one situation what is called for is a T that someone has had; in another, a T that may not have been had by anyone but is still something that it is reasonable to imagine someone as having; in another, a T had by leading scientists of today; and so forth. Accordingly, from the fact that there is a person A who satisfies the six conditions with respect to some T, it does not follow that T can always be counted as a theory. Moreover, I have said that these conditions are semantically relevant for having a theory but (with the possible exception of the fourth) are not logically necessary. So what we can say about the conditions is this: if an A

[4] In the discussion that follows I am indebted to Stephen Barker.

does satisfy (all or most of) them, then he has what in appropriate contexts can be classified as a theory; and if he has what in some context is classifiable as a theory, then he satisfies (all or most of) them. In short, these conditions, together with contextual considerations, are semantically relevant for having a theory.

The following characterization of a theory can now be offered. To say that some T is a theory is, depending on the context, to say one or more of the following: that (at least) some person A now satisfies conditions (1) through (6) with respect to T; or that some person at a previous time satisfied these conditions with respect to T; or that some person now satisfies these conditions with respect to T, and T is a live option today; or that it is plausible to imagine some person as having satisfied these conditions with respect to T; and so forth. Another way of putting this, although truncated and rough, is as follows: T is a theory, relative to the context, if and only if T is a set of propositions that (depending on the context) is (was, might have been, and so forth) not known to be true or to be false but believed to be somewhat plausible, potentially explanatory, relatively fundamental, and somewhat integrated.

2. OTHER CONCEPTIONS OF THEORIES

Let me now contrast the conception of a theory just developed with four others to be found in the philosophy of science.

The first I shall call the *axiomatic* account. It is held by those defending the Positivist position on interpretation discussed in Chapter Three, but I shall formulate it in a more general way that will be neutral on topics such as partial interpretation and the theoretical-nontheoretical distinction. On the axiomatic account a theory is no more and no less than a set of sentences ("axioms") stated in a specified vocabulary (containing primitive and defined terms) together with all the consequences ("theorems") of this set plus the proofs of these consequences. In short, a theory is a hypothetico-deductive system. This conception is usually embellished with further requirements that concern the *adequacy* of the theory rather than whether or not it is a theory; that is, for a theory to be an adequate one, on this account, it must contain at least some general statements, it must be simple, confirmable and confirmed by observations, and capable of generating new consequences.

What is involved in having a theory? Champions of the axiomatic account do not address themselves directly to this question. Some might want to say that for A to have a theory (though not necessarily an adequate one) is simply for A to have formulated or to be willing to formulate (in a specified vocabulary) a set of sentences as axioms, another as theorems, and proofs of the latter. I shall call this the weaker version of the axiomatic account. However, in the light of considerations in the previous section, others might want to say that for A to have a theory T, it is not sufficient simply for A to have formulated or be willing to formulate axioms, theorems, and proofs. A must also not know or be readily able to know that T is true; and he must not know or believe T to be false, but, on the contrary, must think T reasonable or plausible in some measure at least. I shall call this the stronger version.

Let us consider this account in the light of the conception I have suggested. On the weaker version, one who has a theory T can know that T is true or false, as the case may be, thus ignoring my first and second conditions relevant for having a theory; the stronger version was of course constructed so as not to violate these conditions. Since, on the weaker version, for A to have a theory is simply for A to have formulated or to be willing to formulate a set containing axioms, theorems, and proofs, it is not required or relevant that A believe that one of the main functions of these is (or will be) to provide some understanding of something, thus violating my third condition. Nor is this condition satisfied even if, following the stronger version, we add requirements concerning A's knowledge and beliefs regarding the truth and falsity of T. Proponents of the axiomatic account may reply, however, that an *adequate* theory, that is, one that satisfies the further conditions they specify, does provide explanations. For something is explained, on this view, if a statement describing it is deduced from an adequate theory.[5] The deductive model of explanation assumed by the axiomatic account is a complex topic which cannot be explored here. However, there are, I think, numerous examples of "adequate" theories, in the axiomatic sense, that could not justifiably be said to explain something described in the theorems of such theories. Let me cite just one example.

When an electric discharge is passed through hydrogen, light is given off that, when analyzed with a spectroscope, is shown to consist

[5] See Carl G. Hempel and Paul Oppenheim, "Studies in the Logic of Explanation," *Philosophy of Science*, 15 (1948), 135–75.

of a series of sharp lines of definite wavelengths. This has been known since 1860. In 1885, Balmer proposed the following simple relationship between the wavelengths of the lines: $\frac{1}{\omega} = R\left(\frac{1}{2^2} - \frac{1}{\tau^2}\right)$, $\tau = 3, 4, 5, \ldots$, where ω is the wavelength of the line and R is a constant for hydrogen. From this "axiom," together with the further "axiom" that $R = 109,677 cm^{-1}$, the wavelength of each of the known lines can be derived. Moreover (as it actually happened), by substituting $\tau = 7, 8, \ldots$ in the above formula, and using the value for R, the existence of new lines was predicted and later observed. This, then, is, or can be put in the form of, an axiomatic system (indeed one that satisfies the criteria for an acceptable theory indicated by proponents of the axiomatic account: it is general, empirically testable and confirmed, simple, and capable of being used to make new predictions). However, it provides no explanation whatever of the existence of the observed lines, of why the wavelengths are what they are, of their discreteness, and so forth. At most, it organizes the known data in such a way that we are in a better position to seek a theory to explain the initial phenomena.

On either version of the axiomatic account, one who has a theory T may have some more fundamental theory from which he knows T to be simply and directly derivable. In short, any subset of propositions in (or implied by) a theory is itself a theory; and this ignores my fifth condition relevant for having a theory. On either version of the axiomatic account there is no "working together" requirement, so that any unrelated propositions one may string together can constitute a theory, and the conjunction of any two theories can itself be a theory—thus violating my sixth condition. Finally, on either version of the axiomatic account something counts as a theory independently of the context. Any set T consisting of axioms, theorems, and proofs is a theory irrespective of whether anyone has (had, might have had, and so forth) T; indeed, it is a theory irrespective of whether anyone ever contemplated or could have contemplated such a set. This ignores contextual considerations relevant in deciding what is to count as a theory.

Supporters of the axiomatic account may reply that they are not concerned with how the concept of a theory is normally employed. They want to replace it with another concept that they think will be more satisfactory for certain purposes. This replacement of one concept by another regarded as more satisfactory is what Carnap calls explication.[6]

---

[6] See Chap. Three, sec. 4, where this is explained.

By Carnap's own admission, one explicates a concept, that is, replaces concept C by C', only where C leads to certain difficulties (inconsistencies, unclarities, paradoxes). But those defending the axiomatic account never even try to show what difficulties are generated by using what they call the "pre-analytic" concept of a theory. Indeed, they never consider this concept at all. I have tried to point out the differences between their concept and what I regard as one standard concept of a theory employed within (as well as outside) science.

A second view about theories has achieved recent popularity through the writings of Feyerabend.[7] Unlike the axiomatic account, it distinguishes theories from mere empirical generalizations. The latter are considerably restricted in their application, arrived at by observing instances, and refutable in a simple and direct way by conflicting evidence. Theories, on the other hand, are very general unrestricted assumptions. They are ones to which we are deeply committed and would abandon not simply in the light of conflicting evidence but only when we become deeply committed to other such assumptions. They are not arrived at merely by observing instances. Indeed observations are made in the light of a theory; terms used in reporting observations depend for their very meanings on the theory. Feyerabend includes in the set of theories not only those recognized as such in science (Newton's theory of mechanics, the special theory of relativity), but also certain "ordinary beliefs (e.g., the belief in the existence of material objects), myths (e.g., the myth of eternal recurrence), religious beliefs, etc." [8]

Part of this view, having to do with the meaning-dependence of terms, was discussed in the previous chapter. What I want to note here is that this conception of a theory ignores a number of the conditions in section 1. For example, it makes no requirement that one who has a theory not know that it is true; that is, it omits the speculative or conjectural element. Nor is there a requirement that one who has such a theory believe that it does or will provide understanding of something and that this is one of its main functions. Any deep general commitment refutable only by another deep general commitment would count as a theory on this view, whether or not such a commitment is sup-

[7] "Explanation, Reduction, and Empiricism," *Minnesota Studies in the Philosophy of Science,* ed. H. Feigl and G. Maxwell (Minneapolis. 1962), III, 28–97. See also Thomas Kuhn, *The Structure of Scientific Revolutions* (Chicago, 1962).
[8] "Problems of Empiricism," *Beyond the Edge of Certainty,* ed. R. G. Colodny (Englewood Cliffs, N.J., 1965), p. 219, note 3.

posed to provide understanding. Furthermore, classifying any such commitment as a theory ignores contextual considerations of the sort noted earlier. The account also fails to provide a necessary condition. To have a theory T, it is not required that T be criticizable only in the light of other theories and that T be incapable of refutation by conflicting evidence, independently of alternative theories.

However, as with the axiomatic account, the claim may not be that this represents a standard use of the term "theory," even in science. So I want to note two proposals about theories that do appear to be making such a claim.

The first is that of Hanson, who developed it in part in reaction to the axiomatic approach.[9] Hanson rejects the latter on the ground that scientists do not start from hypotheses and then deduce the data; they begin with the data and then search for hypotheses to explain them. Thus, Kepler did not begin with the hypothesis of an elliptical orbit for Mars. He began with observations recorded by Brahe and "struggled back from these, first to one hypothesis, then to another, then to another, and ultimately to the hypothesis of the elliptical orbit." [10] Now a theory is something that organizes initially puzzling observed data into an intelligible pattern, so that these data are "explicable as a matter of course." Hanson writes:

> What is it to supply a theory? It is to offer an intelligible, systematic, conceptual pattern for the observed data. The value of this pattern lies in its capacity to unite phenomena which, without the theory, are either surprising, anomalous, or wholly unnoticed.[11]

To compare Hanson's account with mine, let us suppose that one who has a theory is now supplying it for some purpose. If, as seems quite possible, Hanson means to be suggesting a sufficient condition for supplying a theory, then his account is too liberal. For example, one condition that I suggested as relevant for having a theory but that seems irrelevant for Hanson is that A does not know, and cannot (or could not at first) readily come to know, that T is true. Suppose that A and B are walking in the woods and B observes something that he finds very puzzling moving on a distant tree. Once this is called to his attention, A informs B that it is a bear climbing a tree, though all that is

[9] *Patterns of Discovery,* Chap. 4.
[10] *Ibid.,* p. 72.
[11] *Ibid.,* p. 121.

visible from the present vantage point are the bear's paws clinging to the tree.[12] Here *A* has organized what *B* observes into an "intelligible, systematic, conceptual pattern" so that what *B* observes is no longer "surprising" or "anomalous." *A*, however, is not (at least in my example) supplying some *theory* that he has, since he knows that it is a bear, and even if he did not, he could (have) come to know this in a simple and direct way. Nor, it seems to me, would we speak here of *A*'s theory, though what *A* says does explain what *B* sees, does remove *B*'s puzzlement, and so forth.

If, on the other hand, Hanson means to be suggesting only a necessary condition for supplying a theory, then, one is prompted to ask, What else is relevant? The text does not say. Even so, the condition he does propose is too stringent, and the reason why was suggested earlier.

His account implies that the supplier of a theory must have observed or be aware of certain phenomena for which the theory offers an explanation. This, of course, will frequently happen, but what a theory explains, or is supposed to explain, need not be any phenomena that have been observed but may be items of other sorts, even ones not yet observed. Indeed there might be cases in which the proponent of a theory is unable to produce actual explanations of anything (observed phenomena or otherwise), though he is committed to believing that his theory can be used in explanations (or at least to promote some sort of understanding) of various things and that this will be one of its main functions.

The final conception of a theory I want to discuss is more complex than any of the others. It is that of Sylvain Bromberger.[13] He first introduces the notion of a *p*-predicament ("*p*" for puzzled or perplexed) for which he gives this definition: "*A* is in a *p*-predicament with regard to [question] *Q* if and only if, on *A*'s views, *Q* admits of a right answer, but *A* can think of no answer to which, on *A*'s views, there are no decisive objections." [14] For example, Bromberger informs us that he happens to be in a *p*-predicament with regard to the

---

[12] This bear example is used by Hanson himself in illustrating what he means by "seeing the pattern" in the phenomena. *Ibid.,* p. 12.

[13] Sylvain Bromberger, "A Theory about the Theory of Theory and about the Theory of Theories," *Philosophy of Science: The Delaware Seminar,* ed. Bernard Baumrin (New York, 1963), II.

[14] Bromberger, "An Approach to Explanation," *Analytical Philosophy,* ed. R. J. Butler (Oxford, 1965), II, 82.

question, "Why do teakettles emit a humming noise just before the water begins to boil?" but not with regard to the question, "What is the height of Mt. Kilimanjaro?", although he knows the answer to neither. The point is that he can think of nothing as an answer to the first that is not ruled out by his views about the world, whereas he can think of several possible answers to the second (for example, 15,000 feet, 8,000 feet), no one of which is precluded by his views.

Using the notion of a *p*-predicament, Bromberger provides the following definition of a theory. For *T* to be a theory, it is necessary and sufficient that *T* be a known proposition (or set of propositions) but not known to be true and not known to be false; and that *T* provide an answer to a question *Q* with regard to which it is in principle possible to be in a *p*-predicament; or that *T* provide one among many such answers which are mutually exclusive, where each such answer, in the absence of the others, would contain the only answer to *Q* not precluded by the conditions set by the question; or else that *T* be the contrary of some presupposition of *Q*.[15]

One problem with this conception stems from its requirement that for *T* to be a theory, it must not be known to be false. This would rule out theories now known to be false (for example, the phlogiston theory). Recognizing this to be an unfortunate aspect of his definition, Bromberger proposes that we think of the definition as specifying only what it means to be an "acceptable theory." But he fails to indicate the respect or respects in which he is considering acceptability. Not every set of propositions meeting his criteria would count as an acceptable theory in all relevant respects. On his conception, a theory not known to be false, but for which a considerable amount of disquieting evidence exists, could be an acceptable theory; or similarly, a theory could be an acceptable one, on this conception, even though the answers that it provides to questions, although not known to be false, are generally regarded as implausible, much too complex, and so forth. Furthermore, the requirement that the theory not be known to be true is too stringent. A set of propositions whose truth was once not known, but now is, might legitimately be classified as a theory.

Nor is Bromberger's proposal sufficient for a theory. Suppose B in 1965 raises the question, "Who will be the Republican Presidential nominee in 1968?"; and suppose that he happens to be in a *p*-predicament with respect to this question because he can think of no answer

[15] "A Theory about the Theory of Theory," p. 102.

to which, on his views, there are no decisive objections. *A*, who hears *B*'s question but does not know of his *p*-predicament, proposes the answer "Charles Percy," someone unknown to *B* but not decisively precluded by his views (and where it is not known whether this answer is true or false). According to Bromberger's definition, in proposing this answer, *A* would be proposing a theory. However, if my conception of a theory is correct, then this need not be so. *A* may not be serious in his answer: even though he may not know whether it is true or false he may believe it to be false. Also, not knowing of *B*'s *p*-predicament, *A* did not propose the answer for the purpose of explaining, removing puzzles, and so forth; nor did he think of this as potentially one of the main functions of his answer.

Indeed, if Bromberger's conditions are taken to be sufficient for being a theory, then almost any known proposition not known to be true or to be false is a theory. According to his proposal, for *T* to be a theory, it is sufficient that *T* be a known proposition not known to be true or to be false and that a question *Q* be formulatable with regard to which it is in principle possible for someone to be in a *p*-predicament, where *T* provides an answer to *Q* (or one among several such answers); it is also sufficient that *T* be the contrary of some presupposition of *Q*, where *T* is not known to be true or to be false. Suppose I say, "The cat is on the mat," where this is not known to be true or to be false. A question can now be formulated ("Where is the cat?") such that it is in principle possible to describe someone as being in a *p*-predicament with regard to that question. (For example, such a person believes that there is no mat on which the cat could be and, having looked everywhere else without success, can think of no place the cat could be.) Since my original proposition ("The cat is on the mat") provides an answer to the question "Where is the cat?" with regard to which it is in principle possible for someone to be in a *p*-predicament, and since we are supposing that this proposition is not known to be true or to be false, it is a theory on Bromberger's account. This is not to deny that it could be a theory in some contexts (provided other conditions of the sort mentioned in the previous section are satisfied). The point is simply that, on Bromberger's account, in any context, and no matter what other conditions obtain, if this statement is made and is not known to be true or to be false, it is classifiable as a theory.

Should Bromberger not agree that the question "Where is the cat?" could, even in principle, generate a *p*-predicament, we can choose another question, namely, "How come the cat is on the mat?" Surely it is in principle possible for someone (who, for example, believes he has just put the cat on the mat and now believes the cat is no longer there) to be in a p-predicament with regard to this question. But the proposition "the cat is on the mat" is a contrary of a presupposition of the question just formulated; so, on Bromberger's definition, it is a theory (if it is not known to be true or to be false).

Suppose, then, we try to strengthen Bromberger's requirements as follows. We require not that in principle it be possible to formulate a question to which the theory is an answer (or is the contrary of a presupposition of the question), but that such a question actually have been formulated by the proponent of the theory or by others and that the theory be proposed to answer this question, among others. Furthermore, let us require not that in principle it be possible for someone to be in a p-predicament with respect to that question, but that some people actually be in that p-predicament. Such conditions would obviously not be satisfied by virtually every known proposition not known to be true or to be false.

However, these requirements would be much too stringent. They would not be necessary for a theory. Suppose that in answer to the question "How was the solar system formed?" a group of leading astronomers pondering the latest evidence unanimously agree on three possibilities no one of which is definitely precluded by their views. Then the Astronomer Royal arrives, carefully examines all the evidence, and proposes a fourth quite different answer to this question. I think it is perfectly clear that the Astronomer Royal might have proposed a theory even though no one is in a p-predicament with respect to the question "How was the solar system formed?" and even though he knows that no one is in such a predicament. In general, a person A may propose a theory T in answer to a question Q even though those for whom he is proposing this theory can generate a number of possible answers none of which is precluded by their views and even though A knows this to be so.

3. THE PRESENTATION OF A SCIENTIFIC THEORY

The account of theories in section 1, as well as alternative accounts in section 2, are meant to be applicable to theories in general, not only to scientific theories. To call a theory "scientific" might be to say simply that it is arrived at or justified scientifically. More typically, however, it is to say that it is a theory *in science,* one that makes or purports to make a contribution to science itself. In what follows I turn specifically to theories of the latter sort. My concern will be the nature of their presentations. I want to dispel the idea that a theory is always presented in some one way or that there is one ideal sort of presentation. The discussion should yield insights into what philosophers of science have called the *structure* of a theory, but I shall propose a way of construing such structure different from that provided by the conceptions discussed in the previous section.

There are various types of presentations in science, and what will be suggested is a general schema of their ingredients. The ones I shall abstract are: (1) the central and distinctive assumptions of the theory; (2) the motivation for the theory; (3) the development of the theory; and (4) the discussion of confirmation.

1) *The central and distinctive assumptions of the theory.* These have already been mentioned. They are the assumptions regarded as expressing the most important ideas of the theory and as distinguishing that theory from others. Sometimes they will be explicitly formulated and identified as such. In the course of presenting his special theory of relativity, Einstein formulates two principles as follows:

a) The laws according to which the nature of physical systems alter are independent of the manner in which these changes are referred to two coordinate systems which have a translatory motion relative to each other.

b) Every ray of light moves in the "stationary coordinate system" with the same velocity c, the velocity being independent of the condition whether this ray of light is emitted by a body at rest or in motion. . . .[16]

Einstein calls (*a*) the principle of relativity, and (*b*) the principle of the constancy of the velocity of light; and he obviously regards them as the most distinctive and central assumptions of his theory (though, to be sure, he also regards as central a definition of *synchronism* which [*b*] presupposes).

However, in many presentations the central and distinctive assump-

[16] Einstein, "On the Electrodynamics of Moving Bodies," *Great Experiments in Physics,* ed. Morris H. Shamos (New York, 1962), p. 321.

tions of a theory are not formulated together and labelled as such. They may be formulated and developed separately or even utilized without being explicitly stated. In presenting his wave theory of light Huygens does not gather together his fundamental assumptions or even label them as such. However, by examining the arguments in his treatise one might formulate these as candidates for such a set: (a) light consists of a wave motion in the ether; (b) the wave motion is not communicated instantaneously but travels with a finite velocity through the ether; (c) in different media it travels with different velocities.[17]

Numerous assumptions may be made by a scientist in the course of presenting his theory. Some will be more central for the theory or more distinctive of it than others. In his theory, Einstein seeks to derive transformation equations that give the positions and times of bodies in one coordinate system as functions of those in another moving uniformly with respect to the first. To do so he assumes that such equations must be linear, otherwise one event in one coordinate system would correspond to two or more events in the other. This assumption, although necessary for the theory, is less distinctive of it than the two principles formulated above.

Since there will be differences in centrality and distinctiveness of assumptions, it will be a question of degree which and how many of the assumptions actually made can be said to constitute the class of central and distinctive ones. Moreover, there will be different ways to formulate these assumptions, depending on the level of sophistication and the emphasis desired. One presentation may use highly technical concepts, another may not; one may offer a more complete and detailed formulation of each assumption than another. Also, in one presentation a proposition may be treated as an assumption, in another, as something derived from assumptions. Therefore, which propositions of the theory are taken as assumptions, and how these are formulated, will depend in part on the aims of the presentation: treating certain propositions as assumptions, and formulating them in one way rather than another, may simplify the presentation, make it more revealing, more elegant, or more rigorous.

2) *The motivation for the theory.* In presenting his theory the scientist may also indicate what leads him to make the assumptions he does. He may note various factors to be understood and problems to be solved. He may indicate other theories that attempt to deal with

---

[17] Christiaan Huygens, *Treatise on Light* (Chicago, 1945).

these and show how they fail to do so adequately. He may cite principles accepted in other domains and argue that these need to be applied to the domain in question. He may draw analogies between this domain and others already understood. These considerations will not establish or prove the assumptions but will make them appear something less than arbitrary. They will indicate why a theory is needed and some of the reasons for proposing this particular one.

Consider how Bohr presents his theory of the hydrogen atom.[18] He begins by noting that in order to explain experiments on the scattering of alpha rays Rutherford proposed a theory of the atom. Observing that most alpha particles are not scattered upon striking gold atoms, whereas those that are have large scattering angles, Rutherford suggested that the mass of the gold atom is concentrated in a small nucleus around which electrons revolve. However, Bohr notes, the principles of classical electrodynamics, if applied to Rutherford's atom, yield unacceptable results; for on classical principles a moving electric charge should radiate energy continuously, and this would continually decrease the radius of the electron orbit as well as produce a continuous increase in frequency of radiation from the atom. This is unacceptable, Bohr points out, since spectral experiments show that atoms have fixed dimensions and fixed frequencies of radiation.[19] Bohr then indicates the relevance of Planck's theory of radiation for the problem in question. Planck assumed that "the energy radiation from an atomic system does not take place in the continuous way assumed in the ordinary electrodynamics, but that it, on the contrary, takes place in distinctly separated emissions, the amount of energy radiated out from an atomic vibrator of frequency v in a single emission being equal to $\tau h v$, where τ is an entire number, and h is a universal constant." [20]

It is only after he has said all this that Bohr introduces his own assumptions, and he does so by indicating what suggests them to him. Since experience seems to indicate stable atoms, hence stable orbits for electrons, Bohr assumes that "the electron after the interaction [with the positive nucleus] has taken place has settled down in a stationary orbit around the nucleus" in which no radiation is emitted.[21] Since experience also suggests that atoms do emit radiation, it might be reason-

---

[18] "On the Constitution of Atoms and Molecules," *Philosophical Magazine,* 26 (1913).

[19] *Ibid.,* p. 4.

[20] *Ibid.*

[21] *Ibid.*

able to assume that during the binding of an electron, and also during its transition from one stable orbit to another, radiation is emitted of frequency v. "Then, from Planck's theory, we might expect that the amount of energy emitted by the process considered is equal to $\tau h v$, where h is Planck's constant and τ an entire number. If we assume that the radiation emitted is homogeneous, the second assumption concerning the frequency of radiation suggests itself, since the frequency of revolution of the electron at the beginning of the emission is O." [22]

In short, before presenting the central and distinctive assumptions of his theory, Bohr is motivated to set the stage: to cite experiments and observations that call for a theory of the structure of atoms; to explain the weaknesses of alternative theories (he cites not only Rutherford's but also that of J. J. Thomson); to note principles from other domains that might be applicable to the one in question; to show, that is, that his assumptions are not arbitrary or fortuitous.

3) *The development of the theory.* This frequently occupies the most space in a presentation; it may include many different sorts of things:

a) Introducing additional assumptions that, although not maximally central for or distinctive of the theory, are required or at least very helpful. Often they will not be introduced explicitly and labelled as assumptions but will be implicitly made. They may be principles appropriated from other theories (for example, Bohr assumed principles of classical mechanics for the stable electron orbits in the atom); they may be assumptions that on intuitive or aesthetic grounds seem reasonable to make (for example, Einstein's assumption that the transformation equations are linear).

b) Reformulating assumptions in a more manageable way, often in mathematical terms. Clausius, in formulating the principles of thermodynamics (what he calls "the mechanical theory of heat"), first expresses the fundamental assumptions in a qualitative way. He states the first principle as follows:

> In all cases where work is produced by heat, a quantity of heat is consumed proportional to the work done; and inversely, by the expenditure of the same amount of work the same quantity of heat may be produced.[23]

[22] *Ibid.,* p. 5.
[23] R. Clausius, *The Mechanical Theory of Heat* (London, 1879), p. 23.

141

In a section entitled "Development of the First Main Principle," he then offers several mathematical formulations for this principle, for example, $dQ = dH + dL$, where dQ is an infinitesimal quantity of heat imparted to a body, dH an infinitesimal increment of the total heat existing in the body, and dL an infinitesimal quantity of work done. Another standard mathematical formulation of this law is this: $\oint dW \propto \oint dQ$, where $\oint dW$ signifies the algebraic sum of work transfers through a complete cycle of a system and $\oint dQ$ is the algebraic sum of heat transfers.

c) Explaining the meaning of the assumptions by citing illustrations or analogies or by defining concepts employed. One standard way of explaining the first principle of thermodynamics is by the use of examples. We may be asked to imagine a gas within a cylinder fitted with a movable piston and a source of heat applied to the gas; the gas expands, pushing the piston and thus doing work. If the gas is allowed to return to its initial state by having a body of lower temperature applied to it, then, in accordance with the first principle of thermodynamics, the total work done by the system is proportional to the total heat communicated to it.

d) Introducing new concepts. Clausius, for example, after expressing the first principle of thermodynamics in both a qualitative and quantitative manner, introduces a new concept—that of the energy of a body (now usually called internal energy). This he defines as the sum of the quantity of heat of the body and the quantity of work done by the molecules of the body. The introduction of this concept allows him to offer other quantitative formulations of the first principle, for example, $Q = U_2 - U_1 + W$, where Q is the total heat imparted to the body, W is the external work done, and U_1 and U_2 are the initial and final values of the energy of the body.

e) Deriving general principles as direct consequences of the central and distinctive assumptions. One important proposition derivable from the first principle of thermodynamics is that there is a *thermodynamic property* of a system such that a change in the value of this property is equal to the difference between the heat supplied and the work done during any change in state. It is a thermodynamic property in the sense that it has a definite value when the system is in a particular state, and this value is independent of how the system arrived at that state. (The property is in fact the one that Clausius calls energy.) This principle, though not derived by Clausius, can be generated directly from the first principle of thermodynamics expressed in the form $\oint dW \propto \oint dQ$. The derivation is typically found in modern textbooks developing the theory.

f) Applying the central and distinctive assumptions or their direct consequences to systems satisfying special conditions and working out the results. After developing the first principle of thermodynamics, Clausius applies the resulting formulas to a perfect gas, that is, one satisfying the equation of state $PV = nRT$. In the case of a reversible process, the first principle can be expressed as follows: $dQ = dU + pdV$, where p is pressure and dV an infinitesimal change in volume. Clausius applies this formula to a perfect gas and derives a number of relationships, for example, that for a perfect gas $\dfrac{dU}{dV} = 0$, which means that in a perfect gas the energy U is independent of the volume and is a function only of the temperature.[24]

g) Using the central and distinctive assumptions of the theory or their direct consequences as a basis for working out certain problems about the entities, properties, or relationships postulated by these assumptions; where the solution to such problems does not follow immediately or solely from these assumptions or their direct consequences. Consider how Maxwell develops the kinetic theory of gases. In his paper "Illustrations of the Dynamical Theory of Gases," he begins by stating very briefly the distinctive assumptions of this theory (for example, that the "minute parts of gases," the molecules, are in rapid motion; that they move with uniform velocity in straight lines; that they strike each other; and so on).[25] The bulk of his paper, however, is devoted to showing how the assumption that gases are composed of such particles can be used as a basis for solving problems such as finding the probability of a molecule reaching a given distance before striking another, finding the mean path of molecules in a mixture of two gases, finding the average number of particles whose velocities lie between given limits, showing how viscosity of gases (internal gaseous friction) can be interpreted in molecular terms, and so forth. Solving such problems may involve (*i*) proposing a method of analyzing or structuring the situation that is only suggested but not implied by the central and distinctive assumptions of the theory; (*ii*) introducing new assumptions; (*iii*) introducing mathematical techniques not indicated when the original assumptions are proposed.

[24] *Ibid.*, pp. 43–46.
[25] *The Scientific Papers of James Clerk Maxwell,* ed. W. D. Niven (New York, 1965), I, 377–409.

All three of these are illustrated when Maxwell develops his theory for the viscosity of gases. He proposes that we analyze the phenomenon of viscosity by thinking of the gas as divided into layers that can slide across one another with different velocities; we can then consider the possibility of molecules entering and leaving a given layer. An assumption is now introduced that although not implied by the central and distinctive assumptions of his theory is suggested by them in the light of the above manner of structuring the situation:

> The explanation of gaseous friction, according to our hypothesis, is that particles having the mean velocity of translation belonging to one layer of the gas, pass out of it into another layer having a different velocity of translation; and by striking against the particles of the second layer, exert upon it a tangential force which constitutes the internal friction of the gas.[26]

Having introduced this hypothesis, Maxwell is now in a position to raise and answer questions such as these: What is the number of particles that, starting from one layer, reach and stop in the next layer? What is the mean momentum communicated by each such particle? Using techniques of integral calculus, Maxwell can then determine the friction between a given layer and all the layers below and above.

Because of the introduction of novel ways of structuring situations, new assumptions, and mathematical techniques, none of which may be contained in or implied by the central assumptions of the theory, this cannot be described simply as deriving general principles as direct consequences of such assumptions, that is, as (e). Nor is this what I have called applying the basic assumptions or their direct consequences to systems satisfying special conditions, that is, (f). In the latter situation the scientist takes the central assumptions (or their direct consequences), usually expressed in quantitative form, substitutes in them relationships that obtain for a special system, and then deduces a new set of relationships holding only for the system in question. The procedure described in (g) is different.

4) *The discussion of confirmation.* If A has a theory T, he cannot now, or could not at the inception of his belief in T, come to know immediately and readily that T is true; there is an element of indirectness involved. Especially in science, where typically a fairly large

---

[26] *Ibid.,* p. 390.

and complex set of propositions will constitute a theory, the process of coming to know whether the theory is true will involve drawing inferences from the assumptions and comparing what is inferred with what is establishable by experiment and observation; this, rather than comparing each assumption individually with what is so establishable. Moreover, the inferences tested are typically those that follow not from the central and distinctive assumptions alone but from these together with other less central assumptions or other propositions established independently of the theory.

Not all the inferences from the theory, not even all those drawn by the scientist in his presentation, are actually tested or proposed for testing. There may be no means available for testing some. Others, as I shall explain later, may not be considered as offering the most important or even any tests of the theory. Accordingly, in his presentation the scientist will frequently indicate which consequences, for purposes of confirmation of the theory, are to be compared with what is established or establishable.

Consider some of the inferences from the Bohr theory that Bohr himself treated as relevant for its confirmation. From the central and distinctive assumptions of his theory and the assumption of principles of classical mechanics (for stationary states of the atom), he deduced the formula $v = \dfrac{2\pi^2 m e^4}{h^3} \left(\dfrac{1}{\tau_2^2} - \dfrac{1}{\tau_1^2} \right)$, where v is the frequency of radiation emitted or absorbed by the hydrogen atom, m and e the mass and charge of the electron, and τ_1 and τ_2 whole numbers. Letting $\tau_2 = 2$ and $\tau_1 = 3, 4, 5, \ldots$, we get the known formula for the Balmer series connecting the lines in the spectrum of hydrogen.[27] This agreement between theory and what is established is noted by Bohr as adding in some measure to the confirmation of his theory.[28] In this case the fact that hydrogen does have a spectrum containing discrete lines whose relationship is described by the Balmer formula was part of the motivation for the theory; that is, Bohr sought to develop a theory that could account for the discreteness of these lines. But the fact that he could derive the exact form of the relationship between these discrete lines (that is, Balmer's formula) is taken by him as counting in favor of his theory.

Bohr, however, does not rest his case on the derivation of estab-

[27] See p. 131.
[28] "On the Constitution of Atoms and Molecules," p. 9.

145

lished relationships. Suppose, in the above equation, we let $\tau_2 = 1$ and $\tau_1 = 4, 5, \ldots$. Then, Bohr predicts, we will obtain a series in the ultraviolet region. This series had not been observed at the time but was later discovered (the so-called Lyman series). In the same passage Bohr claims another "agreement between the theoretical and observed values" as counting toward the confirmation of his theory. Consider the expression $\dfrac{2\pi^2 m e^4}{h^3}$. Using values for e, m, and h obtained experimentally, Bohr concluded that $\dfrac{2\pi^2 m e^4}{h^3} = 3.1 \times 10^{15}$. In the Balmer formula the value for the corresponding Rydberg constant R for hydrogen, as obtained by experiment, is 3.290×10^{15}. Bohr considers this agreement between theory and observation to be "inside the uncertainty due to experimental errors in the constants entering in the expression for the theoretical value." [29] He mentions this agreement obviously supposing it adds to the confirmation of his theory.

This does not mean that any established consequence of a theory confirms that theory. Three considerations are relevant here. First is the precision with which the consequence is expressed. The more precise the expression, the more confirmation its deduction tends to give to the theory, provided of course that the consequence is found to hold. One of the reasons why the deduction of Balmer's formula from the Bohr theory could be taken as adding to the confirmation of this theory is that the proposition deduced expresses a precise relationship between certain physical quantities; it is not a vague, qualitative description of discrete lines coming closer together at one end of the spectrum.

A second consideration concerns the availability of alternative, incompatible theories. Suppose that consequence C is derivable from theory T, but that there is an alternative theory T' from which C or something approximating it can also be derived, where T' is considered more adequate than T, or at least equally adequate. Then the fact that C can be derived from T and that C is established cannot be appealed to as confirmation for T, unless T' is somehow discredited. One of the reasons why Bohr could claim that the deduction of the Balmer formula, as well as the agreement between the theoretical and observational values for the Rydberg constant, tended to confirm his theory was because of the absence, at the time of his paper, of any other theory having the relevant consequences.

[29] *Ibid.*

The third consideration relates to how C is actually derived from the theory. The more assumptions of the theory that need to be utilized in the derivation, especially the central and distinctive ones, that is, the more that the derivation of C is a joint effort on the part of such assumptions, the more the establishment of C tends to add to the confirmation of the theory. If C is a consequence of just one of many central assumptions in a theory, or if it is a consequence simply of additional assumptions added to T for certain purposes, then the establishment of C cannot be claimed to confirm theory T (but at best only one of the central assumptions of T or only some of the ancillary assumptions needed for T). Bohr could cite the derivation of Balmer's formula as support for his theory because it used all the central and distinctive assumptions of his theory, not just one, and not ancillary assumptions alone.

Accordingly, the issue of confirmation is not decided simply by pointing to all the consequences of the theory, even to all those considered established. The scientist, if he discusses the question of confirmation at all, will need to be selective.

How is the discussion of confirming consequences different from what I have called the motivation for the theory? The former may indeed be part of the motivation. What may have led scientists to propose certain assumptions is the fact that if they made them, they could derive conclusions known to be correct. But usually not all, if indeed very many, confirming consequences of the theory will actually have motivated scientists to propose that theory, for not all of these will be known to be consequences of the theory at the time it is proposed; and even among those that are, many will not be known or believed to be true when the theory is first proposed. Moreover, factors other than confirming consequences are part of the motivation for the theory. In short, the class of confirming consequences is neither included within nor does it include the class of motivating factors; at best these classes will overlap.

I have outlined four ingredients in the presentation of a theory. Not all will be found in every presentation, nor will each occur neatly distinguished from the others or receive equal treatment. There may be several different presentations of the same theory, some emphasizing certain ingredients, while making casual or even no reference to others. Some will be more historically oriented, indicating as part of the motivation a chronological account of the theoretical and experimental origins of the theory. Other presentations may de-emphasize or omit motivating factors in favor of a detailed formulation of the assumptions and the development of their consequences. In his "Illustrations of the Dynamical Theory of Gases," Maxwell offers quite a different sort of presentation of the kinetic theory from the one in his lecture on molecules delivered before the British Association at Bradford.[30] The former is almost exclusively concerned with the development of the theory and proceeds at a mathematically sophisticated level. The latter is presented in a much more elementary and qualitative way (not a single equation or symbol appears); it covers much less ground as far as the development of the theory is concerned; and it contains numerous motivating considerations including references to the theories of Anaxagoras and Democritus. Yet it succeeds in presenting the theory to an audience with little or no knowledge of physics. Many presentations of the kinetic theory, even for those with a background in physics, are different from either of these.

Obviously, in typical presentations of a theory, even in those containing all four ingredients, not all the assumptions will be formulated, motivating factors cited, aspects of the theory developed, or potentially confirming consequences derived and compared with what is established. Within a given category, which aspects are chosen, as well as the sophistication and completeness with which they are presented, will depend on the particular sort of presentation desired; and this can vary with the aims of the scientist (or whoever is presenting the theory) and the audience intended.

4. THE AXIOMATIC PRESENTATION OF A THEORY

All this does not mean that any presentation is as good as any other. The point is that to evaluate a presentation one must first consider the sort of information it is trying to impart and the emphasis, if any, attempted. Given this, of course particular presentations can be evaluated with respect to how well they will serve these aims. Moreover, even if one presentation is acceptable given the aims in question, it is possible to indicate why, for other purposes, it would be inadequate.

This can be illustrated by considering the presentation of a theory suggested by the axiomatic account. Those who speak of hypothetico-

[30] *Scientific Papers,* II, 361–77.

deductive systems suggest that a theory is to be presented by citing all the assumptions made or at least needed by its proponents. These include not only what I have called the central and distinctive assumptions of the theory but also others, possibly from different theories, introduced in developing the theory in question. All assumptions not derived from any others are to be presented together under a heading marked "axioms." They are to be stated using only those terms of an initially agreed-upon vocabulary containing primitive terms and ones defined by reference to these. Propositions which follow deductively from the set of axioms are to be indicated and their proofs to be given with logical and mathematical inferences made explicit. In short, to present a theory axiomatically it is necessary and sufficient to supply a vocabulary of primitive and defined terms and to cite axioms, theorems, and proofs.

Proponents of axiomatic presentations need not maintain that theories are actually presented in this way in science. They may propose this as a desirable though often difficult goal to achieve. Nor need they claim that there is only one way to axiomatize a theory: only one set of propositions to take as axioms, one set of terms to treat as primitive, one set of definitions to use, or one set of proofs to construct. Alternative axiomatizations may be possible and equally valuable. Moreover, there may be differences in the degree to which actual presentations approximate the ideal. Some may formulate a set of axioms and proofs but omit certain obvious assumptions, fail to distinguish between primitive and defined terms, or assume but not explicitly formulate logical and mathematical rules of inference. Others will be much more complete and rigorous, using techniques of formal logic.[31]

An axiomatic presentation has several potential advantages. Assumptions actually employed or needed by the proponent of the theory are made explicit. By contrast, in actual presentations it is sometimes not clear what is being assumed and what is taken as proved from assumptions; or again, in actual presentations assumptions are sometimes implicitly made, especially in the development of a theory, that if explicitly stated could be recognized at once to be implausible or even inconsistent with others. Also on the axiomatic approach, the logical structure of the theory becomes more apparent in the following sense:

---

[31] For a range of such axiomatizations of some actual theories in science, see *The Axiomatic Method,* ed. L. Henkin, P. Suppes, and A. Tarski (Amsterdam, 1959).

one can determine exactly from what assumptions, using what mathematical techniques and principles of inference, theorems are supposed to follow; and all deductions can be verified in an objective step-by-step manner. Another advantage is the organization provided for the set of terms in the theory: a term is recognized as one whose definition can be given using other terms in the theory, in which case the connections are indicated explicitly, or else as one for which no such definition is to be given, in which case it is listed as "primitive." Finally, showing how a large number of propositions of the theory can be derived by suitable choice and formulation of others as axioms can be a gain in elegance, another obvious advantage.

Yet an axiomatic presentation has potential disadvantages. First, by indiscriminately including under the list of axioms *all* the assumptions actually needed for the theory, it may become difficult to discern which are especially central for and distinctive of the theory; which present the characteristic ideas of the theory, by contrast with ones that are less central, are needed only for the solution of certain problems, are appropriated from other theories, or are formulated ad hoc simply to handle these problems. With respect to assumptions the axiomatic account is completely democratic: all are treated as equally central, equally distinctive. Second, since it need include no motivating factors for the theory, an axiomatic presentation can make the assumptions seem perfectly arbitrary; it can leave one completely puzzled as to what sorts of problems they were meant to solve or why these rather than other seemingly plausible ones were made. Third, in an axiomatic presentation proofs of theorems may promote relatively little understanding of why what is proved is so—by explicitly including all the assumptions needed and all the steps in the proofs, and by failing to indicate which assumptions are central to the theory and which ancillary, one following such a proof may not see the forest for the trees. Although such a person may be in a better position to check the validity of the proof,[32] he may not discern its overall pattern, central ideas, or crucial steps. Fourth, in an axiomatic presentation at least one important aspect of the development of a theory is omitted—namely, explaining the meaning of some of the assumptions in ways other than by giving definitions; for example, by providing illustrations and analogies.[33] Fifth, in such a presentation al-

---

[32] But not always. In some axiomatizations the steps included are not needed to check validity, being painfully obvious.

[33] Some, though not all, who defend axiomatic presentations do introduce analogies as part of the presentation; their position on analogies will be discussed in Chap. Eight.

though the theorems of the theory can be derived from the complete set of assumptions, and even though a set of such theorems will be formulated, it need not be indicated which of these are treated as consequences actually tested, or likely to be, to confirm the theory. As indicated earlier, not all theorems can be used in confirming the theory; even among those which can, not all will actually be employed. With respect to confirmation an axiomatic presentation is too completely democratic: all theorems are relevant and each is as relevant as any other.

This is not to deny that discussion giving differences in centrality, motivating factors, amplification of proofs, illustrations, and important aspects of confirmation could be added to an axiomatic presentation; but those who espouse axiomatic presentations tend to ignore these and treat them as unnecessary baggage, of use perhaps only to the slow thinker; and their examples of axiomatizations usually omit most if not all such considerations. The reasoning seems to be this: since a theory *is* just a system of assumptions, theorems, and proofs, that is the way it should be presented.

Let me comment finally on the use of a special vocabulary. In Chapter Three, I criticized the view that requires all definitions to provide logically necessary and sufficient conditions; so let us construe the present doctrine more liberally to include not only such definitions but also others described in the first two chapters. It might be that those who advocate the use of a special vocabulary have in mind simply listing together all terms that have actually been utilized in a presentation of a theory, indicating which are supposed to be defined by reference to others and how the definitions are to be expressed. Such a procedure can obviously be useful and will not be discussed further. However, the advocate of a special vocabulary might be suggesting something stronger. He might be suggesting not that a list of terms is to be compiled *after* completing a presentation but *before* embarking upon one; that to begin with, a list of acceptable terms be provided and that a presentation of a theory proceed by using only terms on the list. This might be construed in two ways: (1) Anything in the presentation must use this vocabulary. (2) Certain parts of the presentation must use it.

If (1) is the claim, then the use of such a vocabulary can have a stifling effect on the presentation of a theory. Suppose that before presenting his theory the scientist constructs a list of terms and proposes to use these and only these throughout. However, in offering his presentation, there may be new and unforeseen considerations calling for the introduction of new terms. For example, in developing the theory the scientist may apply his assumptions to special systems not discovered or even envisaged when his original list was composed, where the description of such systems requires new terms that cannot be defined using those on his original list. In citing motivating factors he may invoke other theories not expressible using the terms proposed; he may wish to offer reformulations of his assumptions employing at least some new technical or even nontechnical terms; or he may explain some of his assumptions by providing illustrations or analogies using other terms. All of this would be precluded if he must present his theory confining terms to some basic vocabulary.

Suppose then we adopt alternative (2) and require only that certain parts of the presentation utilize terms in a specified vocabulary. Such a proposal, I think, can be useful. For example, because of the problematic nature of certain terms in Newton's theory of mechanics, it can be of some value to try to formulate the central and distinctive assumptions with only a certain set of terms. Following Hertz, these might be terms for mass, time, and space, which are considered to be clearer than others (such as force).[34] The attempt would then be made to define the problematic terms using these. This limited task does not commit one to employing this restricted list throughout the entire presentation of Newtonian mechanics. For example, it does not commit one to using only these terms (or those defined by reference to them) when applying the fundamental assumptions to celestial systems (here Newton needed to introduce terms like "sun," "planet," and "star"); or when explaining the fundamental principles by citing illustrations and analogies, or when formulating motivating factors.

What do proponents of an axiomatic presentation say on the question of vocabulary? Not simply that after the completion of a presentation a list of all the terms and definitions is to be compiled. They demand that before embarking upon a presentation a list of terms be compiled and that these and only these be employed in the presentation. However, they would probably espouse alternative (2) rather than (1) and argue that only certain parts of the presentation need be given using terms from the fixed vocabulary. Many of those who accept the axiomatic account of theories agree at least that explanations of the meaning of assumptions (explanations proceeding by use of a metalanguage), as well as analogies employed, require terms not on the

[34] Heinrich Hertz, *The Principles of Mechanics* (New York, 1956).

fixed vocabulary. But just what part of the presentation must be given using this vocabulary? The answer seems to be that all assumptions made in presenting the theory (not just the central and distinctive ones) and all the theorems generated (including those for special systems) must be expressed using this vocabulary. Such a requirement, although more acceptable than (1), is too stringent. For example, special assumptions regarding systems not yet envisaged may need to be made, and these as well as the new theorems they generate may employ terms not on the original list or definable using just these. To compose a list of acceptable terms before developing the theory may stifle any such development.

I have tried to suggest several advantages as well as disadvantages of an axiomatic presentation. The fact that there are disadvantages should not debar theories from being presented axiomatically. It all depends on the aim of the presentation. If what is wanted is an elegant, precise, and complete formulation of all the assumptions made or needed, one that will provide a completely rigorous basis for verifying logical inferences of the theory, an axiomatic presentation is in order. Yet by characteristically omitting motivating factors, failing to distinguish assumptions with respect to centrality and distinctiveness, failing to contain reformulations of various assumptions in other terms (not restricted to those on some fixed vocabulary), and failing to indicate which consequences are relevant for confirmation, such a presentation can hinder an understanding of the theory. Therefore, if the aim is to teach the theory to one ignorant of the subject and to avoid the pitfalls above, a different sort of presentation, emphasizing other ingredients and developed at an appropriate level of completeness and rigor, may be necessary. If the aim is to present the development of a theory and to do so mainly for one's colleagues (as in Maxwell's "Illustrations of the Dynamical Theory of Gases"), a still different mode of presentation may be called for. If the aim is a mixed one, to provide some advantages of each, as often happens in a textbook on the theory, various approaches may be tried separately or together. The point is that no single type of presentation of a theory will satisfy all intellectual needs that might be felt.

Let me revert, finally, to conceptions of theories discussed in section 2. Roughly speaking, Feyerabend, Hanson, and Bromberger, respectively, construe theories as deep, general commitments, conceptual organizers, and potential puzzle-removers; yet these philosophers do not provide, and perhaps do not seek to provide, any deeper analysis of the elements or "constituent parts" of theories. On the other hand, supporters of the axiomatic account, especially contemporary Positivists, do insist on analyzing theories into components: an uninterpreted deductive calculus and rules of interpretation (the latter including correspondence rules and semantical rules). But such an analysis carries with it commitments regarding the interpretation of terms that I reject.[35] It also carries the implication that there is one ideal way to present a theory—namely, axiomatically. In abstracting the ingredients described in the previous section, I have provided an alternative way of structuring a theory. It is more general than that provided by the axiomatic account and allows us to understand better how a theory can assume quite different but equally valuable forms.

5. A BROADER CONCEPT OF THEORY

We have been speaking about that use of the term "theory" illustrated in science by "the kinetic theory of gases" or "the Bohr theory of the atom"; but there is a somewhat different, and broader, use of this term illustrated by expressions such as "physical theory," "nuclear theory," and even "Newtonian theory" (by contrast with "Newton's theory").[36] In the narrower sense to speak of theories is to speak of propositions; at least it is to refer to those distinctive of the theory and central in it. However, as we have seen, the question, "Which propositions are the theory?" has no simple answer; and there is a sense in which propositions derived from T, as well as laws and principles from other theories that are used in T, are part of the theory. At any rate, to use "theory" in the narrower sense is to view what is being talked about in a "propositional" way as a set of claims or assertions. To use "theory" in the broader sense is to view what is being talked about as a field or subject matter. A theory, in this sense, might be construed as a set containing not only propositions but also concepts, methods of analyzing or structuring situations, methods for solving problems, applications to various systems, and so forth.

For example, when one studies Newtonian theory one studies con-

---

[35] See Chap. Three.

[36] The distinction I shall outline here is somewhat akin to one Bromberger has made. See "A Theory about the Theory of Theory."

cepts such as angular velocity, conservative system, coriolis acceleration. One studies methods for analyzing and structuring situations such
as vector analysis, methods for analyzing systems of bodies into com-
ponent forces, methods for finding the center of mass. One studies special systems to which the principles are applicable, for example, freely
falling bodies, Atwood's machine, perfectly rigid bodies. To be sure,
these may all be introduced in the course of presenting Newton's theory
of mechanics (narrower sense). But to use the term "theory" in the
latter way is to view them simply or primarily as part of a set of propositions (constituting Newton's theory). To use the term "theory" in the
broader sense is to view these not simply or primarily in this way but
as items to be considered separately. If we were to represent a theory in
the broader sense schematically we might do so as follows: $P_1, \ldots,$
P_m; $C_1, \ldots, C_n$; $M_1, \ldots, M_o$; $A_1, \ldots, A_p$—where P's are
propositions, C's concepts, M's methods of analysis and computation,
and A's various applications. If, then, we were to represent a theory in
the narrower sense schematically, we might do so simply as $P_1, \ldots,$
P_m—thinking of the C's, M's, and A's as part of, or primarily in connection with, the P's. Moreover, a theory in the broader sense (for example, physical theory) may contain a number of different and even
conflicting theories in the narrower sense. On the other hand, it may
contain no theories in the narrower sense but simply methods of analysis
and computation (for example, the theory of equations).

In some cases "theory" will be used in both ways. If so, a simple
grammatical difference may signal the distinction, namely, that between
"*the* theory of X" (or "*the* X theory") and "theory of X" (or "X theory"). Usually to speak about *the* Newtonian theory is to speak about
a certain set of propositions. To speak about Newtonian theory is to
speak about a broader set containing not only these but, in addition,
concepts, methods of analysis, idealized systems, and so forth. Other
examples would be "the kinetic theory" vs. "kinetic theory," "the atomic
theory" vs. "atomic theory," "the genetic theory" vs. "genetic theory."
There are, however, uses of "theory" where "the" cannot occur, for example, "physical theory," "chemical theory," "nuclear theory."[37] Here
"theory" is being used in the broader sense. There are also uses of "the
theory of X" in the broader sense where "theory of X" does not usually
occur, for example, "the theory of the microscope." My point is only

---

[37] Except, of course, in expressions such as "the physical theory of Newton."
But this is the narrower use of "theory."

that when "theory of X" can be used both with the definite article and without it, and when it is used in both a broader and narrower sense, the use of the definite article typically signals the narrower sense, its omission, the broader one.

There are certain similarities between the two senses of "theory." One of the primary functions of theory (broader sense), as well as a theory (narrower sense), is to provide an understanding of various things (via explanation, interpretation, analysis, and so forth). Of course it need not be the case that one who makes a specific contribution to theory (broader sense) or to a theory (narrower sense) does so primarily for this purpose; all I am claiming is that this is one of the primary functions of theory or a theory considered as a whole. Second, as in the case of a theory, a speculative element, or something akin to it, is typically involved in theory. To refer to principles, concepts, methods, and so forth, as part of a theory is to imply that it is (or was) not certain that they afford the correct or most satisfactory understanding of those things for which theory was developed or provide the most illuminating answers to problems that prompted theory in the first place. Although there may be some reason to believe they do, this can be subjected to doubt or questioning; hence theory is always subject to modification. Principles, concepts, methods, and so forth, developed for providing understanding but treated as indubitable and unalterable, are more likely to be called dogma than theory.

6. CONCLUSIONS

I began this chapter by suggesting conditions semantically relevant for having a theory and then, by reference to these, characterizing what it is to be a theory. Using this as a basis, it is possible to show why several alternative accounts of theories are inadequate. Also using this as a basis, it is possible to consider the presentation of theories. This I did by distinguishing several ingredients within presentations and by showing how, depending upon the aim of the presentation, some can be emphasized and developed rather than others. Finally, I have tried to distinguish a narrower from a broader concept of theory. We are now in a position to examine a question raised in Chapter Three while discussing the Positivist account: with respect to theories can a distinction be drawn between theoretical and nontheoretical terms?

CHAPTER FIVE

OBSERVATIONAL TERMS

1. THE DISTINCTION BETWEEN THEORETICAL AND NONTHEORETICAL TERMS

A fundamental assumption of many contemporary philosophers of science is that there is a distinction between theoretical and nontheoretical terms, one crucial for a proper understanding of the concepts and methods of science. Here are some examples drawn from the writings of those who make the distinction.

theoretical terms		*nontheoretical terms*	
electron	mass	red	floats
electric field	kinetic energy	warm	wood
atom	electrical resistance	left of	water
molecule	temperature	longer than	iron
wave function	gene	hard	weight
charge	virus	volume	cell nucleus

Scientists employ terms from both lists. Terms classified as nontheoretical are often used in describing experiments, but they are also found in the principles of theories that these experiments test. When Bohr formulated the principles of his theory of the atom he used terms such as "particle," "moves," and "distance," which many authors might place on the nontheoretical list. Conversely, terms called theoretical are used not only in the principles of a theory but also in the descriptions of experimental results. Chadwick, in describing experiments that led to his neutron hypothesis, employed terms such as "ion," "radiation," and "proton." [1]

The theoretical-nontheoretical distinction is made for several reasons. First, for those who want to explore the "logic of science" and do so by characterizing the language of the scientist, a classification of terms becomes desirable. Second, such a division allows certain questions about science to be put in a more general, philosophical way. Concern with the logic of science might prompt the questions: What meaning can the terms "electron," "field," or "gene" have if the items to which they refer cannot be observed? How can a scientific theory that purports to be empirical employ the terms "charge," "mass," and "kinetic energy," which refer to quantities not directly measurable? What is the relationship between concepts expressed by the terms "electron" and "molecule" and those expressed by "red," "warm," and "hard," which the layman ordinarily uses to describe the world? These questions mention specific terms, but philosophers of science want to raise the same issues in a much more general way. Accordingly, they invoke broad categories and formulate the previous questions to refer to "theoretical" and "nontheoretical" terms generally. The issue then becomes not simply what significance particular terms such as "electron" and "warm" have, but what significance theoretical and nontheoretical terms have, what roles they play in theories, and what their relationships are to each other. The division of terms into these broad categories allows questions to be put in this more general form. Third, this distinction is considered essential by those defending the contemporary Positivist view considered in Chapter Three. The proposal is that terms in each category be treated in fundamentally different ways: theoretical terms, as symbols in a calculus for which no semantical rules are given; nontheoretical terms, as ones interpreted by means of semantical rules or else as explicitly defined using terms having semantical rules. Such a position, it must be emphasized, is founded upon a *prior* classification of terms as theoretical or nontheoretical. In Chapter Three I considered difficulties in this account that arise when terms called theoretical by Positivists are treated as uninterpreted or "partially" interpreted. Now I want to ask whether, indeed, any basis can be found for the general division presupposed.

For Positivists, the distinction depends on the criterion of observa-

---

[1] J. Chadwick, "The Existence of a Neutron," *Foundations of Nuclear Physics,* ed. Robert T. Beyer (New York, 1949), pp. 5–21.

bility: terms on the theoretical list are supposed to refer to unobservables, those on the nontheoretical list to observables. But other proposals have also been made: according to one, terms on the former list are theory-dependent, those on the latter are not; there are also proposals appealing to conceptual organization, conjecture, precision, and degree of abstractness. My purpose in this chapter and the next is to examine these criteria and show that each generates not one but many different distinctions under which the classification of terms varies markedly.

If my general conclusion about the present distinction is correct, one might ask: Why are philosophers so often in agreement about the terms to be placed in each group? It is not clear that there is general agreement here, since those who invoke the distinction cite very few examples and even then differences emerge; but suppose we grant some agreement on classification. This might not be difficult to explain on a superficial level. In many cases philosophers might be classifying as theoretical terms used and understood mainly by scientists and those acquainted with science; and as nontheoretical those used and understood equally by scientists and nonscientists. In short, lists might be generated by reference to the type of person who typically uses and understands the terms, just as one could distinguish surgical instruments from nonsurgical ones by saying that they are instruments used typically by the surgeon. However, this merely postpones the issue of fundamental concern to those constructing theoretical and nontheoretical lists. Now the problem would be formulated as follows: What is characteristic of those terms used and understood typically by scientists and those acquainted with science, by contrast with terms used and understood by scientists and nonscientists alike? (Just as in the surgical example one might want to know what is characteristic of instruments used typically by the surgeon.)

It will be my contention that unobservability, theory-dependence, conceptual organization, conjecture, precision, and degree of abstractness, are not features the possession or lack of which generates either list. But my aim is not simply to establish this negative conclusion; I want to examine the concepts of observability, theory-dependence, and so forth, for these are frequently invoked but not sufficiently studied in the philosophy of science.

2. OBSERVATION

The first proposal is that the basic distinction is between observables and unobservables. Thus, according to Carnap, we have on the one hand "terms designating observable properties and relations," and on the other, "terms which may refer to unobservable events, unobservable aspects or features of events." [2] Carnap does not here explain what he means by "observable" and "unobservable." Presumably he is not using these terms in an unusual manner, for he believes that his readers will understand in at least a general way the distinction intended. I want to begin by considering the concept of observation in order to clarify its use as well as to indicate possible reasons why Carnap chooses it; then I shall ask whether observation can provide a basis for the distinction.

"Observe" has a number of senses with which I shall not be concerned. It can mean "to keep or abide by" (a law or custom); it can also mean "to remark." I want to consider the concept in the sense in which observing involves visually attending to something.

1) To observe something, in this sense, is to engage in an activity. It is something that can be done carefully or carelessly, quickly or slowly. What does the activity involve? If I am observing something, I am attending to (looking at or for) various *aspects* or *features* of it. Suppose I stare at a blank wall; normally, of course, I could be described as looking at it and seeing it, but I am not observing it unless I am looking at or for its cracks, its color and texture, its position with respect to other objects, or something of the like. This need not imply any special interest in what is being observed. The shy man has no special interest in the flowered pattern on the rug, although he may be observing it. Nor need it imply that the observer intends to find out something in particular about what he is observing. I may be asked to observe something without having any idea what, if anything, I am supposed to find out about it. There is no particular number or set of aspects of an item I must attend to before I can be said to have observed that item. How many and which ones I do attend to will depend on my concerns and my knowledge. The detective, the physician, and the

---

[2] Carnap, "The Methodological Character of Theoretical Concepts," *Minnesota Studies in the Philosophy of Science*, ed. H. Feigl and M. Scriven (Minneapolis, 1956), I. In other writings Carnap offers somewhat different accounts, which will be noted subsequently.

sculptor may be observing the same person, although each in the course of his job is attending to different features or aspects of him. And whether we say that someone has observed X or that he has observed only *some* aspects or features of X will depend on the context. Observing X is just observing those aspects or features of X that it is appropriate to attend to, given the concerns in question.

2) "Observe" can be contrasted with several related verbs, for example, "see," "detect," and "recognize." Seeing, unlike observing, does not require attending to aspects or features of something. (As I sit at my desk I may see a man walk quickly by my door without observing him.) "Observe," then, is a term particularly appropriate to science, where attention to the various aspects and features of items is often required. Usually the term refers to attending that is visual (or at least partly so). There is a slight oddity in speaking of observing something solely by touching it, smelling it, tasting it, or listening to it. If I am observing Glenn Gould performing Bach's *Goldberg Variations,* the suggestion is that I am observing Mr. Gould and not simply listening to the music. Observing can also be distinguished from detecting, since the latter implies that what is detected is hidden or not immediately obvious in some way, whereas what is observed need not be either of these. Observing does not imply recognizing, as it is possible to observe X and have no idea what X is, or even to mistake it for something else. The savage may carefully observe the airplane, thinking all the while that it is a giant bird.

3) One can observe X, or observe X doing something, even though X is present but in a certain sense "hidden from view." A ranger in a tower on the top of the mountain may be observing a fire on a distant mountain, though all he can see is smoke. The airplane watcher may observe jets flying overhead, though all that is visible are white trails. From the top of a cliff I may be observing boats moving in the river, though all I see are their wakes. I may observe the corn in the field, though all that is visible are husks.

In such cases one observes X by attending to something Y associated with X in a certain way. Three conditions normally obtain if one speaks of observing X in these cases. (*a*) The Y associated with X is something produced by X (such as smoke, tracks, wake) or something that covers X more or less closely (such as a garment or husk). If X is an individual object (for example, an airplane), by contrast to a stuff (for example, fire), then the Y associated with X will be associated with a *single* X, not a group of X's. If we observe a single bomb produce a flash when it explodes, we can claim to have observed the bomb explode; but if the flash we observe is produced by more than one bomb, then we cannot claim to have observed any one bomb explode (though we can, of course, claim to have observed the bombs explode). (*b*) The Y associated with X is within X's "general vicinity," where what counts as X's general vicinity can vary depending upon the location of the observer and the relative distances involved; and the Y continues to remain within X's general vicinity as X moves (if it does). (*c*) Attending to Y, given the present position of the observer and the means he is using, is one standard way, possibly the only way, to visually attend to X from that position, given those means. With the naked eye, the only way to observe a high flying jet from the ground is to attend to the trail it produces as it moves. If the jet flies low enough so that both it and its trail are visible, and I attend only to the trail, then it would be incorrect or misleading for me to claim to be observing the jet.

This is obviously relevant for items on the theoretical list, since, with respect to many of them, these three conditions are satisfied. Consider electrons, electric fields, and temperature. An electron can be observed passing through a cloud chamber. This is because it ionizes gas molecules on which water droplets condense, and these droplets form a visible track; the track produced is in the "general vicinity" of the electron; and, given the cloud chamber method, attending to the track is a standard way (indeed, the only way) to observe the electron passing through the chamber. An electric field causes the leaves of an electroscope in its midst to diverge, this being a standard test for the presence of such a field; it is by observing the divergence of the leaves that one observes the electric field. Finally, the rise in temperature of a substance will cause the mercury in a thermometer in contact with it to expand; and the expansion of the mercury provides a standard method for observing the rise in temperature. In these cases, given the contexts in question, it is perfectly appropriate to speak of observing electrons (in cloud chambers), observing electric fields (with electroscopes), and observing changes in temperature (with thermometers). Indeed, physicists speak in just such ways.

I have said that one observes X by attending to various aspects or features of it; and that the physicist can observe the temperature of a substance by attending to the thermometer in contact with it. Yet it seems odd to say that the physicist is attending to various aspects or features of the temperature. However, there is a point to this way of speaking: to say that the physicist is observing the temperature is to imply that he is attending not merely to what it is but to whether it is changing or has changed and if so how. It places him in a situation in which he is paying attention to what has been and will be happening. In this sense he is attending to "various aspects" of the temperature.

If I observe X, it does not necessarily follow that what it is that I am *seeing* or *looking at* is X. I can observe the temperature of a substance by looking at the thermometer in contact with it, but it is odd to speak of seeing or looking at its temperature (though I can see what its temperature is by looking at the thermometer). It is even odder to speak of seeing the kinetic energy or the entropy of a substance, though when one observes kinetic energy or entropy one does look at something. The point is that what one looks at and sees in such cases is distinguishable from the quantity itself. Accordingly, "observing (the) X" does not necessarily imply *seeing* (*the*) X, although where it does not, it does imply seeing something associated with (the) X in the ways described.

4) There is a second type of case in which X may be "hidden from view" yet where one may speak of observing X, namely, when one is attending to X's reflection in a mirror or to X's image produced by a lens or to something of the like. In such cases the following conditions normally obtain. (1) That which is attended to (the reflection or the image) is produced by X. (2) It is a likeness of X. (3) It changes as X does, when X moves. (4) It exists at the same time as X (at least when X is not too distant from that which it produces). If some of these conditions do not obtain, it can be misleading to speak without qualification of observing X.

Consider a case in which the last three conditions are satisfied but not the first. Suppose that as the astronauts maneuver their spaceship around the earth a model in the laboratory is made to simulate its motion. If one observed only the latter, it would be misleading to speak of observing the spaceship, though one could speak of observing a model of it. Something that violates (2) but satisfies the other conditions would be a configuration produced by X-ray diffraction. This is not a likeness of the item diffracting the X-rays, so scientists tend to speak here not of observing the item but of observing the diffraction pattern it produces. A photograph of X would be a violation of (3), although it could satisfy the other conditions. If I am looking at a current photograph of Lyndon Johnson, then it would be somewhat misleading to say that I am observing him, though I can certainly claim to be observing him in a photograph (or to be observing a photograph of him). Something that might satisfy the first three conditions but not the fourth is a motion picture of X. If I have seen only an old movie of Woodrow Wilson, then it is somewhat misleading for me to claim that I once observed him, without adding: on a motion picture screen.

The qualifications mentioned may be obvious in context, so I might not need to add that what is being observed is a model, photograph, or motion picture. There will also be intermediate cases. If what is observed is produced by X but the production becomes indirect and involved, one might add a qualification, for example, I observed him on television. Again, what counts as a likeness is a matter of degree, and there may be borderline cases (for example, observing shadows of objects).

Notice, on the other hand, that when one observes X via the production of a concurrent image of X, it is not misleading to speak of observing X. We need not, though of course we can, add: through the telescope or through the microscope. There is nothing misleading when someone claims to have observed a certain specimen, and it turns out that he did so with a microscope where an image was produced. Nor is it misleading when someone claims to have observed the moon, and it turns out that he did so through a reflecting telescope in which the moon's image is produced on mirrors.

5) I can describe what I am observing in many different ways. Suppose that while sitting by the roadside at night carefully attending to the road ahead I am asked what I observe. I might reply: a car, a pair of automobile headlights, two yellowish lights, and so on. Or, when driving on a dirt road in the daytime I might, in one and the same situation, claim to be observing a car, a trail produced by a car, or just a cloud of dust. In each case what I will actually say that I observed depends upon factors such as the extent of my knowledge and training, how much I am prepared to maintain in the circumstances about the object, and the type of answer my questioner might want.

Turning to scientific contexts, suppose that an experimental physicist, acquainted with the sorts of tracks left by various subatomic particles in cloud chambers, is asked what he is now observing in the chamber. He might reply in a number of ways, for example, electrons passing through the chamber, tracks produced by electrons, strings of tiny water droplets that have condensed on gas ions, or just long thin lines. Similarly, to the question "What does one observe in a cathode-ray experiment?" the physicist might answer: electrons striking the fluorescent zinc sulfide screen, light produced when molecules of zinc sulfide are bombarded, a bright spot, and so on. In each case what the physicist actually claims to have observed will depend upon how much he knows and is prepared to maintain, the knowledge and training of the questioner, and the sort of answer the physicist thinks appropriate under the circumstances.

Analogous considerations hold for other terms on the theoretical list. Thus, the physicist may report having observed the electric field in the vicinity of a certain charge, or he may describe what he did as having observed the separation of leaves in an electroscope. He may report to be observing the rise in the temperature of a given substance, or simply the increase in length of the column of mercury in the thermometer. Each such way of describing what is observed may be perfectly correct, unmisleading, and informative. Which is most appropriate will depend on the particular situation.

I have made five points about the concept of observation in order to shed light on its use and indicate why Carnap and others regard it as especially appropriate for the theoretical-nontheoretical distinction (more appropriate, for example, than "see"). Let me summarize those points particularly relevant for this distinction.

The proposal is that terms in the nontheoretical category refer to observable items, those in the theoretical category to unobservable ones. This I find objectionable on two grounds. First, it rests on the claim that one cannot report observing items such as electrons, fields, and temperature; and this I would reject [see points (3) and (4)]. Second, those who make the proposal assume that what is observable is describable in some unique way, by using some special vocabulary (Carnap's "observational vocabulary" by contrast to his "theoretical vocabulary"). This I should also reject [see point (5)]. What scientists as well as others observe is describable in many different ways, using terms from both "vocabularies."

3. QUALIFIED OBSERVATION

Some writers do not base the theoretical-nontheoretical distinction on observation plain and simple, but introduce qualifications. One suggestion is to invoke the distinction between *observing* and *observing that:* whereas it is possible to *observe that* theoretical items are doing such and such, it is not possible to *observe* these items doing anything. When the physicist sees the tracks forming in a cloud chamber, it might be said he *observes that* electrons are passing through, he does not observe the electrons passing through.[3]

"Observe that," like "observe," is sometimes used in the sense of "remark that." But, like "observe," it is also used in the sense of "visually attend to something." In the appropriate sense, if I observe X doing Y, then I observe X or something associated with X (for example, tracks, smoke, covering), where this relationship satisfies the conditions noted earlier;[4] but if I observe *that* X is doing Y, there is no such implication. The airplane pilot may observe *that* his airplane is passing through a given region by observing his instrument panel and his charts, but if he does so, he is not observing his airplane pass through this region. Similarly, the physicist may observe *that* electrons are now passing through the cloud chamber simply by observing a radioactive substance placed in the chamber. If so, he is not observing the electrons pass through the chamber. If the physicist does claim to be observing electrons now passing through the chamber, there is an implication not carried by the expression "observe that," namely, that he is now attending to something that (in this case) electrons characteristically produce in their general vicinity as they pass through the chamber, something that provides a standard means for observing electrons pass through the chamber. So, there is an important difference between "observe" and "observe that," and, contrary to the present suggestion, there are circumstances in which it is correct and even more appropriate to use the former for electrons as well as other items on the theoretical list.

Suppose it is acknowledged that the term "observe" functions in this way and that one can speak of observing subatomic particles in cloud chambers, electric fields in the vicinity of charges, temperature, and so forth. Still, it might be urged, the situation will be entirely differ-

---

[3] Cf. Bruce Aune, "Feigl on the Mind-Body Problem," *Mind, Matter, and Method,* ed. P. K. Feyerabend and G. Maxwell (Minneapolis, 1966), p. 24.

[4] See sec. 2, pts. (3) and (4).

ent if we consider, *strictly speaking,* what is observed. Strictly speaking, what the physicist observes is not the electron but only its track, not the electric field but only the separation of leaves in an electroscope, not the temperature but only the column of mercury, and so forth. In short, there is a strict way of speaking in accordance with which none of the items on the theoretical list is observable.

This proposal is unacceptable, for what counts as "strict" depends upon how much is known and what is allowed and not allowed to be taken for granted; and this will vary with the situation. Suppose one asks, "Strictly speaking, can the physicist say that he observes electrons in the cloud chamber?" Someone might reply, "No, he is entitled to say that he observes only some charged particles." "But, strictly speaking, can he say even this?" "No, only that he observes water droplets that have condensed on gas ions." Whether we stop earlier, here, or later (going on to: strictly speaking he can say only that he observes a track, or only this wavy line) depends upon standards appropriate for the context.

A more plausible approach is to claim that items on the theoretical list are not *themselves* observable. What the physicist observes is not the electron *itself* (but only its track, or a flash of light); and when he detects the presence of an electric field, what he observes is not the field *itself* (but only the separation of leaves in the electroscope). At least one writer adopts this way of speaking (though he talks of "concepts" rather than "objects"):

> . . . in all interesting cases the initial hypotheses of the theory will contain concepts which are . . . not themselves observable (call these theoretical concepts); examples are electrons, Schrödinger wave functions, genes, ego-ideals.[5]

To begin with, if I report that I did not (or could not) observe a certain object *itself,* I imply or at least suggest that I did (could) observe something; and a claim that an object is not itself observable will seem incomplete unless what *is* observable is indicated by contrast or is obvious in the context. If I report that I did (or could) not observe the President's car itself, the natural reply is: What then did (could) you observe? A replica of it in a museum, its tracks on the ground,

[5] R. B. Braithwaite, "Models in the Empirical Sciences," *Logic, Methodology, and Philosophy of Science,* ed. E. Nagel, P. Suppes, and A. Tarski (Stanford, 1962), p. 227.

only the swarms of people around it, or what? The point of using the emphatic "itself" here can best be brought out by indicating what it is that I did (could) observe, by contrast with what I did (could) not.

Consider now the case of a virus examined by means of an electron microscope. Suppose I say that the microbiologist does not observe the virus itself. What claim am I making (what contrast would I invoke to explain my claim)? I might be saying that since (let us suppose) he employs a staining technique (by attaching heavy molecules to the virus), he observes not the virus itself but only the staining material known to be present in certain parts of the specimen. Or, I might be saying that what he observes is the image of the virus on a screen, not the virus itself (which, of course, is not on the screen). On the other hand, comparing electron microscopy with X-ray diffraction, I might conceivably claim that in the former case he *is* able to observe the virus itself (since what he observes is a likeness of it), whereas in the latter case he observes only the effects of X-rays on the virus (a pattern unlike the virus itself). On different occasions any of these contrasts, and possibly others, might underlie the claim that the virus itself cannot (or can) be observed.

Furthermore, even if one particular contrast seems most natural for a given item on the theoretical list, other items will require different contrasts. Suppose the point of saying that electrons themselves are unobservable is to contrast observing an object by seeing its track with observing it (for example, as a speck) together with or apart from its track, which cannot be done with electrons. However, the situation is different in the case of molecules, especially larger ones, whose *shapes* can even be observed with the aid of electron microscopes. Here one would need to invoke a different sort of contrast, for example, that between seeing an image projected on a viewing screen and seeing the object with the naked eye.

I do not deny that one could supply a context for at least some items on the theoretical list in which it might be appropriate to invoke the expression "not itself observable." However, these contexts and the sorts of contrasts they may involve will in general be quite different. If such contrasts must be invoked to indicate the *point* of classifying an item as not itself observable (that is, if to classify an item in this way we must say what sort of thing *is* observable as well as what is not), then not one but many distinctions will emerge. For example, we might distinguish objects such as electrons and alpha particles, which are observed by means of their tracks, from objects such as cars and airplanes, which can be observed together with or apart from their tracks; objects such as smaller molecules, which must be stained in order to be observed, from larger objects for which staining is unnecessary; objects that must be observed by producing images on a screen from those that can be observed apart from such images; and so forth. Each of these distinctions is different and will yield quite varied classifications of terms.

Still, it might be replied, the fact that different contrasts are possible with the expression "not itself observable" does not require that these be made explicit or imply that this expression means something different each time it is used. Would it not be possible to characterize items as not themselves observable no matter what the particular contrast? Admittedly such a characterization would not convey as much information as one in which the contrast with what *is* observed is given, yet this might be sufficient for purposes of a general division of terms. We must therefore say more about the expression "not itself observable."

This expression is normally used only when one distinguishes, or can distinguish, X from something that it produces (tracks, smoke), that represents it (a picture or replica), or that is associated with it in some other particularly intimate way, where what is observable is something only of the latter three sorts (though this relationship, since it includes that of picture to original, is broader than the one discussed in point 3 of section 2, and so need not satisfy the set of conditions stated there). Even so, the claim that X is not itself observable can be understood in one of two ways.

It might be meant as a contingent claim about X and the method of observation in that context or at the present state of science. (X's are too small to be observed with instruments presently used, they are too far away, the items with which they react are not yet known, and so on.) In this sense if I claim that X is not itself observable, I am implying that given appropriate methods of observation (which we may not be using in the present context, or have not yet been discovered), X is the sort of thing that *could* be observed independently of what it produces, and so forth. For example, to claim that abominable snowmen are not themselves observable in the Himalayas is to imply that no one has yet been able to observe the creatures that allegedly produce tracks in the snow, although someday someone might.

However, this sort of claim could not be made for many items on the theoretical list. Suppose someone says that temperature is not itself observable. He could not mean that temperature is the sort of thing that, given appropriate methods of observation, could be observed independently of things like thermometers, thermocouples, parts of the body, and so forth. Temperature, in this respect, is unlike abominable snowmen, items that may one day be observed independently of what they produce. Accordingly, if "not itself observable" is to be understood in a contingent sense (and also as implying: has not itself yet been observed in *any* context), then this label will be inapplicable to temperature (as well as to other items on the theoretical list, such as electric fields, charge, and mass) and applicable to some items that would presumably appear on the nontheoretical list (such as abominable snowmen).

There is another sort of claim, a logical one, that might conceivably be made using the expression "not itself observable." In teaching the use of the concept entropy one might point out that it is a property of a system and not itself an object or system. So one might say, although the entropy of a particular system is observable, entropy is not itself observable. But if this is how the expression "not itself observable" is to be used, then the point expressed can be put more felicitously, simply by talking about properties of things by contrast with the things that have them. This surely is not the distinction desired by those who construct theoretical and nontheoretical lists. There is another logical claim that might conceivably be made using the expression "not itself observable." Electric fields, it might be said, are the sorts of things observable only by observing charged objects within them. An electric field is not (the sort of thing that is) itself observable. Again, however, the point can be put more felicitously by saying something like this: electric fields are not items with mass and volume but simply regions wherein charged bodies do or would receive accelerations. So, we might distinguish objects such as electric fields, which are not the kinds of things to which mass and volume are ascribed, from objects such as solids to which they are. This, again, would not provide the desired theoretical and nontheoretical classifications.

The distinction between contingent and logical uses of "not itself observable" will have borderline cases. How shall we understand the claim that electrons are not themselves observable in the cloud chamber? Is this claim logical or contingent? On the one hand, we are perhaps willing to envisage what it would be like to observe electrons themselves in a cloud chamber (for example, observing small specks, as we do in certain cases when we see both an airplane and its trail, specks we could identify as the electrons). This, we might say, counts in favor of its being a contingent claim. On the other hand, according to quantum theory, such a state of affairs is impossible. We might say that it is or becomes semantically relevant for being an electron that such observations are impossible. If so, the claim that electrons are not themselves observable in a cloud chamber could express a logical point somewhat akin to the claim that electric fields are not themselves observable, though of course the *particular* point would be somewhat different in each case. In a logical spirit, by saying that electrons are not themselves observable (as specks) in a cloud chamber, one might wish to convey the information that electrons are not particles in the classical sense.

I noted that the expression "not itself observable" is normally used only where one distinguishes, or can distinguish, X from something it produces, something that represents it, or from something associated with it in some other particularly intimate way. Now there are cases where the method for observing X requires that something produced by X be observed but where it is not clear whether to say that X is or is not itself observable by such a method. With a reflecting telescope, is the moon itself observable or only its image in the telescopic mirror? With the electron microscope, is the virus itself observable or only the staining material attached to the virus (or only the image on the screen)? Images can be distinguished from the objects that produce them, staining substances from the objects they stain.[6] Yet these images and stains (unlike tracks) provide a likeness of the object (at least a likeness of its shape) and change as the object does. Accordingly, what is observed in such cases may be identified as the object itself. However, in some contexts it may be important to distinguish an object from its image or reflection in a mirror, where otherwise error or confusion may arise. If so, we *might* say: Remember, what you are observing is not the object itself, which is in *that* direction, but only its image in the mirror, which has a different direction (if it has a direction at all). In other contexts, where no such confusion will arise, we may claim that what we are observing (using the mirror) is the object itself (and not, for

---

[6] Earlier I claimed that it is correct and unmisleading to speak of observing X when we are observing an image produced by X. The question now is whether, even though it is correct to speak of observing X in such cases, it is incorrect to speak of X *itself* as being observable.

example, a replica of it). Accordingly, if particular contrasts and contexts are not made explicit when the expression "not itself observable" is employed, there will be a number of terms (those referring to items observed by the production of images or by the use of stains) for which the question of classification will remain unsettled.

Let me now summarize my conclusions about the use of the expression "not itself observable" for the classification of terms.

1) The claim that an item is "not itself observable" will seem incomplete and cannot convey much information unless some particular contrast is invoked that clarifies the point of such a classification by indicating what *is* observable. On the basis of such contrasts, which can differ from item to item, and even in the case of a single item, from context to context, many different classifications of terms are possible.

2) Two nonequivalent sorts of claims can be made with the expression "not itself observable": contingent and logical. If used in a contingent sense, it would be inapplicable to many items on the theoretical list (temperature, mass, and so on) and so would not generate the distinction desired. If used to make a logical point, then a number of distinctions emerge, but none is the desired one.

3) A classification of terms using the expression "not itself observable" is problematic with respect to those items on the theoretical list typically observed by the production of images in microscopes and telescopes or by the use of stains, where likenesses can be observed. Whether we should say that such items are not themselves observable will vary with the context.

4. DIRECT OBSERVATION; THE NUMBER
OF OBSERVATIONS

There are two further qualifications some authors place on the criterion of observation. The first introduces the idea of *direct* observability. Hempel, for example, writes:

> In regard to an observational term it is possible, under suitable circumstances, to decide by means of direct observation whether the term does or does not apply to a given situation. . . . Theoretical terms, on the other hand, usually purport to refer to not directly observable entities and their characteristics.[7]

[7] "The Theoretician's Dilemma," *Minnesota Studies in the Philosophy of Science,* ed. H. Feigl, M. Scriven, and G. Maxwell (Minneapolis, 1958), II, 42.

In offering this criterion, Hempel, like Carnap,[8] mentions no special or technical sense that he attaches to the phrase "direct observation." [9] Nor does he elaborate upon its meaning, except to cite a few examples.[10] He admits that his characterization does not offer a precise criterion and that there will be borderline cases. Yet the problem is more complex than Hempel seems willing to allow, and, contrary to his suggestion, does not turn just on the question of drawing a more precise line of demarcation.

The expression "directly observable" is one whose use is not firmly entrenched in English. Austin claims that in the case of perception, "the notion of not perceiving 'directly' seems most at home where . . . it retains its link with the notion of a kink in direction." [11] If I claim not to be directly perceiving (or observing) something, I am contrasting this with the case where the item is in the line of sight, where I am looking straight at it. For example, I might say that someone is not directly observing the sun if his observations are confined to studying its reflection in a mirror.

However, "directly" can mean not only in a straight line but also without something or someone coming between, without some intermediary (as in "I contacted him directly"). When so used, there are two general ways something might not be "directly observable," for in observing something the "intermediary" might be of two sorts. It might be something needed to observe *with*. Thus, if the physicist claims that electrons cannot be directly observed, he may mean simply that instruments such as cloud chambers, cathode ray tubes, or scintillation counters are necessary. On the other hand, the "intermediary" might be some item that must be observed in order to observe X. Thus when the physicist claims that electrons cannot be directly observed, he may mean that when one observes an electron in a cloud chamber one observes only its track but not, for example, a speck one would identify as the electron itself. Again, in thermodynamics physicists sometimes speak of

---

[8] In "The Methodological Character of Theoretical Concepts."

[9] In his later work, *Philosophical Foundations of Physics* (New York, 1966), Carnap (pp. 225–26) suggests that there are two uses of "observe," the scientist's and the philosopher's. The scientist means "anything that can be measured in a relatively simple way." The philosopher means anything that can be "directly perceived by the senses." In this work Carnap chooses the "philosopher's" use.

[10] Observations of "readings of measuring instruments, changes in color or odor accompanying a chemical reaction, utterances made . . . " ("Theoretician's Dilemma," p. 42).

[11] J. L. Austin, *Sense and Sensibilia* (Oxford, 1962), p. 16.

entropy as not being a directly observable property of a system. Here they mean that in order to observe the entropy of a system one must observe other quantities such as temperature and specific heat, from which the entropy is calculated.

Neither the "straight line" nor the "no-intermediary" use of "directly observe" will generate the sort of theoretical list desired. It makes no sense to speak of a direction of sight with respect to many items on the theoretical list (for example, mass, kinetic energy, temperature); and with respect to others, it is not clear that observation involves a *kink* in the direction of sight (for example, observing alpha particles in the cloud chamber). The no-intermediary use depends on what counts as an intermediary, and this may vary with the context and with some particular contrast one may wish to make. Thus, neutrons and neutrinos are sometimes spoken of as not directly observable in a cloud chamber, since they do not produce tracks but must cause the ejection of alpha particles that do. Given this contrast, electrons and alpha particles (which, being charged, produce tracks) are directly observable in a cloud chamber. In short, the label "not directly observable" will be applied to an item with one contrast in mind, whereas "directly observable" may be applied to that same item on the basis of a different one.

Instead of judging "intermediaries" relative to a context, would it be possible to speak of them in some absolute sense? For example, could we define "X is not directly observable" to mean X is not observable without instruments, or to mean X is observable only by observing something distinct from it?

The latter is similar to "not itself observable" discussed in section 3 and is subject to the same difficulties. Is an item observed only by the production of images and reflections observed "only by observing something distinct from it"? Also, this expression, like "not itself observable," might be used to make two sorts of claims: contingent and logical. In the contingent sense the label "observable only by observing something distinct from it" (where this implies "*could,* in principle, be observed without observing anything distinct from it") is inapplicable to many items on the theoretical list (for example, temperature, mass); whereas if used to make a logical point, various distinctions emerge.

Consider, then, "X is not observable without instruments." Whether this is applicable to an item depends on what features or aspects of the item, or facts about it, are in question; and this can vary with the situation. For example, many facts about items on the nontheoretical list (items such as wood, water, weight, and even red) can be ascertained only by using instruments. If we mean (a) "*no* aspect of X is observable without instruments," then many items on the theoretical list will need to be reclassified. Just by looking and feeling, without the use of instruments, we can in many cases observe changes in temperature, kinetic energy, entropy, mass, charge, and so forth. If we restrict this to (b) "instruments are generally required to detect the *presence* of X," this will be inapplicable to those items on the theoretical list for which talk about "the presence of X" is inappropriate (temperature, kinetic energy, wave function). And if we change this to (c) "instruments are generally required to *measure* X or its properties," this will be applicable to many items on the nontheoretical list. I do not deny that (a), (b), and (c) generate distinctions. My point is that they will not generate the one desired. With (a) the theoretical list will be diminished considerably; with both (b) and (c) we will have two classes each containing some terms from the theoretical list and some from the nontheoretical list, while other terms on these lists will be in neither class.

The final qualification on observability I want to discuss concerns the *number* of observations necessary to correctly apply a term or expression. In "Testability and Meaning," Carnap writes:

> A predicate 'P' of a language L is called *observable* for an organism (e.g. a person) N, if, for suitable argument, e.g., 'b', N is able under suitable circumstances to come to a decision with the help of a few observations about the full sentence, say 'P(b)', i.e., to a confirmation of either 'P(b)' or '~P(b)' of such high degree that he will either accept or reject 'P(b)'.[12]

Carnap's proposal leaves some important questions unanswered. Is the number of observations to mean the number of times the object must be observed (or, if an experiment is in question, the number of times the experiment needs to be repeated) before a property can definitely be ascribed to the object? Or does Carnap perhaps mean the number of different characteristics of the object that need to be observed? Again, he may be thinking of the amount of preliminary investigation necessary before a final observation can be made.[13] Perhaps all of these considerations are relevant.

---

[12] Reprinted in *Readings in the Philosophy of Science,* ed. H. Feigl and M. Brodbeck (New York, 1953), p. 63. Cf. Carnap, *Philosophical Foundations of Physics,* pp. 225–26.

[13] According to Carnap, when instruments are used we have "to make a great many preliminary observations in order to find out whether the things before us are instruments of the kind required" ("Testability and Meaning," p. 64).

However, whether an observation or experiment will need to be repeated, or many different characteristics of the item examined, or considerable preliminary investigation undertaken, depends not only on the nature of the item observed but also on the particular circumstances of the investigator and his investigation. One relevant factor will be the type of instrument employed and how readily the scientist has learned to manipulate it. The physicist familiar with electroscopes need make few, if any, repetitions of an experiment with this instrument to determine the presence of an electric charge and hence of an electric field. Nor need he observe many characteristics of the field (for example, its intensity and direction at a certain point) to determine its presence. And he will not always need to make extensive preliminary observations on the instruments (but only a few). Yet charges and electric fields are alleged to be unobservable.

Another factor determining the facility with which an observer will identify an object or property is the extent of his knowledge regarding the particular circumstances of the observation. If the physicist knows that a radioactive substance has been placed in a cloud chamber, he may readily be able to identify the particles whose tracks are visible in the chamber. If he knows nothing about the circumstances of the experiment, or, for example, if he is simply shown a photograph of its results, successful identification may be a more complicated task. In short, under certain "suitable circumstances," to use Carnap's phrase, quite a number of terms classified by him as nonobservational can be correctly applied "with the help of [just] a few observations."

Furthermore, if nonobservability in Carnap's sense is held to be sufficient for a *theoretical* classification, additional difficulties emerge. For many ordinary expressions more than a "few observations" might well be required before correct application is possible, for example, "is chopped sirloin," "is a bridge that will collapse," "was composed by Corelli." Yet these are not expressions Carnap wishes to call theoretical. Even with color words, which are supposed to be paradigm cases of "observation terms," if sufficiently narrow classifications are employed (for example, "dark ultramarine"), more than a few observations may be required to determine whether they are applicable.

On the other hand, if following Scheffler,[14] Carnap's criterion for "non-observability" is to be construed simply as a necessary but not a sufficient condition for being theoretical, then unless further criteria

[14] Israel Scheffler, *The Anatomy of Inquiry* (New York, 1963), pp. 164ff.

are proposed (which they are not by either Carnap or Scheffler) we will have no general basis for separating theoretical from nontheoretical terms.[15] If the above criterion concerning the number of observations is to be construed as a sufficient one for a *non*theoretical classification (as Carnap and Scheffler suggest), then, we have seen, many terms classified by these authors as theoretical will require reclassification.

5. CONCLUSIONS ON OBSERVATION

I have considered attempts to found the theoretical-nontheoretical distinction upon observation. Those who defend this basis for the distinction seem captivated by certain examples they regard as typical of each list. They seem to be considering medium-sized objects encountered every day, such as tables, and the properties typical of these, and to be contrasting them with submicroscopic entities, such as electrons and their properties. Behind the classification of tables as observable and electrons as unobservable lies the following sort of reasoning.

If a table is present, then we can observe it and do so simply by looking; we can observe the table *itself* (not just some of its effects, as the marks it leaves on the rug); we can observe the table *directly* (without the use of instruments); we can determine that it is a table on the basis of at most a *few* observations. Electrons (so it is said) cannot be observed at all, or at least not simply by looking; when electrons are determined to be present what is observed are not the electrons themselves (but only their tracks); instruments are required for their detection, as are numerous observations.

These claims underlie "observable" and "unobservable" classifications. What I have been arguing is that they are different; that they are heavily dependent upon the context and some intended contrast, so that in one context they may be applicable to certain terms, in others not; that too much attention is given to examples such as "electron" and "table" and not enough to others on both lists for which such claims may not be suitable; that some of the claims are not even suitable for electrons; and that, in any case, no one of these claims will serve as grounds for the proposed distinction.

[15] Scheffler concludes (p. 164) that the only thing left to do is simply to specify an exhaustive list of primitive terms to be called "observational" (and presumably a corresponding list of those to be called "theoretical"); but this leaves the question of the basis for this separation unanswered.

The thesis that a list of "observational" terms can be compiled is defended by those envisaging the possibility of constructing an "empiricist language." An underlying assumption of this program is that there exists a unique (or at least a most suitable) way to describe what is or can be observed—a special "physical object" or "sense-datum" vocabulary eminently fit for this task. But there are numerous ways to describe what one observes in a given situation, some more infused with concepts employed in various theories than others. This does not preclude classifying certain reports as observational. The point is simply that there is no special class of terms that must be used in describing what is observed. Words from the previous theoretical list, such as "electron," "field," and "temperature," are frequently employed for this purpose. Still, it might be urged, even though terms on both lists can be used in descriptions of what is observed, those on the first list are more "theory-dependent" than those on the second. Whereas it may not be possible to draw the intended large-scale distinction on the basis of observation, it is feasible and important to separate terms on the basis of their "theoretical" character. It is to the latter position that I shall now turn.

CHAPTER SIX

THEORETICAL TERMS

Of various senses associated with the word "theoretical" three might be relevant for the theoretical-nontheoretical distinction: part of a theory; depending upon a theory; and conjectural or speculative (whether or not a theory is involved). Accordingly, the label "theoretical term" might be used to refer to a term occurring (primarily) in scientific theories; or to a term dependent in some way on scientific theories (beyond simply occurring in them); or to a term associated with conjecture and speculation. Will any of these senses provide an adequate basis for the distinction between theoretical and nontheoretical terms?

The last sense I shall consider in section 4. "Theoretical term," if taken in the first sense, might generate a distinction, but one that merely postpones the important issue, namely, what is characteristic of those terms occurring primarily in scientific theories? (This criterion would be like the one noted at the beginning of Chapter Five: "used typically by scientists and those acquainted with science.") It is the second sense that concerns several writers on this topic, such as Hanson and Ryle, and will be discussed next. To begin with, I shall use the narrower concept of "theory" described in Chapter Four; later, I shall say something about the broader one.

1. CONCEPTUAL ORGANIZATION

According to Hanson there is a distinction between terms that "carry a conceptual pattern with them" and those "less rich in theory, and hence less able to serve in explanations of causes";[1] or, in Ryle's

[1] N. R. Hanson, *Patterns of Discovery* (Cambridge, England, 1958), p. 60.

words, between expressions "more or less heavy with the burthen of [a particular] theory . . . [and those that] carry none [of the luggage] from that theory." [2] As an example of a term that carries with it a conceptual pattern Hanson cites the word "crater":

> Galileo often studied the Moon. It is pitted with holes and discontinuities; but to say of these that they are craters—to say that the lunar surface is craterous—is to infuse theoretical astronomy into one's observations. . . . To speak of a concavity as a crater is to commit oneself as to its origin, to say that its creation was quick, violent, explosive. . . .[3]

"Crater," then, carries with it a conceptual pattern not borne by (nontheoretical) terms such as "hole," "discontinuity," or "concavity."

Two notions underlie these suggestions, one stressed more by Hanson, the other by Ryle. The first is that a theoretical term is one whose application in a given situation can organize diffuse and seemingly unrelated aspects of that situation into a coherent, intelligible pattern; terms that carry no such organizing pattern Hanson sometimes calls "phenomenal." The second notion is that theoretical terms are those that depend on theories. "The special terms of a science," Ryle asserts, "are more or less heavy with the burthen of the theory of that science. The technical terms of genetics are theory-laden, laden, that is, not just with theoretical luggage of some sort or other but with the luggage of genetic theory." [4]

The first proposal fails to provide a sufficient characterization of those terms Hanson calls "theory-laden" (or "theory-loaded"), for almost any term can be employed in certain situations to produce the type of pattern envisaged. Indeed, Hanson himself offers many examples of this. Early in his book he presents a drawing whose meaning is incomprehensible until it is explained that it represents a bear climbing a tree.[5] In this context, the term "bear," or the expression "bear climbing a tree," is one that organizes the lines of the drawing into an intelligible pattern. Moreover, one could describe contexts in which Hanson's "phenomenal" terms such as "hole," "concavity," or "solaroid disc," might be employed to organize certain initially puzzling data. Conversely, there

---

[2] Gilbert Ryle, *Dilemmas* (Cambridge, England, 1956), pp. 90–91.
[3] Hanson, *Patterns of Discovery*, p. 56.
[4] Ryle, *Dilemmas*, p. 90.
[5] Cf. Chap. Four, sec. 2.

are situations in which terms such as "crater," "wound," "volume," "charge," and "wavelength," which Hanson calls "theory-loaded," are used to describe initially puzzling data that require "conceptual organization."

Hanson, at one point, grants that terms can have this dual function:

> It is not that certain words are absolutely theory-loaded, whilst others are absolutely sense-datum words. Which are the data-words and which are the theory words is a contextual question. Galileo's scar may at some times be a datum requiring explanation, but at other times it may be part of the explanation of his retirement.[6]

This admission is a large one, for it means that the rendering of "conceptual organization" is not a special feature of terms on the theoretical list that sets them apart from those on the nontheoretical list. Whether a term provides an organizing pattern for the data depends on the particular situation in which it is employed. In some contexts, the term "electron" will be used to organize the data (for example, tracks in a cloud chamber); in others, to describe certain data requiring organization (for example, the discontinuous radiation produced by electrons in the atom). But even a term on the nontheoretical list, such as "warm," can be used in certain contexts to organize data thereby producing an explanation, and in others, to describe something that itself demands explanation.

Hanson does make reference to the "width" of terms, claiming that some terms are "wider" theoretically than others and hence presumably "carry a [greater] conceptual pattern with them." [7] So despite the fact that most terms can serve explanatory functions, distinctions might still be drawn on the basis of "width." However, it is not clear how this metaphor should be unpacked. Sometimes there is the suggestion that one term is "wider" than another if it can be used to explain situations descriptions of which contain the latter term. Thus, referring to the Galileo example just quoted, the term "scar" would be wider than the term "retirement" because it can be used to explain something designated by the latter. Yet this is not satisfactory since we might imagine a case in which a man's retirement constituted part of an explanation of a scar he incurred. Analogously, the term "electron" can be employed in

[6] Hanson, *Patterns of Discovery*, pp. 59–60.
[7] *Ibid.*, p. 61.

explanations of magnetic fields; yet the presence of a magnetic field can explain motions of electrons.

Perhaps the reference to "width" should be understood in connection with the thesis, proposed by Ryle (and shared by Hanson), that certain terms depend for their meanings upon a theory, whereas others do not or at least are much less dependent. I turn now to this proposal.

2. THEORY-DEPENDENCE

Ryle cites as an analogy the situation in games of cards. To understand the expression "straight flush" one must know at least the rudiments of poker, whereas this is not so with the expression "queen of hearts," which is common to all card games and carries with it none of the special "luggage" of any of them. In a similar manner certain terms used by scientists are such that to understand the concepts they express one must have at least some knowledge of the theory in which they appear. These are the "theory-laden" terms.[8] Other expressions utilized by scientists can be understood without recourse to that theory.[9]

Before examining the criterion of theory-dependence, some preliminary points should be noted. First, Ryle often seems to suggest that a theory-laden term "carries the luggage" of one particular theory (". . . one of them carries the luggage of a specific theory, while the other carries none from that theory"). Yet quite a few of the terms he and Hanson classify as theory-laden—terms such as "temperature," "wavelength," "electron"—appear in, and might be thought to be infused with the concepts of, *many* scientific theories. Such terms are not restricted to just one theory, as in the case of games, "straight flush" is to poker.

[8] Cf. Hanson, *ibid.,* pp. 61–62: " 'Revoke,' 'trump,' 'finesse' belong to the parlance system of bridge. The entire conceptual pattern of the game is implicit in each term. . . . Likewise with 'pressure,' 'temperature,' 'volume,' 'conductor,' 'charge' . . . in physics. . . . To understand one of these ideas thoroughly is to understand the concept pattern of the discipline in which it figures."

[9] Hempel has recently suggested a criterion for the division between theoretical and nontheoretical terms somewhat akin to Ryle's. In *Philosophy of Natural Science* (Englewood Cliffs, N.J., 1966), p. 75, Hempel relativizes the distinction to a particular theory by distinguishing those "terms that have been introduced prior to the theory and can be used independently of it" from those that depend on the theory for their characterization. Much of what I say about Ryle's proposal is applicable to Hempel's as well.

Second, it is certainly not a feature characteristic only of terms Ryle calls "theory-laden"—or only of such terms and those from card games—that the concepts they express must be understood by reference to some scheme, system of beliefs, or set of facts. Following Ryle's lead one might draw up many sorts of classifications, for example, "university-laden" terms, such as "hour examination," "credit," and "tutorial," that cannot be understood without some knowledge of universities and their procedures; or, referring to scientific contexts, "instrument-laden" terms, such as "dial," "on," "off," that presumably would not appear on the theoretical list yet require at least some knowledge of instruments. Thus the present proposal must not be construed simply as a criterion for distinguishing terms that must be understood in the context of a set of beliefs from those that can be understood independently of any such set, though Hanson's "theory-loaded" versus "sense-datum" labels might suggest this.

Third, one must always specify the theory with respect to which a given term is or is not "theory-laden." A term might receive this classification with reference to one theory but not another, though it occurs in both, for in one theory, but not another, the concept it expresses might not be understood unless the principles of the theory are known. "Mass" might be considered theory-laden with respect to Newtonian mechanics but not with respect to the Bohr theory of the atom in which it also appears. (Thus, presumably, not every term occurring in a given theory T will be T-laden, just as not every term found in standard formulations of the rules of poker—for example, "sequence," "card"—will be "poker-laden," to use Ryle's expression.) If a theory must always be specified with respect to which a given term is deemed theory-laden, and if a term can be classified in this way with reference to one theory and not another in which it appears, then we have a choice when constructing theoretical and nontheoretical lists. We can cite particular theories and for each one compose such lists indicating which terms are to be considered theoretical and which not *for that theory*.[10] Or, we can say that

---

[10] At many points Ryle does seem to be pressing for a distinction between terms appearing within the context of a given theory (or system) that are "theory-laden" and those that may also appear in the same context but are not. This is suggested by the sorts of examples he chooses ("light wave" versus "blue"; "straight flush" versus "queen of hearts") and also by the questions he raises ("How are the special terms of Bridge or Poker [for example, 'trump'] logically related to the terms in which the observant child describes the cards that are shown to him [for example, 'hearts']?"). So, relativizing the distinction to terms employed in

a term will be classified as theoretical if it is theory-laden with respect to at least one theory and as nontheoretical if it is not theory-laden with respect to any theory. I shall discuss the former procedure first.

According to Ryle, terms are theory-dependent if "knowing their meanings requires some grasp of the theory" in which they occur. This might suggest that a theory-dependent term is one of the following sort:

1) A term denoting some item X such that the semantically relevant (including logically necessary and sufficient) properties of X are attributed to X by the principles of the theory in question and only by these principles (or by other theories only if they presuppose the principles of this one). In short, a theory-dependent term is one whose semantical aspect of use would need to be learned by learning the theory.

When Ryle and Hanson speak of theory-dependent terms I would take them to be including terms of type (1);[11] but they may be including other sorts of terms as well. They might argue that knowing the semantical aspect of the use of "X" is not all that is important for understanding the concept of an X, or at least for having a full or deep understanding. So let us construe "theory-dependence" more broadly and consider other possible ways an understanding of concepts might depend on knowledge of a theory. Suppose we are given a particular theory. Within it the following sorts of terms might also be considered theory-dependent.

2) A term that denotes an expression that appears in a formula whose *derivation* in the theory will not be understood unless certain laws of that theory are known. Often a concept in a theory will not be fully understood unless one knows how the expression it designates arises, that is, how certain formulas containing this expression are derived from the principles of the theory, even though the derivation might not be considered semantically relevant for the concept in question. "Enthalpy" in thermodynamics is defined as $U + pV$, where U is the internal energy of a system, p its pressure, and V its volume. One standard method for introducing this concept is by considering a constant pressure process and applying the first law of thermodynamics, arriving at an expression containing $U + pV$. Here, the definitions of U, p, and V

---

the context of a particular theory is not completely foreign to Ryle's thought, though on some occasions he does suggest that he intends a broader distinction, as between terms "laden" with a theory and those dependent on no theory whatever.

[11] In Chap. Three I considered Feyerabend's thesis that all terms in a theory are dependent for their meanings on that theory in just this way.

can be given independently of the theory, though the standard derivation of the formula containing $U + pV$ cannot.

3) A term referring to some X that the theory is designed to describe and explain in certain ways and for which the question "What is (an) X?" could be answered, at least in part, by considering principles of that theory. Very often this question will be asked when one is attempting to understand the concept of X; and an answer may be given by reference to principles of a theory that attribute properties to X, even though these properties may not be semantically relevant for X. Suppose one asks, "What are electrons?" Many sorts of replies could be given depending upon the knowledge and interests of the inquirer. References might be made to the Bohr or quantum theories, which describe the various energy states of electrons within the atom; to the band theory of solids, which uses quantum mechanical results in describing properties of electrons in conductors; to the theory of the chemical bond, which describes the sharing of electrons by atoms; and so forth. By characterizing various properties of electrons, even though many of these may not be semantically relevant for electrons, such theories provide answers to the question "What are electrons?" and thereby an understanding of the concept of an electron.

4) A term whose actual range of application (the objects and situations to which it in fact applies) can be known only if principles of the theory are understood. Expressions will sometimes be introduced into theories in abstract ways, so that, although one can cite properties that are semantically relevant and even general characterizations involving nonsemantically relevant properties, one may still be in doubt about what actual items satisfy the conditions cited. A logically necessary and sufficient condition for "irreversible process" can be given in thermodynamics, and various properties of such processes can be characterized. However, to have a full understanding of this concept one should be able to produce examples of actual processes that are irreversible, an ability that in this case depends upon, or at least is considerably enhanced by, knowledge of the second law of thermodynamics. (A process is irreversible if a perpetual motion machine of the second kind, that is, one violating the second law of thermodynamics, results from its being assumed reversible.)

5) A term expressing a concept whose *role* in the theory can only (or best) be appreciated by considering principles in which it is employed. To fully understand a scientific concept it may be important to consider

the role or roles it plays in a theory, even though these may not be se-mantically relevant for the concept. In most theories the roles of con-cepts can be examined from several points of view. One might simply consider whether and how a given concept is needed for the purpose of *formulating* some of the principles of the theory (for example, how the concept of a quantum of energy is used in the formulation of two funda-mental postulates of the Bohr theory). Once a theory has been stated one might ask whether and how a certain concept affords a *simplification* or *concise expression* of other principles (for example, how the concept of energy facilitates the formulation of principles of classical mechan-ics), or how it is used in *proofs* of important theorems. From a wider viewpoint, the role of a concept might also be studied by considering how principles in which it functions *explain* various phenomena (how, for example, the concept of resonance potential in the Bohr theory is used in the explanation of electron transitions to different energy levels). Conversely, one might consider the manner in which principles of the theory are used to explain various phenomena that the term itself desig-nates.[12]

3. THEORY-DEPENDENCE AND THE CLASSIFICATION OF TERMS

I have considered several ways in which terms might be deemed theory-dependent. Each type of dependence, if employed to generate a classification of terms, will yield different results; and none will yield the broad category of theoretical terms desired.

On the basis of the first type of dependence we could distinguish between (*a*) terms denoting items most of whose semantically relevant properties are attributed to them only by the theory in question, and (*b*) terms denoting items most of whose semantically relevant properties are attributed to them independently of the theory. (In thermodynamics "entropy" might be considered a term of the former sort, "enthalpy" of the latter.)

On the second type, we could distinguish between (*a*) expressions

---

[12] Hanson, it might be noted, suggests at one point that terms referring to some-thing explained by a theory are dependent in meaning upon that theory. Thus, he claims, Tycho and Kepler, because they had different theories about the move-ment of the sun, attached different meanings to "sun" (*Patterns of Discovery*, p. 7).

usually introduced by reference to formulas whose derivations will not be understood unless principles of the theory are known, and (b) expressions not introduced in this manner but appropriated with unchanged definitions from other theories. (In thermodynamics "enthalpy" would fall into the first category, "pressure" into the second.)

On the third type, we could distinguish between (a) terms referring to items that the theory describes in such a way that the question "What is (an) X?" could be answered by considering principles of that theory, and (b) terms occurring in that theory for which this question would not usually be answered by reference to the theory itself (but perhaps to others). (In the Bohr theory terms such as "electron" and "atom" would fall into the first category, terms such as "velocity" and "acceleration" would not.)

On the fourth type, we could distinguish between (a) terms (such as "Newtonian system") whose range of application cannot be known unless principles of the theory are understood, and (b) terms (such as "velocity") whose range of application is known more or less independently of that theory.

In the case of the fifth dependence several nonequivalent classifications are possible depending upon the type of role considered. If we group together those terms expressing concepts whose (principal) role is simply to enable the formulation of certain postulates, in general we will get a different classification from that obtained by grouping together terms expressing concepts introduced mainly for simplifying certain formulations. (In the Bohr theory, Planck's constant h might be classified in the first manner, $\hbar$ [h divided by 2π] in the second.) If we consider all the different roles cited earlier and attempt to draw a distinction between (a) terms expressing concepts at least some of whose roles cannot be fully understood without knowledge of principles of the theory, and (b) terms expressing concepts for which this is not necessary, we will find no distinction left to be drawn, since every term in the theory would be theory-dependent.

Accordingly, the various types of dependence generate several distinctions between terms in a given theory. In the case of some of these the class of terms to be considered theory-laden might be quite small (for example, terms denoting items most of whose semantically relevant properties are attributed to them by the theory and only by that theory); in other cases it might be larger (for example, terms designating items that are such that the question "What is [an] X?" could be answered by reference to principles of the theory); and in still other cases it would include practically every term employed by the theory (terms expressing concepts serving at least one role that cannot be understood without a knowledge of some of the principles of the theory). As should be evident from the examples cited, a term classified as theory-laden in one of these senses would not necessarily be so classified in another. And on some distinctions many terms in the theory cannot be classified either as theory-laden or as theory-independent. Most important, as is obvious from the examples alone, none of these types of theory-dependence will generate the lists of the previous chapter. On the other hand, if all the various senses in which a term in a theory might be considered dependent upon that theory are lumped together and a term classified as theory-laden if it conforms to any of these, then such a label becomes useless for distinguishing between terms occurring in a theory, since it would apply to all of them.

I have considered the question of theory-dependence with respect to a given theory. What has been said is relevant also for the broader distinction between terms laden with the principles of some theory or other and terms dependent upon no theory whatever. Since there are various sorts of theory-dependence many distinctions become possible. Should any of the criteria outlined earlier be sufficient to render a term theoretical, then many terms philosophers have placed on the nontheoretical list would need to be reclassified. This would be true since for such terms there are theories that can be used to answer the question "What is (an) X?" (where X is wood, iron, red, volume, solid body, liquid); as well as theories in which some of these terms play various roles (for example, in the formulation of statements describing phenomena to be explained or even in the formulation of principles).

In Chapter Four, broader and narrower uses of "theory" were distinguished. Up to this point I have been using the narrower "propositional" sense. Let me say something finally about theory-dependence when "theory" is used in the broader sense to refer to a field or subject matter. Here we might classify as theoretical those terms expressing concepts used in some theory, whether or not they occur in, or depend in some way on, a set of principles that may constitute a part of that theory. But then many terms on the nontheoretical list would need to be reclassified: they express concepts often used in some theory. We might try to strengthen this criterion by saying that they must express concepts of particular relevance or importance for a theory, but since there are different respects in which concepts are relevant and important, various distinctions would be possible. And if *any* respect in which it is relevant or important for the theory were sufficient to render a term theoretical, then, as before, numerous terms from the nontheoretical list would need to be reclassified.

4. CONJECTURE

I have been asking whether the concept of a theoretical term can be explicated when "theoretical" is understood in the sense of "depending on a theory." Now I turn to a broader sense of "theoretical," namely, conjectural (whether or not what is conjectural is associated with a theory). It might be claimed that terms on the theoretical list involve a conjectural element in a way that those on the nontheoretical list do not. Typically, a conjecture is or involves an inference on the basis of meager data. However, I mean to use the term in a broader way to include not only this but also related criteria suggested by philosophers who speak of theoretical terms as designating "hypothetical" or "inferred" entities.[13]

The root concepts here—conjecture, hypothesis, and inference—can be distinguished from one another, yet all three involve a "going beyond or further than" what is given or established. This common feature has led philosophers to invoke them when speaking of theoretical entities. It is a sense of "theoretical" to be contrasted with "established," and it suggests a number of possible bases for the theoretical-nontheoretical distinction.

1) To refer to something as conjectural is to imply, at least, that a claim is involved whose truth has not yet been established. So, in drawing up theoretical and nontheoretical lists one might distinguish items claims about which are established from items claims about which are not. The problem is that a given item may be deemed conjectural in different respects: one might consider claims regarding its existence, its properties, its presence (or magnitude) on particular occasions (whether it is generally difficult to identify or measure accurately), and so on. Are electrons conjectural (that is, are claims about electrons established by

[13] For example, Hempel, "The Theoretician's Dilemma," *Minnesota Studies in the Philosophy of Science,* ed. H. Feigl, M. Scriven, and G. Maxwell (Minneapolis, 1958), II; Lewis White Beck, "Constructions and Inferred Entities," *Readings in the Philosophy of Science,* ed. H. Feigl and M. Brodbeck (New York, 1953), pp. 368–81.

the evidence)? Their existence is presumably not conjectural, although it once was. Some of their properties are, some not. The presence of electrons on particular occasions (in a particular cloud chamber experiment) may or may not be conjectural, depending upon the circumstances.

Suppose, then, we consider only *existence* and attempt to draw a distinction on the basis of whether or not the existence of the item has been established. Electrons would then be nontheoretical since their existence is established by the evidence, whereas abominable snowmen, flying saucers, and the knights of King Arthur would be theoretical (or at least more theoretical than electrons). Moreover, many items could not be classified on this basis at all. Kinetic energy, for example, is not something whose existence is established (or not established) by the evidence; it is defined in such a way that bodies must have it. Suppose we broaden the criterion by allowing a term to be theoretical if it refers to something concerning which numerous claims of various sorts (including, possibly, existence claims) are not yet established. Electrons would still be classified as nontheoretical, abominable snowmen, and so on, as theoretical. Moreover, problems of classification would remain with terms like "kinetic energy," "instantaneous velocity," "mass," and "temperature," which refer to quantities. Many claims made by invoking these terms may not yet have been established, whereas many others have. This is not to deny the possibility of useful distinctions between *claims* with respect to the amount of supporting evidence in their favor. My point is only that a general division of *terms* into theoretical and nontheoretical cannot be drawn on this basis.

2) There is another possible sense of "going beyond or further than" what is given or established and hence another use of "conjectural" for drawing the intended distinction. It might be claimed that when used to describe a given phenomenon, terms on the theoretical list commit one to more than do terms on the nontheoretical list. Consider experimental situations in which the presence, magnitude, or effects of an item designated by a "theoretical" term are said to be observed. Phenomena will occur that can be described by using terms on the nontheoretical list, or at least by using terms less—or not very—theoretical. An inference is then made to the existence or presence of some entity or property that explains these observed phenomena and whose existence or presence is not definitely established by the phenomena alone: it is more

conjectural than the phenomena. A term that refers to such an item is theoretical by contrast with terms used in the original description of the phenomena.[14]

To examine this proposal let us turn to three different sorts of terms on the theoretical list: "molecule," "charge," and "kinetic energy." The presence (or effects) of molecules is said to be observed in the following experimental situation. Fine particles are suspended in a liquid, and haphazard motion of these particles can be seen with a microscope. Given this phenomenon, so-called Brownian motion, the physicist infers the existence of molecules whose random motion produces the observed Brownian motion, but whose existence is not definitely established by this motion alone, and thus is more conjectural than the latter. The term "molecule," then, is theoretical by contrast with (or is more theoretical than) the term "Brownian motion." This fits the above account well.

Consider now the term "charge," as used in classical electrostatics, and an experimental situation in which the presence of charge (or a charged object) is said to be observed. A rod made of hard rubber is rubbed with fur, rendering it capable of attracting bits of light material such as paper and cork. The physicist speaks of the rod as charged with electricity. When he does so (in the context of electrostatics), is he inferring the existence or presence of something that explains the phenomenon or capability of attraction (and something whose existence is not definitely established by the phenomenon of attraction)? The answer is not clear. The expression "charged (with electricity)" might be said to carry with it a *suggestion* that "capable of attracting bits of light material" does not. It suggests that there may be something with which the rubber rod is "burdened," something responsible for the observed phenomenon of attraction, though there is no indication what this might be. However, in electrostatics when the physicist uses the expression

---

[14] Hempel ("The Theoretician's Dilemma," p. 41) distinguishes between "two levels of scientific systematization: the level of empirical generalization and the level of theory formation. . . . [In the second level] research is aimed at comprehensive laws, in terms of hypothetical entities, which will account for the uniformities established on the first level." Again, one of Hanson's examples of a "theory-loaded" word is "crater," the corresponding "datum-word" being "concavity." To describe the lunar surface as filled with craters, Hanson claims, commits one to more than does the description of it as filled with concavities; in this case it commits us to a certain range of possible causes (*Patterns of Discovery*, pp. 56ff.).

"charged (with electricity)" it is not clear that he is definitely inferring the existence of this something.[15] This is different from the case of Brownian motion, where the physicist uses the term "molecule" to make a definite inference concerning the cause of the Brownian motion.

The term "kinetic energy," in classical mechanics, is different from either of the above. Suppose a particle (of negligible size) is determined to have a mass m and to be moving with a constant velocity v. The physicist will then conclude that its kinetic energy is $\frac{1}{2}mv^2$. The introduction of the term "kinetic energy" in this situation does not, however, carry with it an inference to something that accounts for the velocity or mass of the particle (as the introduction of the term "molecule" accounts for the Brownian motion). Nor is there an inference to something that cannot definitely be established on the basis of the observed phenomena alone (that is to say, once the mass and velocity are known). And, unlike the case of "charge," there is no suggestion that there might be some common though as yet undiscovered cause of motion. This is not to deny that the term "kinetic energy" (like most terms) can play a part in explanations of phenomena. The point is only this: it is not true that whenever the kinetic energy of an object is determined on the basis of observed phenomena, an inference is made to something that explains these phenomena and is not definitely established by them.

Given the present criterion for being conjectural, and considering standard experimental contexts, although a term such as "molecule" (as well as "electron," "alpha particle," and so forth) will fall clearly into the theoretical class (by contrast with "Brownian motion," "thin track," and so forth), "charge" ("heat," "internal energy of a thermodynamic system") will be borderline, and "kinetic energy" ("instantaneous velocity," "mass") will be nontheoretical. Accordingly, although "conjectural," in the present sense, may be used to generate one sort of classification, it will not do as a basis for the lists envisaged.

3) There is a third possible use of "conjectural" for the desired distinction. Items on the theoretical list might be said to be more conjectural than those on the nontheoretical list insofar as claims involving them require reasoning of a more complicated or intricate sort for their

---

[15] This is true for some physicists but not others. It seems to have been so for Gray in the early part of the eighteenth century but not for certain other more mechanistically inclined physicists of that century. See Roller and Roller, "The Development of the Concept of Electric Charge," *Harvard Case Histories in Experimental Science,* ed. J. B. Conant (Cambridge, Mass., 1957), II, 589; and my previous quotation in Chap. Three, sec. 6.

defense. Such claims "go beyond or further than" what is given or established in a more involved way than do claims about items on the non-theoretical list. To defend a claim about the mass of electrons would require a more intricate chain of reasoning than that necessary to defend a claim about the color of swans.

This criterion is different from the first two. Claims defended by intricate reasoning may or may not be less firmly established by the evidence than those defended by less complex reasoning; they may or may not postulate the existence of something that explains observable phenomena. Whether this criterion will generate the desired classification is another matter.

To begin with, the relevant notion of complexity is by no means clear. Shall we include the *number* of assumptions and inferences involved in the defense? Shall we also consider the complexity of each of these? If so, how is this to be done, and how are the various factors to be combined? These questions are not meant to demonstrate the impossibility of the task but only to suggest one major difficulty in classifying terms on this basis. Moreover, as noted before, different sorts of claims are possible using terms on either list: for example, claims concerning the existence of (certain) items on both lists, their properties, the presence of the items (or their magnitudes) on specific occasions. The complexity of the defense can vary considerably with the particular sort of claim made.

Whether or not a defense is complex will also depend on the type of challenge offered in the context or on the type that might be expected to be offered. The physicist defending his claim that a rod is charged with electricity might note simply that it makes the leaves in an electroscope separate. Depending upon the interest and knowledge of those concerned, further challenges could be made, necessitating more and more complex arguments. But this is also true of items on the nontheoretical list. The assertion that this wooden building is the oldest one in town might be defended simply by pointing out that the date stamped on it is 1743. Yet many different challenges could be offered: How do you know the date stamped on it represents the date it was built? How do you know this *is* the date stamped on it? How do you know that other buildings do not have an earlier date? These challenges might prompt arguments of very complex sorts.

In short, complexity of defense depends not simply on what term is used but on the character of the assertion and on the type of challenge in question. Complex as well as simple defenses can be given for assertions made with terms on both lists.

5. PRECISION

Another criterion invoked in making the theoretical-nontheoretical distinction is precision. Some authors may not wish to recognize this as sufficient for the distinction, but precision might be deemed a necessary or at least frequent characteristic of terms on the theoretical list. Contrast this with the unprecise character of terms on the nontheoretical list, which are found in low-level empirical generalizations and in ordinary discourse. Hempel, for example, writes:

> The vocabulary of everyday discourse, which science has to use at least initially, does permit the statement of generalizations, such as that any unsupported body will fall to the ground; that wood floats on water but that any metal sinks in it. . . . But such generalizations in everyday terms tend to have various shortcomings; their constituent terms will often lack precision . . . , and as a consequence, the resulting statement will have no clear and precise meaning. . . .[16]

What is precision? In a general way, we attribute it to something that permits the recognition or use of sharply as well as narrowly defined boundaries. For example, a precise method of measurement is one that permits the recognition of sharp differences in the magnitude of a quantity, even when small differences of degree are concerned. A precise description of an object is one that permits someone to distinguish it sharply from others, even from those only slightly different. Under what conditions can we speak of a term as a precise one?

We might speak this way if the definition of the term is based upon, or introduces, a numerical scale that allows the recognition of sharp as well as small differences in degree. It is for this reason, presumably, that "temperature," as defined by the physicist, is said to be a precise term, whereas "odor," as defined in standard dictionaries, is not. Of course, merely having a scale allowing for small differences in degree is not sufficient for precision. The scale must be capable of being used so that actual differences can be discerned objectively.

[16] *Fundamentals of Concept Formation in Empirical Science* (Chicago, 1952), p. 20.

We might also speak of a term as a precise one if it is part of a precise system of classification. In this system definite criteria for the use of terms are provided in such a way that items are more or less sharply distinguished and more or less fine distinctions are recognized. A term used within this system might be said to be more precise than some counterpart from ordinary language, especially if the former is based on criteria delimiting the class of items designated more sharply than criteria associated with the latter. Thus it might be said that *"Homo sapiens"* is a more precise term of classification than "man." Again, one term within a given system of classification might be said to be more precise (or to offer a more precise classification) than another within that same system if it is more specific, for example, if it gives species as well as genus (*"Viola triloba"* versus *"Viola"*). The system of classification need not, however, be one in science. Austin, for example, notes that "duck-egg blue" is a more precise term than "blue";[17] and one might say that "four-door sedan" is a more precise term of classification than "sedan."

I have noted two related criteria of precision: (1) A term is said to be a precise one if its definition is based on, or introduces, a numerical scale that allows the recognition of sharp as well as small differences in degree; (2) a term is said to be a precise one—usually more precise than another—if it is part of some precise system of classification and more sharply delimits a class of items, or is more specific, than another term. Only the first criterion allows anything resembling an absolute division of terms. The second is best utilized by comparing two terms or expressions that, like "man" and *"homo sapiens,"* apply to the same sorts of things. When there are radically different applications, comparisons can become futile. (Whereas "duck-egg blue" is a more precise term of classification than "blue," and "four-door sedan" more precise than "sedan," which, if either, is more precise, "duck-egg blue" or "four-door sedan," and how are we to decide?)

With respect to the second criterion, some terms on the theoretical list might be said to be more precise than others, whereas comparisons in many if not most cases will be impossible. The same is true of terms on the nontheoretical list, whether comparisons are made only between terms on this list or between these and terms on the theoretical list. Moreover, many terms on the theoretical list (for example, "field," "wave function," "mass") could not be described as part of a precise

---

[17] *Sense and Sensibilia* (Oxford, 1962), p. 127.

system of classification in the way that terms such as *"Homo sapiens"* and *"Viola triloba"* can. Suppose, then, we attempt to classify terms according to whether they are based upon, or carry with them, a finely graduated scale for measuring degrees. This will put terms like "temperature," "mass," and "kinetic energy" on one list and "red," "warm," and "wood" on another. The problem is that numerous terms on the theoretical list (for example, "electron," "molecule," and "field") do not refer to quantities capable of degrees. Such terms do of course refer to entities with various properties capable of finely graduated (and measurable) degrees; but this is true as well of terms that appear, or would appear, on the nontheoretical list (for example, "wood," "desk," "pencil"). Moreover, at least some terms philosophers have placed on the nontheoretical list are based upon scales of the sort envisaged (for example, "volume," "weight," "hard").

Finally, "precise" is sometimes used to mean simply "not vague." In this sense one might wish to claim (and indeed many philosophers often suggest) that terms on the theoretical list are precise insofar as they are clearly and unambiguously defined or explained by the scientist; by contrast, many terms on the nontheoretical list are not defined at all or have meanings that are not as clear or unambiguous.

Two brief comments. First, some terms philosophers put on the theoretical list are not clearly defined (for example, "superego"), whereas many on the nontheoretical list could not be construed as vague (or more vague). (Is "red" a vague term? Is it more vague than "superego"?) Second, admittedly, because the scientist often introduces new words, he is usually careful when he defines or explains them, whereas he may make no special effort at definition or explanation in the case of terms (such as "red") used by scientists and nonscientists alike. But this does not make the latter terms less clear or more ambiguous or show that they are less capable of clear definitions.

In sum, although the label "precise" is applicable in certain respects to some terms on the theoretical list, in other respects (and with reference to other terms) it is not. The same can be said of terms on the nontheoretical list. Precision, then, does not generate the desired distinction.

6. ABSTRACT TERMS

The final category I want to mention is designated by the label "abstract terms." Carnap, in one of his writings,[18] divides the "vocabulary of science" into abstract terms and elementary terms, a division that corresponds to his (later) one between theoretical and observational terms.

One sense for the expression "abstract term" is "a term expressing a quality apart from any subject of which the quality is predicated" (*Webster's*). Examples are "honesty," "whiteness," and "beauty" (so-called abstract nouns). This is obviously not the sense intended when the label "abstract" is applied to terms on the theoretical list. On the other hand, a division is frequently made between so-called abstract (or pure) sciences (for example, theoretical physics) and applied sciences (for example, engineering). This division is between sciences concerned primarily with the application of principles to actual objects and systems and those whose primary aim is the formulation and development of the principles themselves without concern for particular applications. However, such a distinction does not provide a means for classifying *terms*, since many terms ("mass," "velocity," "force") appear in the formulas of applied engineering as well as in the "abstract" principles of the theoretical physicist. Such terms can be considered both "abstractly" (independently of applications to actual instances) and "concretely" (as applied to actual instances).

To claim that a term is abstract, in a sense that would seem most appropriate for present purposes (whether or not this is exactly an "ordinary" sense), might be to claim this: that it refers to something removed from everyday experience (and hence that it refers to something more difficult to understand, an implication frequently carried by "abstract"). But there are different respects in which items can be so "removed." Carnap mentions only one, observability:

> We find among the concepts of physics—and likewise among those of the whole of empirical science—differences of abstractness. Some are more elementary than others, in the sense that we can apply them in concrete cases on the basis of observations in a more direct way than others. The others are more abstract; in order to find out whether they

[18] *Foundations of Logic and Mathematics*, p. 61.

hold in a certain case, we have to carry out a more complex procedure, which, however, also finally rests on observations.[19]

Using this as a criterion, one term would be more abstract than another if it refers to something whose observation requires more indirect methods. Thus, "entropy" would be abstract by contrast with "temperature," since determining entropy changes requires determining specific heats, temperatures, and pressures, and then calculating—a procedure obviously more indirect than that involved in determining temperature changes.[20]

On the other hand, one might consider abstractness with respect to definition. In thermodynamics a standard definition of "temperature" as a certain function of the pressure and volume of a system is abstract in that it involves an abstract mathematical argument for its establishment. This is true also of concepts such as kinetic energy in classical mechanics and partition function in statistical mechanics. Such notions are abstract in that methods employed to introduce their definitions involve mathematical derivations and manipulations divorced from familiar experimental situations.

Another consideration would be the types of objects to which the term applies. We could contrast terms such as "pressure" and "velocity," applicable to ordinary, familiar objects, with "gravitational potential," which applies only to fields in which conservative forces are acting (items that might be considered more abstract than those to which the former terms apply). *Perhaps* one might also consider a term abstract from the point of view of the role it plays in a given theory. Thus, although the definition of "pressure" and the method of measuring pressures might not be considered abstract, the concept of pressure plays a fundamental role in certain abstract differential equations of thermodynamics.

As is evident from the examples, a term abstract in one respect may not be so in another. Accordingly, we do not have a label that will generate the type of distinction envisaged nor one that will provide even a necessary condition for classification on the theoretical list.

[19] *Ibid.*
[20] The notion of indirect observation was discussed in Chap. Four, where difficulties in using this for the classification of terms were noted.

7. GENERAL CONCLUSIONS ON THE
THEORETICAL-NONTHEORETICAL DISTINCTION

In this as well as the previous chapter, I have considered the widespread doctrine that there exists a fundamental distinction between two sorts of terms employed by scientists. On one view the distinction rests upon observation; on another, upon conceptual organization, theory-dependence, or conjecture; still other criteria are precision and abstractness.[21] What has been shown is not that divisions are impossible but that, using any one of these criteria, many distinctions will emerge; these will be fairly specific ones applicable only to certain classes of terms employed by the scientist; and each will be different, so that a term classified as observational (or theory-dependent, and so forth) on one criterion will be nonobservational (or theory-independent, and so forth) on another. In short, none of these labels will generate the very broad sort of distinction so widely assumed in the philosophy of science.

Of what use, if any, are the labels "observable," "theory-dependent," "precise," and so forth? The answer will depend on the particular issues we raise. Suppose that from a philosophical point of view we want to investigate Newtonian mechanics or the quantum theory and the concepts employed. We might be concerned with how concepts such as force, field, psi-function, or electron should be understood. Given this concern, the previous labels can play an important role. Their importance lies in the fact that they can be used to refer not to single characteristics (or sets of characteristics) of terms but rather to *categories of questions* that can be raised about terms.

We may wish to study the manner in which particular terms are tied to observation. To do so we must recognize that despite some similarities there are important differences. "Electron" is tied to observation in a manner different from that of "field," "temperature," or "molecule," so that labels such as "unobservable," "not directly observable," or "not themselves observable" are bound to prove unhelpful insofar as one expects them to describe some definite characteristic or set of characteristics shared by these terms and others on the theoretical list. Instead, such labels should serve as invitations to consider the particular methods

---

[21] For a somewhat different treatment of some of these as well as related criteria, see Marshall Spector, "Theory and Observation," *British Journal for the Philosophy of Science*, 17 (1966), Part I, pp. 1–20; Part II, pp. 89–104.

of observation and to contrast them with others. How, for example, is the observation of electrons similar to and also unlike the observation of high flying jets, large molecules, neutrons, chairs and tables? Each such contrast can be invoked to bring out a definite point concerning electrons and observation. Employing a series of contrasts one could also examine the senses in which terms are theory-dependent, conjectural, precise, or abstract. In short, if asked to characterize particular terms employed by the scientist, we can proceed by raising questions concerning observation, theory-dependence, conjecture, and so on. Our questions, however, will not be "Is the term observational?," "Is it theory-dependent?," "Is it conjectural?," but instead "In what ways (by contrast with others) is it observational, theory-dependent, conjectural?" To be able to answer questions of this sort is to go some way toward understanding the concept expressed by the term.

A characterization of terms that proceeds by raising such questions can also provide a basis for evaluating particular theories and their presentations. It will reveal whether and in what respect a term has been introduced without indication of relevant methods of observation; without definite or clearly outlined connections to other terms in the theory; in a manner that makes what is said too conjectural in various respects or too abstract. The procedure I am outlining will be of particular value for theories employing concepts considered unclear or otherwise deficient in these ways. This is often said of force and mass in Newtonian mechanics. Instead of presenting this theory by dividing its terms into observational and nonobservational, theory-dependent and theory-neutral, conjectural and nonconjectural, or abstract and elementary, we might consider the various ways in which its terms are tied to observation, depend on the theory, are conectural, and are abstract. We consider possible methods for observing forces and determining whether two bodies are equal in mass. We show whether and how the theory supplies semantically relevant conditions for force and mass and what roles they play in the formulation and development of the theory. We consider which claims involving these terms are established and in what ways claims with these terms make deeper commitments or involve more intricate reasoning for their defense than claims using other terms. If our original puzzlement concerned the observational, theory-dependent, conjectural, or abstract nature of such terms, it will remain if we simply classify them using one of these labels.

I have mentioned the philosophical interest in issues concerning specific terms and theories and have suggested what value the labels "unobservable," "theory-dependent," and so forth, can have with respect to these issues. Philosophers of science, however, raise questions not only about terms in particular theories but also about terms generally. They formulate these questions about broad categories of terms, and ask, for example, how nonobservational terms can be significant or how theory-dependent terms are related to theory-neutral ones. The position I defend precludes general questions of these sorts, for the categories presupposed are a myth. But can these questions be formulated without appeal to such categories? Suppose we consider terms used especially by the scientist and those who understand science. We might ask how they are tied to observation and to theories. Let us grant that there exists a rough distinction between such terms and those used by scientists and nonscientists alike.[22] The problem here is that when questions about observation and theory-dependence are reformulated about terms used especially by the scientist, no *general* answer can be given. Such terms are exceedingly varied in their relationships to observation and to theories, as well as with respect to conceptual organization, conjecture, precision, and abstractness.

My position does not prevent a recognition and examination of categories of terms, even if labels such as "observational," "theory-dependent," and so forth, fail to pick them out. Under each of these labels, however, it is possible to invoke more specific categories that may prove helpful in understanding, evaluating, and presenting theories. In the case of observation, one might invoke a category of terms designating "items too small to be detected with the naked eye," or "properties whose magnitudes are generally determined by means of instruments," or any of the other more or less specific ones mentioned earlier. In each such case certain terms can be grouped together and attention to relevant similarities may prove instructive; but in each such case, any criterion placing terms into one of two categories will apply only to certain terms, not to all terms used in science or even to all those in a particular theory.

Accordingly, I do not deny the possibility or importance of categories for marking similarities. I emphasize only that if such categories are invoked, they will be much more numerous and specific than those too often presupposed in the philosophy of science.

[22] See Chap. Five, sec. 1.

CHAPTER SEVEN

ANALOGIES AND MODELS

The present subject is a thorny one. Philosophers as well as scientists tend to make sweeping and often confusing claims about analogies and models without devoting sufficient attention to the kinds of conceptions in the sciences they seek to characterize. Some accord analogies and models a more central role in science than others; but all agree that these conceptions are frequently employed by scientists in the formulation and development of theories as well as for the interpretation of scientific terms. In the present chapter I want to characterize analogies and models in science, and in Chapter Eight I will examine a widely accepted theory that attempts to provide a unifying scheme for them.

1. ANALOGIES

The following are typical analogies that have been employed in science:

1) The analogy between an atom and a solar system, in which the nucleus is likened to a sun and the electrons to planets revolving about it in elliptical orbits:

> The alternative [to a harmonic model of the atom] was to copy the motion of the planets around the sun. The reason planets do not fall into the sun is that they have reached stable orbits in which the centripetal force required to constrain them in their orbits is exactly the force of gravitation pulling them in. . . . Similarly in the atom, a

revolving electron if moving fast enough would not fall into the positively charged nucleus.[1]

2) The analogy drawn by Huygens between waves of light, sound, and water:

> I call them [light and sound] waves from their resemblance to those which are seen to be formed in water when a stone is thrown into it, and which present a successive spreading as circles, though these arise from another cause, and are only in a flat surface.[2]

3) The analogy between a gas and a container of billiard balls, in which the molecules in the gas are likened to perfectly elastic billiard balls striking the sides of the container as well as each other.

4) The analogy between nuclear fission and the division of a liquid drop into two smaller drops:

> On account of their close packing and strong energy exchange the particles in a heavy nucleus would be expected to move in a collective way which has some resemblance to the movement of a liquid drop. If the movement is made sufficiently violent by adding energy, such a drop may divide itself into two small drops.[3]

5) The analogy between the atomic nucleus and extranuclear electron shells:

> Bartlett's interpretation . . . drew upon an analogy with the structure of the extra-nuclear atom. He assumed that neutrons and protons formed 'shells' containing $2(2l + 1)$ particles of each kind where $\dfrac{lh}{2\pi}$ is their orbital angular momentum.[4]

6) The analogy drawn by Maxwell between the electric field and an imaginary incompressible fluid flowing through tubes of variable section:

[1] Rogers Rusk, *Introduction to Atomic and Nuclear Physics* (New York, 1958), p. 161.

[2] Christiaan Huygens, *Treatise on Light* (Chicago, 1945), p. 4.

[3] Lise Meitner and O. R. Frisch, "Disintegration of Uranium by Neutrons: A New Type of Nuclear Reaction," *Nature,* 143 (1939), 239.

[4] B. H. Flowers, "The Nuclear Shell Model," *Progress in Nuclear Physics,* ed. O. R. Frisch (New York, 1952), p. 235.

If we consider these curves [Faraday's lines of force] not as mere lines, but as fine tubes of variable section carrying an incompressible fluid, then, since the velocity of the fluid is inversely as the section of the tube, we may make the velocity vary according to any given law, by regulating the section of the tube, and in this way we might represent the intensity of the [electrical] force by the motion of the fluid in these tubes.[5]

7) The analogy noted by Kelvin between electrostatic attraction and the conduction of heat:[6]

Kelvin began by imagining a point to be a certain distance from a source of heat and then computed the temperature at the point as a function of the distance and the intensity of the heat source. For heat source he substituted a source of electricity and for the point at a certain distance from the heat source he substituted a unit charge. He then computed the potential at the point as a function of the distance and the magnitude of the charge on the source. Both situations can be represented by similar mathematical equations. (This analogy, as well as the previous one, will be discussed in more detail later.)

Using these examples as a basis, can we say what is typically the case in science when someone, call him A, draws an analogy between two things X and Y?

a) One obvious point is that A is suggesting the existence of certain similarities between X and Y. The items he claims to be similar can be of various sorts, for example: physical objects (the analogy between molecules and billiard balls), stuffs (the analogy between Maxwell's fluid and the electric field), or phenonema (the analogy between nuclear fission and the division of a liquid drop into two smaller drops).

The similarities noted can also be of various sorts. Indeed, the term "analogy" is sometimes used in a broad sense to include almost any similarity.[7] However, it is also used in a more restricted way to cover only certain types. Let me mention three that are especially important in science. X and Y may be similar in virtue of satisfying the

[5] Maxwell, "On Faraday's Lines of Force," *Scientific Papers,* ed. W. D. Niven (New York, 1965), I, 158–59.

[6] See Lord Kelvin, *Papers on Electrostatics and Magnetism* (London, 1884), pp. 1–14.

[7] One of the entries for "analogy" in the *Oxford English Dictionary* is "more vaguely, agreement between things, similarity."

same physical principles. Both gas molecules, of the sort envisaged in example (3), and perfectly elastic billiard balls operate on principles of classical mechanics. Electrostatic force is analogous to the velocity of Maxwell's fluid (6) in that both quantities vary inversely as the square of the distance from respective sources, whereas the potential of the electric field at a given point is analogous to the pressure of the fluid at a given point in that both quantities vary inversely as the first power of the distance. In other cases the principles may be similar but not identical; for example, principles governing the atomic nucleus and those governing the extranuclear electron shells (5). Another type of similarity that provides a basis for analogies is similarity in geometrical configuration. One way a Bohr atom is analogous to a planetary system is that in both a relatively light object is revolving about a relatively heavy one in an elliptical orbit with the heavy object at one of the foci of the ellipse. Still another type of similarity generating analogies is similarity in function or role; for example, the similarity between the gill of a fish and the lung of a quadruped.[8]

Two points should be noted about the similarities just mentioned. First, they are somewhat abstract ones by contrast, say, with similarities in color, shape, or size. And, indeed, typically, at least in science, similarities of the latter sort do not generate analogies, or do so only insofar as they are relevant for the more abstract similarities noted. Second, the similarities that generate the analogy between X and Y involve physical principles, geometrical considerations, or functions regarded as important in understanding how X (and possibly Y) operates or behaves. Both gas molecules and billiard balls are subject to conservation laws of classical mechanics. This similarity is one that helps generate the analogy, since such principles can be appealed to in explaining the behavior of gases. On the other hand, gas molecules as well as billiard balls are subject to gravitational forces; but this is not significant in the analogy, since such forces, being quite weak, have little effect on the behavior of either sort of item.

All the similarities I have noted may be involved when, as frequently happens, X and Y are similar in their *relationships* or in their *structure:* parts, aspects, or properties of X are related to X in ways

---

[8] Biologists distinguish analogy from homology, where the latter, but not the former, is based on considerations of evolution. See E. Mayr, E. G. Linsley, and R. L. Usinger, *Methods and Principles of Systematic Zoology* (New York, 1953), p. 42.

similar to those in which parts, aspects, or properties of Y are related to Y. The parts similarly related are said to correspond, and in describing such an analogy it will typically be said what in Y corresponds to what in X. The billiard balls in the box correspond to the molecules in the gas; the electrons in the atom correspond to the planets in the solar system; the velocity of Maxwell's fluid corresponds to the force of attraction of the electric field. On the other hand, of course, X may be analogous to Y in virtue of the fact that X is a part, aspect, or property of some larger system X' to which it bears relationships similar to those borne by Y to some larger system Y'.

b) Despite various similarities X and Y are, in other respects, unlike. You cannot draw an analogy between two boxes of identical billiard balls in virtue of, say, similar behavior, since, in other respects, they are also alike. The more similar are X and Y in all respects, the odder it becomes to talk about an analogy or analogies between them.

c) Frequently, especially in science, when A draws an analogy between X and Y, he suggests that X can be thought of and described, in certain ways and to some extent, from the point of view of Y, using Y as a basis; and that this can be done by employing concepts and ways of speaking appropriate to Y, where it might not have been obvious that these are appropriate to X. A may ask those for whom the analogy is intended to think of X's *as* Y's ("Think of molecules in a gas as tiny billiard balls in a box"); or to think of X's as something like Y's ("Think of atoms as something like miniature solar systems"). In such cases A is suggesting that certain concepts (for example, mechanical concepts) are appropriate in thinking about and describing gases as well as billiard balls, atoms as well as solar systems. Of course the analogy need not be presented in this way. A may draw the analogy between X and Y simply by suggesting certain similarities between X and Y. But when he does so, there is often the implicit claim that these can be used as a basis for thinking about and describing X and that the possibility of doing so might not have been obvious.

d) A's point in drawing an analogy between X and Y may simply be to depict X in a vivid or striking way. This is typically so in literary uses of analogy. On the other hand, A may have no point or purpose in mind, beyond noting certain similarities between unlike items. In the sciences, however, A will typically have some further aim. He may intend to illuminate X, to help provide some, or a better, understanding or grasp of X. And he may believe that Y will be considered more familiar, better understood, or more easily grasped than X by those for whom the analogy is intended. In Maxwell's day hydrodynamic phenomena were better understood than electrical ones; hence Maxwell thought it enlightening to compare the latter with the former. Again, the proponent of an analogy may want to make some claim about X appear plausible, and he may do this by citing an analogy with Y, claims about which have already been established. Such is the use of analogy in argument. For example, the assumption that a nuclear force field should be accompanied by a particle (the so-called pi-meson) was made to seem more plausible when an analogy was drawn between such a field and the electromagnetic field, which is accompanied by the photon.[9] The plausibility of any such assumption will depend of course on the extent of the similarities between the X and Y in question.

I have indicated four conditions that generally obtain in science when someone draws an analogy. Using these we can characterize an analogy in science as the sort of thing such that if it is drawn between X and Y, then these conditions are generally satisfied; and if they are satisfied, then an analogy is drawn. But what sort of "thing" is this? The term "analogy" is used in two slightly different senses. It is used to refer to certain types of similarities between two items. When so used, analogies are said to exist and to be discovered. The term is also used to refer to something like a comparison, something one draws, makes, constructs, or formulates. However, in a comparison one is looking for both similarities and differences (distinguished from a contrast, in which one *emphasizes* the differences); whereas in an analogy one is looking only for similarities. Briefly, then, to speak of an analogy between X and Y is to speak of (certain types of) similarities between otherwise unlike items X and Y (or of a noting of such similarities), attention to which may enable one to think of and describe X from the point of view of Y (a point of view that might not have been obvious), and thus to depict X in a more enlightening way, one that may help to make plausible certain claims about it.

Analogies are employed in science to promote understanding of concepts. They do so by indicating similarities between these concepts and others that may be familiar or more readily grasped. They may also suggest how principles can be formulated and a theory extended: if we have noted similarities between two phenomena (for example, be-

---

[9] See Hideki Yukawa, "On the Interaction of Elementary Particles," *Foundations of Nuclear Physics*, ed. Robert T. Beyer (New York, 1949).

tween electrostatic and gravitational phenomena), and if principles governing the one are known, then, depending on the extent of the similarity, it may be reasonable to propose that principles similar in certain ways govern the other as well. (It may be reasonable to propose an inverse square law for electrostatic attraction on the analogy with gravitation.[10])

I shall return to some of these points in Chapter Eight when considering a widespread theory about analogies. Now I want to turn to models.

2. REPRESENTATIONAL MODELS

Although the items called models in the sciences are a varied lot, three broad types can be distinguished. I turn first to the representational model, a three-dimensional physical representation of an object which is such that by examining it one can ascertain facts about the object it represents. Examples are tinkertoy models of molecules, models of the solar system found in science museums, engineering models of dams, turbomachines, airplanes, ships, an electrical circuit model for an acoustical system, a rolling ball model of radio signals, and so forth. Representational models, although used in all the sciences, are particularly central in engineering. Instead of investigating an object directly, the engineer may construct a representation of it, which can be studied more readily.

Four types of representational models can be distinguished.[11] In characterizing these I shall follow engineering terminology and speak of the object represented by the model as the *prototype*.

1) True models. Here all those characteristics of the prototype of importance to the scientist are reproduced in the model to a set scale (with respect to a given quantity, for example, distance, mass, force), so that by examining the model corresponding characteristics of the prototype can be determined. For example, a model of a bridge is constructed in which length, width, and thickness are reduced by a factor of 100.

2) Adequate models. Here only some characteristics of the proto-

---

[10] Joseph Priestley, indeed, did just this. See Roller and Roller, "The Development of the Concept of Electric Charge," *Harvard Case Histories in Experimental Science*, ed. J. B. Conant (Cambridge, Mass., 1957), II, 613.

[11] Cf. Glenn Murphy, *Similitude in Engineering* (New York, 1950), pp. 61ff.

type of importance to the scientist are reproduced in the model, so that not all characteristics of the prototype can be determined by examining the model. For example, a model of a bridge is constructed in which deflection is made to be a function of the moment of inertia of the cross section rather than of the width and depth. Such a model would enable one to determine bending deflection of the bridge but not shearing deflection.

3) Distorted models. Here all (or some) of the characteristics of the prototype of importance to the scientist are reproduced in the model, although different scales (with respect to a given quantity) are used. For example, a model of a bridge is constructed in which the width is reduced by a factor of 100, the length by a factor of 50. This is done where it is difficult or impossible to change the scale uniformly. When information about the prototype is to be ascertained from such a model, different conversion factors must be employed for different aspects of the model.

4) Analogue models. Here the characteristics of the prototype are not themselves *reproduced* in the model. Instead an analogy is drawn between two essentially unlike objects or systems X and Y, and Y is thought of as representing X by serving as an analogue for it. Y is called the model of X. For example, an electrical circuit is frequently treated as a model for an acoustical system. The engineer may begin with a problem about an acoustical system (for example, an automobile muffler), draw an electrical network that is the analogue of this system, solve the electrical problem, and convert the answer into the original system.[12] This does not mean that whenever any analogy is drawn between X and Y, Y is an analogue model of X. To be so classified, Y must be thought of or treated as something to be studied, considered in some depth, experimented upon (if it is constructed), something with respect to which calculations are to be made—where this is to be done before or in place of studying or experimenting upon X directly. Not every analogy between X and Y involves treating Y in this way. When Maxwell drew an analogy between self-diffusion of molecules in a gas and the movement of a swarm of bees, he did not intend that the latter phenomenon be studied, experimented upon, or subjected to calculation.[13] He treated it as something already familiar, something not re-

---

[12] For details, see Harry F. Olson, *Dynamical Analogies* (New York, 1943), pp. 180ff.

[13] *Scientific Papers*, II, 368. See also Chap. Three, sec. 6.

quiring very deep consideration, something the mere mention of which would provide illumination for the concept of self-diffusion. On the other hand, when he drew an analogy between the electric field and the tubes containing an incompressible fluid, he was describing an analogue model, for the latter was intended as something to be considered in depth, subjected to calculation, and so forth.[14] Obviously, then, when an analogy is drawn between X and Y, the question of whether to view Y as an analogue model of X will be a matter of degree, depending upon the extent to which Y is treated as something to be carefully studied before, or in place of, studying X directly.

Some general observations about representational models are now possible. In all four cases to speak of a model is to speak of an object distinct from the prototype of which it is a model; it is to speak of something intended to represent the prototype and to do so in such a way that facts about the prototype can be ascertained by examining, making calculations with respect to, and possibly experimenting upon, the model. In all four cases if the prototype is three-dimensional, so is the model; a two-dimensional representation would be a picture, diagram, or map. A model of each of the first three types is something actually built. An analogue model need not be built but only described. (The model in such a case is still the three-dimensional object or system described, not the description of it.) Maxwell's description of tubes containing incompressible fluid is a description of an analogue model of the electric field. He "constructed" his model simply by describing these tubes, not by building them. In none of the four cases need the model represent the prototype in all respects. An adequate model of the planets might be constructed to represent only the relative distances of the planets from the sun, not the relative sizes of these bodies. Even when a model represents an object by reproducing certain of its characteristics, the reproduction may involve approximations and simplifications. However, it will involve a minimal amount of *convention*. A representational model is not a mere symbol or set of symbols. It represents something not by symbolizing it but (in the first three cases) by reproducing its properties or (in the last case) by being an analogue of it.

[14] See sec. 1, example (6).

3. THEORETICAL MODELS

The second use of the term "model" is quite different. In this sense, when scientists speak of a model of X they are not referring to some object or system Y distinct from X, but to a set of assumptions about X. Here are some examples of what I shall call *theoretical models*:

1) The billiard ball model of a gas. This postulates that molecules comprising a gas exert no forces on one another except at impact, travel in straight lines except at instant of collision, are small in size compared to the average intermolecular distances, and so forth.

2) The Bohr model of the atom. According to this model, the electron revolves about the nucleus of an atom in such a way that its orbital angular momentum is quantized, as is the energy radiated or absorbed by the atom.

3) The corpuscular model of light, according to which light consists of particles in motion.

4) The shell model of the atomic nucleus. According to this model, the particles in the atomic nucleus are arranged in shells and move in orbits with quantized angular momentum in a nuclear field due to all the other particles in the nucleus.

5) The free-electron model of metals. This postulates that the valence electrons in the atoms of a metal move freely through the volume of the specimen.

6) The hard-sphere model of a fluid, according to which a fluid contains molecules which interact only when they collide.

All these examples come from physics, but the term "model" is used in the present sense in many other fields, such as biology (probability models in genetics), biochemistry (the Crick-Watson model of the DNA molecule), psychology (models of learning behavior), and economics (the multiplier-accelerator model of economic growth). In economics as well as other social sciences they are sometimes referred to as mathematical models.

What are the characteristics of theoretical models?

1) A theoretical model is a set of assumptions about some object or system. The billiard ball model is that set of assumptions according to which molecules in a gas exert only contact forces on each other, travel in straight lines, and so forth. The Bohr model is that set of assumptions ascribing a quantized angular momentum to orbital electrons and a quantized energy to radiation emitted or absorbed by the

atom. Three points deserve notice. First, theoretical models must be distinguished from diagrams, pictures, or physical constructions that, although sometimes useful in presenting the model, are not to be identified as the model itself. Second, it is sometimes though not always true that what is called a model is also called a theory, as in the case of the Bohr model of the atom and the free-electron model of metals. This interchangeability of labels is possible since in such cases the terms "model" and "theory" refer to the same set of assumptions; however, to call this set a model is not to suggest the same things about it as when one calls it a theory. (Some of the differences, as well as the reasons why not all models are called theories and vice versa, will emerge in what follows.) Third, the assumptions comprising the model will often be stated using mathematical equations; hence the use of the term "mathematical model" in the social sciences, where the contrast between mathematical and nonmathematical treatments is often more marked than in the physical sciences.

2) A theoretical model describes a type of object or system by attributing to it what might be called an inner structure, composition, or mechanism, reference to which is intended to explain various properties exhibited by that object or system. The billiard ball model ascribes a molecular structure to gases which enables the derivation of principles relating pressure, volume, temperature, entropy, and so forth. The corpuscular model of light ascribes a particle composition to light that purports to explain properties of light such as reflection and refraction. The Bohr model attributes an underlying mechanism to the hydrogen atom which explains radiation of discrete wavelengths observed when hydrogen is excited. Explanation by appeal to such notions covers a number of similar (though by no means identical) kinds of analyses. The following points should clarify some of the ideas involved.

The distinction between a set of exhibited properties of an object and its inner structure, reference to which can explain these properties, is not to be confused with the distinction between "macro-phenomena" and "micro-phenomena." Many of the properties explained by a theoretical model may themselves be on the "micro-level" (as in the case of atomic and nuclear models). On the other hand, the properties explained as well as the structural components of the model can both be on the "macro-level" (as in the case of "world-models" in cosmology). Moreover, the structure depicted must always be considered with reference to those properties it serves to explain and not as something ultimate or incapable of further explanation. (Thus, the molecular structure invoked in the billiard ball model is itself explained by atomic models.)

Finally, the distinction in question must not be understood simply as the distinction between properties and their explanation, for not every set of principles capable of explaining properties exhibited by an object or system (and hence not every theory) need refer to its inner structure. Some explanations proceed by describing just what relationships obtain among the exhibited properties themselves. In classical thermodynamics changes in some thermodynamic properties of matter, such as pressure, volume, temperature, and energy, can be explained by changes in others of these, although no inner structure (such as that involved in a molecular hypothesis) is ascribed to matter. Other explanations relate properties of the object to properties of quite different objects (as the tides on the earth are explained by the gravitational attraction of the sun and moon). A theoretical model, on the other hand, will proceed by analyzing the object that exhibits certain known regularities into more basic components, not just by expressing these regularities in quantitative terms or by relating the known properties to those of distinct objects or systems. Accordingly, the use of the term "theory" is in this respect broader than this use of "model," since not all theories are designed to provide structural analyses typical of theoretical models.

3) A theoretical model is treated as a simplified approximation useful for certain purposes. One who formulates or utilizes such a model will reason as follows: "It is useful to represent X's as having such and such a structure, for then various known principles can be derived; moreover, the actual structure of X's is something like this, though more complex, since only simple relationships have been assumed and various complicating factors omitted." For example: "It is useful to represent gases as composed of tiny elastic spheres obeying Newtonian laws, for then we can derive the ideal gas law, diffusion and transport equations; moreover, the actual structure of gases is something like this, though more complex because attractive and repulsive intermolecular forces are not considered in this representation." The *value* of a given model, therefore, can be judged from two different though related viewpoints: how well it serves the purposes for which it is employed, and the completeness and accuracy of the representation it proposes. Is the billiard ball model a valuable conception? Yes and No. It does enable a number of important relationships to be derived, though by completely ig-

noring certain intermolecular forces it fails to provide a full or accurate representation.

The fact that a theoretical model is proposed as a way of representing the structure of an object or system for certain purposes explains why there are often alternative models in use: different representations may be employed for different purposes, for example, the billiard ball model for deriving the perfect gas law, the weakly-attracting rigid-sphere model for deriving Van der Waals' equation, the model representing molecules as point centers of inverse power repulsion for facilitating more realistic transport calculations.[15] Here, then, is another difference between the use of the terms "theoretical model" and "theory." To propose something as a *model* of (an) X is to suggest it as one useful way of representing X that provides some approximation of the actual situation; moreover, it is to admit the possibility of alternative representations useful for different purposes. To propose something as a *theory* of (an) X, on the other hand, is to suggest that (it is plausible to believe that) X's *are* governed by such and such principles, not just that it is useful for certain purposes to represent X's as governed by these principles or that such principles are deliberately simplified approximations of those that actually obtain. Accordingly, the scientist who proposes something as a theory of (an) X must hold that alternative theories are to be rejected, modified, understood as holding only for special cases, or something of the like.

This helps to explain why certain sets of principles first called theories (for example, the Bohr theory, the free electron theory) may later be called models. Originally proposed as reflecting the actual structure of the items in question (atoms, metals), they are now recognized as simplified approximations, still useful for certain purposes. Such conceptions may of course continue to be classified as theories, thereby reflecting the historical fact that they were once proposed as theories and not simply as models.[16]

4) A theoretical model is proposed within the broader framework of some more basic theory or theories. By this I mean that when a scientist proposes a theoretical model of X, he appropriates certain principles of some more fundamental and general theory or theories to which he is committed and applies them, along with various new assumptions, to X, where "X" designates some relatively restricted class

---

[15] See R. D. Present, *Kinetic Theory of Gases* (New York, 1958), pp. 108ff.
[16] See Chap. Four, sec. 1.

of objects or systems. Thus the billiard ball model was proposed within the broader framework of Newtonian theory. In this model Newton's three laws of motion are applied to molecules in a gas, and various new and specific assumptions about these molecules are made (for example, assumptions about intermolecular forces). The Bohr model was proposed within the framework of classical electrodynamics and classical mechanics. It uses Coulomb's law as well as Newton's second law of motion, though it does introduce two new assumptions regarding quantization of angular momentum and energy that are inconsistent with these classical theories. The vector model of the atom uses principles of quantum mechanics and quantum statistics in offering a structural account of the atom. The more the assumptions about X are simply principles of some theory or theories applied (in an approximative and simplified way) to a relatively restricted class of items, the more likely are we to speak of this as a model rather than a theory.

There is another sense in which a theoretical model may be proposed within the broader framework of some theory: it may be proposed when a theory is presented. The proponent of a theory may postulate as central and distinctive assumptions some fairly complex set of relationships; yet in the development of the theory he may deliberately simplify these to facilitate calculations. For example, proponents of the kinetic theory may assume as part of their theory that forces between molecules are not simple contact forces. Yet in presenting their theory they may (for a while at least) utilize a billiard ball model that postulates contact forces and treat this as an approximation or idealization useful for certain derivations.

5) A theoretical model is often formulated, developed, and even named, on the basis of an *analogy* between the object or system described in the model and some different object or system. The Bohr model postulates orbiting electrons by analogy with a planetary system. The liquid-drop model of the atomic nucleus explains nuclear fission by utilizing an analogy with the division of a liquid drop into two smaller drops. The nuclear shell model was developed by invoking an analogy between the atomic nucleus and extranuclear electron shells. This conforms with the point, previously made, that theoretical models are intended to provide a useful representation of a system: to do so it is frequently helpful to draw an analogy between the system in question and some known system governed by laws that are understood and to suppose that some of these laws, or similar ones, also govern the

system described in the model. Reasoning of this sort is never sufficient to establish the principles of the model but only to suggest that they may be reasonable first approximations, subject to test and subsequent modification. In each case, however, the model itself can be distinguished from any analogy upon which it might have been developed. The billiard ball *model* consists of those propositions asserting that gases are composed of tiny elastic spheres, and so on. The *analogy* is drawn between gases thus described and perfectly elastic billiard balls.

These, then, are the characteristics of theoretical models. What is the difference between such models and theories? Appealing to what has just been said, as well as to my characterization of theories in Chapter Four, the differences can be summarized as follows:

If a person proposes something as a theoretical model of (an) X, by contrast with a theory of (an) X, he may know or believe that, strictly speaking, his assumptions are false, inaccurate, or applicable only within a very limited range. His theoretical model will typically simplify by using approximations, omitting complicating factors, introducing idealized relationships. Such simplifying assumptions may be useful in affording certain calculations and explanations; but, unlike those constituting a theory of (an) X, they are not proposed as assumptions that, taken literally, actually govern X's. Of course, the proponent of a theory may also recognize that his assumptions are to some extent simplified, inaccurate, or restricted; there is some leeway here, though not of the magnitude allowed in a theoretical model. Second, a theory, unlike a theoretical model, need not attribute to an object an inner structure, composition, or mechanism, reference to which is intended to explain various properties exhibited by that object. It may indicate what relationships obtain among these properties without postulating any inner structure, or it may relate the properties of the object in question to those of a distinct object or system. Third, when someone proposes a theoretical model much of what is proposed will typically be derived from some more fundamental theory or theories; principles of the latter will be applied to a relatively restricted set of objects or systems. Some theories are also like this, but many are not.[17] In many cases when a scientist proposes a theory none of his central and distinctive assumptions will be borrowed or derived from more fundamental theories.

As for *use,* theoretical models serve all the functions that theories

[17] See Chap. Four, sec. 1, pt. 5.

do: they can be used for explanation, systematization, interpretation, prediction, calculations, derivation of laws, and the like. But they provide explanations, and so forth, based on simplified as well as relatively restricted assumptions. Where both a theory and a theoretical model are available and applicable in the same area, explanation and systematization via the theory are often said to be "deeper" and to provide more insight, thus reflecting the belief that the principles constituting the theory are more accurate than those of the theoretical model and take into account more of the known quantities; also that they are more general than many of the assumptions in the model. Why then not always employ a more accurate, complete, and general theory instead of a theoretical model? First, there may be no such theory available, as is presently the case with models of the atomic nucleus; or there may be several more general theories no one of which is considered entirely satisfactory. Second, a theoretical model may be of considerable importance even if there is a more accurate, complete, and general theory. It may afford calculations impossible or exceedingly difficult with the theory. In kinetic theory calculations involving transport phenomena, such as diffusion, heat conduction, and viscosity, become quite difficult unless simplifying assumptions embodied in several models of intermolecular force fields are adopted. Again, by studying the consequences of deliberately simplified assumptions constituting a model, the scientist may gain further insight into the more complex theory and may even be led to extend or modify it. Finally, theoretical models serve an important didactic role. It is frequently a simpler procedure to study the Bohr model before turning to quantum theory or to treat transport phenomena by assuming a billiard ball model before learning the more advanced Maxwell-Chapman transport theory.

4. IMAGINARY MODELS

The third type of model I want to distinguish will be called an imaginary model. It is similar to a theoretical model in some respects and also to one type of representational model, the analogue model, in others. But it is sufficiently different from either to deserve separate classification. Here are two examples.

a) Poincaré's model of a Lobachevskian non-Euclidean world.

In trying to show what such a world could be like, Poincaré described an imaginary sphere concerning which he made a number of assumptions:

> The temperature is not uniform; it is greatest at the center, and gradually decreases as we move towards the circumference of the sphere, where it is absolute zero. The law of this temperature is as follows: If R be the radius of the sphere, and r the distance of the point considered from the center, the absolute temperature will be proportional to $R^2 - r^2$. Further, I shall suppose that in this world all bodies have the same coefficient of dilation, so that the linear dilation of any body is proportional to its absolute temperature. Finally, I shall assume that a body transported from one point to another of different temperature is instantaneously in thermal equilibrium with its new environment.[18]

In this world the postulates of Lobachevsky's geometry are satisfied (as judged from the point of view of an inhabitant). For example, through a point not on a given straight line more than one straight line can be drawn that does not intersect the given line.

b) Maxwell's mechanical model of the electromagnetic field expounded in his paper "On Physical Lines of Force." Here Maxwell introduces a number of assumptions concerning the electromagnetic field, some of which I shall quote:

> (1) Magneto-electric phenomena are due to the existence of matter under certain conditions of motion or of pressure in every part of the magnetic field, and not to direct action at a distance between magnets or currents. . . .
> (2) The condition of any part of the field, through which lines of magnetic force pass, is one of unequal pressure in different directions. . . .
> (3) This inequality of pressure is produced by the existence in the medium of vortices or eddies. . . .
> (4) The vortices are separated from each other by a single layer of round particles. . . .
> (5) The particles forming the layer are in *rolling contact* with both the vortices which they separate, but do not rub against each other. . . .
> These particles, in our theory, play the part of electricity. Their motion of translation constitutes an electric current, their rotation serves to transmit the motion of the vortices from one part of the field to an-

[18] Henri Poincaré, *Science and Hypothesis* (New York, 1952), p. 65.

other, and the tangential pressures thus called into play constitute electromotive force. . . .

(6) The effect of an electric current upon the surrounding medium is to make the vortices in contact with the current revolve. . . .[19]

Maxwell treats these assumptions in a special way, which is brought out when he comments on assumption (5):

> I do not bring it forward as a mode of connexion existing in nature, or even as that which I would willingly assent to as an electrical hypothesis. It is, however, a mode of connexion which is mechanically conceivable, and easily investigated. . . .[20]

The following are important characteristics of such models:

1) In an imaginary model an object or system is described by a certain set of assumptions. Poincaré assumes that in his spherical world the temperature is greatest at the center, decreasing toward the circumference, and so forth. Maxwell makes assumptions regarding vortices and particles comprising the electromagnetic field. The word "model" may refer either to the object described or to the assumptions made about it.

2) The proponent of the model does not commit himself to the truth, or even to the plausibility, of the assumptions he makes; nor does he intend them as approximations to what is actually the case. Maxwell in his model does not commit himself to the view that the electromagnetic field has the structure he describes, even approximately. In some cases, indeed, the assumptions may be entirely fanciful and contrary to what their proponent believes to hold in the actual world. Poincaré was describing what he took to be a purely imaginary world when he introduced special laws of temperature.

3) The point of an imaginary model is to show what the object or system could be like if it were to satisfy certain conditions initially specified; it is to show that if these conditions were to be satisfied, then it would be at least logically possible to suppose the object or system is as described in the model. (In Maxwell's model the condition is set that Newtonian principles of mechanics, and only these, are to be employed and that known electromagnetic phenomena are to be explained by reference to them.) The following question is then raised: How might X be described so that these conditions are met? (How

---

[19] *Scientific Papers,* I, 485–87.
[20] *Ibid.,* p. 486.

could the electromagnetic field be described in such a way that it is subject only to mechanical forces obeying Newtonian laws?) The assumptions of the model provide an answer. Yet there is no commitment to the claim that there is an X that actually does satisfy the required conditions; or to the claim that there is an X that does satisfy the assumptions proposed; or even to the claim that if there is an X that does satisfy these conditions, then it also satisfies the assumptions proposed. In his model Maxwell does not assume that the electromagnetic field is completely mechanical; or that it has the structure he describes; or even that if it is completely mechanical, it has this structure. His point is to show what the structure of the electromagnetic field could be like if it were subject only to mechanical laws.[21]

What can an imaginary model accomplish? Possibly several things. First, it can show that certain suppositions, which might otherwise be thought self-contradictory or inconceivable, are at least consistent; for example, the supposition of a completely mechanical electromagnetic field. Second, by showing that an X subject to conditions C is conceivable, it may provide a basis for further investigation of what X (subject to these conditions) is actually like. Maxwell, for example, intended his demonstration of the possibility of a purely mechanical electromagnetic field to serve as a stimulus to further investigation into the actual structure of this field. Third, an imaginary model can promote understanding of the principles that X is imagined to satisfy. Thus, Poincaré's model provides more of an understanding of abstract Lobachevskian principles by supplying an application for them.

5. COMPARISONS BETWEEN IMAGINARY, THEORETICAL, AND ANALOGUE MODELS

Imaginary models are similar to theoretical models and to analogue models in certain respects but not in others. A theoretical model

---

[21] In his *Treatise on Electricity and Magnetism* (New York, 1954), Maxwell, speaking of this earlier model, writes: "The attempt which I then made to imagine a working model of this mechanism must be taken for no more than it really is, a demonstration that mechanism may be imagined capable of producing a connexion mechanically equivalent to the actual connexion of the parts of the electromagnetic field. The problem of determining the mechanism required to establish a given species of connexion between the motions of the parts of a system always admits of an infinite number of solutions."

221

is, and an imaginary model can be, a set of assumptions. But in a theoretical model the assumptions are treated as giving a plausible, if approximative and simplified, description of what X actually is; there is no such commitment in an imaginary model. An analogue model is, and an imaginary model can be, an object rather than a set of assumptions. Moreover, one who constructs an imaginary model of X, like one who constructs an analogue model of X, is not committed to the belief that X is identical with the object described in his model. However, in an imaginary model the assumption is made (for the special purposes of the model) that X is identical with the system described, although this assumption is not claimed to be true or even plausible. In an analogue model such an identification is never made. Although the analogue model is treated as representing the prototype, as substituting for it for purposes of calculation, the assumption is never made that the two are identical. When he constructs his mechanical model of the electromagnetic field (an imaginary model), Maxwell, by admitting that he does "not bring [the proposed mechanical system] forward as a mode of connexion existing in nature," grants that his system is distinct from the electromagnetic field. Still he is assuming for the sake of the model (in order to show how a purely mechanical field could be described) that the mechanical system he describes actually constitutes the electromagnetic field, that is, that they are not distinct but one and the same thing. In his earlier paper, "On Faraday's Lines of Force," the system he describes is an analogue model, not an imaginary model. Tubes of fluid are never assumed by him, even for the sake of the model, to comprise the electric field but only to serve as an analogue for it.

In short, when the scientist proposes a theoretical model of X, he wants to approximate to what X actually is by making assumptions about it. In an analogue model of X he wants to construct or describe some different item Y that bears certain analogies to X. In an imaginary model of X he wants to consider what X could be like if it were to satisfy conditions he specifies.

Nineteenth century models of the ether and of the electric field provide examples of each of these types. Some were intended as analogue models (Maxwell's fluid model of the electric field), some as imaginary models (Maxwell's mechanical model of the electromagnetic field). An example of a theoretical model of the ether is that proposed in 1899 by George Francis FitzGerald:

222

. . . I have been advocating the hypothesis that the ether is of the nature of a fluid full of vortical motion, and that electromagnetic actions are due to particular arrangements of this motion, which is, in general irregular or at least undirected. . . . What I now desire to call attention to is a hypothesis as to the nature of the wave motion which can be transmitted by a system of vortex filaments.[22]

The hypothesis in question, which attributes spiral vortices to the ether, was not proposed as a mere analogue, and unlike Maxwell (in the case of his imaginary model), FitzGerald made no claim that he did "not bring it forward as a mode of connexion existing in nature." Instead he called it a "hypothesis . . . put forward very tentatively."

There are two complicating factors about models illustrated by nineteenth century ether models. One concerns analogue models. Since the nineteenth century physicist did not claim to know what the ether is actually like, he would very often describe some distinct system that, he thought, *might* bear certain analogies to the ether, although he did not want to commit himself to this in any way. He treated his conception as a *possible* ether analogue. For example, in 1885, Fitz-Gerald formulated a "model illustrating some properties of the ether." [23] "The model," he writes, "consists of a series of wheels rotating on axes fixed perpendicularly in a plane board, and connected by indiarubber bands." FitzGerald made it clear that he did "not intend it to be supposed that the ether is actually made up of wheels and indiarubber bands, nor even of paddlewheels, with connecting canals." [24] He was not proposing a theoretical model, or even an imaginary model, of the ether. Nor was he committing himself to the view that the ether was *like* this in certain respects: "I need hardly say, in conclusion, that I do not in the least intend to convey the impression that the actual structure of the ether is a bit like what I have described." [25] What FitzGerald seems to be doing here is constructing a possible mechanical analogue model of the ether, that is, describing something as a possible ether analogue. This is to be contrasted with Maxwell's hydrodynamic analogue model of the electric field, which was claimed to be similar to the electric field (in the respects he considered relevant). In many analogue models the conception proposed is claimed

[22] *Scientific Writings* (Dublin, 1902), pp. 472–73.
[23] *Ibid.,* p. 142.
[24] *Ibid.,* p. 151.
[25] *Ibid.,* p. 162.

to be *definitely* analogous to the system in certain respects and *possibly* analogous in others.

The second complicating factor illustrated by nineteenth century ether models concerns the problem of identifying the type of model proposed. When the physicist ascribed a structure to the ether was he treating his assumptions as simplified approximations of what he actually believed to be the case? Was he saying what the ether could be like if it were to satisfy certain conditions? Or was he saying that the ether is analogous to the system he described? Did he, in short, propose his conception as a theoretical model, an imaginary model, or an analogue model of the ether? Often we can determine the answer by considering what the physicist himself wrote about his conception or how he in fact used it; but in some cases it is not clear. Lord Kelvin once offered a mechanical description of the ether that at some points he seems to treat as an analogue model:

> . . . imagine for a moment that we make a rude mechanical model. Let this be an infinitely rigid spherical shell; let there be another absolutely rigid shell inside of it, and so on, as many as you please. . . . Let zig-zag springs connect the outer rigid boundary with boundary number two. . . . Suppose we have shells 2 and 3 also connected by a sufficient number of zig-zag springs and so on; and let there be a solid nucleus in the centre with spring connections between it and the shell outside of it.[26]

In other passages he appears to claim reality for his conception and to be treating it as a theoretical model of molecules constituting the ether:

> It seems to me that there must be something in this molecular hypothesis and that as a mechanical symbol it is certainly not a mere hypothesis, but a reality.[27]

How a scientist intends his conception to be taken, that is, what sort of model he is proposing, will obviously make an important difference regarding the standards appropriate in evaluating it. The scientist who actually attributed to electric fields a certain mechanical structure

---

[26] Lord Kelvin, *Baltimore Lectures on Molecular Dynamics and the Wave Theory of Light* (London, 1904), pp. 12–13.
[27] *Ibid.,* p. 14.

could be criticized as proposing a false conception if, on the basis of experiments, it is concluded that electric fields have no such structure, even approximately. Such criticism could not be leveled against one who claimed merely that electric fields could be like this if they were subject only to mechanical laws.

In this chapter several types of models employed in the sciences have been characterized and the concept of an analogy explained. In what follows I turn to a widely accepted theory about models and analogies; it proposes a single unifying scheme for all these conceptions.

CHAPTER EIGHT

ON A SEMANTICAL THEORY OF MODELS

1. THE SEMANTICAL THEORY

There is a widespread theory about models and analogies in science. Its proponents are generally those who defend the contemporary Positivist account discussed in Chapter Three. Following the formal semantics of Rudolf Carnap, these philosophers refer to a set of sentences or formulas all of whose terms are uninterpreted as a *calculus,* and the sentences obtained when all the terms are interpreted as a *model* (or *interpretation*) for that calculus.[1] They then apply Carnap's semantical distinctions to scientific theories, especially to those presented in an axiomatized manner.[2] The axioms of a theory may be considered as uninterpreted strings of symbols or as interpreted propositions. The former would be called a calculus for this theory, the latter a model for the calculus of this theory.

To illustrate these ideas, consider the following set of uninterpreted formulas[3] that might constitute part of a calculus for the kinetic theory of gases (that part expressing principles of classical mechanics for molecules treated as mass points):

(1) The set P is finite and non-empty
(2) The set T is an interval of real numbers
(3) For p in P, s_p is twice differentiable on T
(4) For p in P, $m(p)$ is a positive real number

[1] See Carnap, *Introduction to Semantics* (Cambridge, Mass., 1942), p. 203.
[2] See Chap. Four.
[3] Taken from Patrick Suppes, *Introduction to Logic* (Princeton, 1957), p. 294.

(5) For p and q in P and t in T, $f(p, q, t) = -f(q, p, t)$

(6) For p and q in P and t in T, $s(p, t) \times f(p, q, t) = -s(q, t) \times f(q, p, t)$

(7) $m(p)D^2s_p(t) = \sum_{p \neq q} f(p, q, t) + g(p, t)$

The terms in this calculus are to be interpreted as follows: P is to designate a class of molecules in a gas, T is a class of elapsed times, s_p is the position of molecule p, $m(p)$ is the mass of p, $f(p, q, t)$ is the force that p exerts on q at time t, and $g(p, t)$ is the resultant external force acting on p at time t. Now we can formulate seven interpreted statements that constitute some of the axioms for kinetic theory. For example, (5), on the present interpretation, would be: The force exerted by molecule p on molecule q at time t is equal in magnitude and opposite in direction to that exerted by q on p at time t. Suppose now we let p designate a class of perfectly elastic billiard balls in a box and let the remaining terms have the same interpretations as before. The resulting statements will describe billiard balls as subject to the principles of classical mechanics. Thus, formula (5) would be: The force exerted by billiard ball p on billiard ball q at time t is equal in magnitude and opposite in direction to that exerted by q on p at time t. The set of such statements will constitute a *model for the calculus of the kinetic theory*. We can also say that it constitutes a *model for the kinetic theory* or a *model of a gas*.

On the semantical theory, then, the concept of a model is defined as follows: Let S be a set of statements comprising some theory, and S^* the calculus of this set (what this set becomes by treating each nonlogical predicate constant in S as a predicate variable). Let S' be a set of statements obtained from S^* by substituting an (interpreted) predicate for each predicate variable in S^*. Then S' is a *model* for S^*. Derivatively, we can say that S' is a model for S, and that S' is a model of the items described in S.[4]

[4] There is a different but related account of models in mathematical logic. Here a model is construed not as a set of *statements* obtained by interpreting terms in the calculus, but as a set of *items* (objects, relationships, and so forth) that satisfy the formulas of the calculus. For example, in mathematical logic a model for the above calculus would be an ordered set $< P, T, s, m, f, g >$ that satisfies this calculus. Given such a model, in the sense of mathematical logic, it is possible to formulate a set of statements about the items P, T, s, m, f, g. It is these statements, rather than the ordered set of items they describe, that is usually called the model by the authors I want to consider; and it is this "linguistic" rather than the "set-theoretical" notion of model I propose to discuss.

According to the semantical theory, this definition applies to conceptions characterized in the previous chapter. What I have called theoretical models, representational models, imaginary models, and analogies are all held to be models in the sense of being interpretations of the calculus of some theory. Proponents of this idea cite as examples the Bohr model of the atom, a planetary museum model of the solar system, Maxwell's tubes of fluid as a model of the electric field, Poincaré's model of a non-Euclidean universe, and the analogy between heat conduction and electrostatic attraction. I am concerned with this theory insofar as it claims to apply to these conceptions. It deserves consideration not only because of the eminence of its supporters (for example, Braithwaite,[5] Nagel,[6] Hempel,[7] Brodbeck,[8] Hutten[9]), but also because it is the only theory that attempts to provide a unifying scheme for models and analogies in science.

To discuss this theory we must separate a number of claims it makes:

1) A model is a set of statements ascribing properties to some object or system.

2) The statements that constitute the model describe some item assumed to be distinct from that of which it is a model. When we speak of a model of (an) X (for example, a model of a gas) the X will be the object mentioned in S (see definition above); whereas the object described in S' (the model) will in general be different from X, since the terms used in S' will in general be different from those in S. For example, a model of a gas might describe billiard balls in a box, not molecules in a gas.

3) A model is designed to provide an interpretation for an uninterpreted formalism or calculus. Nagel, for example, speaks of a model as "an interpretation . . . for the abstract calculus which supplies some flesh for the skeletal structure in terms of more or less familiar conceptual or visualizable materials." [10] Hutten asserts that

---

[5] R. B. Braithwaite, *Scientific Explanation* (Cambridge, England, 1953); "Models in the Empirical Sciences," *Logic, Methodology, and Philosophy of Science,* ed. E. Nagel, P. Suppes, and A. Tarski (Stanford, 1962).

[6] Ernest Nagel, *The Structure of Science* (New York, 1961), pp. 90–117.

[7] Carl G. Hempel, *Aspects of Scientific Explanation* (New York, 1965), pp. 433–47.

[8] May Brodbeck, "Models, Meaning, and Theories," *Symposium on Sociological Theory,* ed. L. Gross (Evanston, 1959).

[9] Ernest H. Hutten, *The Language of Modern Physics* (London, 1956).

[10] *Structure of Science,* p. 90.

"the model gives a possible interpretation to the symbols [in an equation or formula] which thereby acquire a meaning, and we can apply the equation or formula and test it." [11]

4) A model is always proposed with reference to some theory, the model having the same formal structure (the same calculus) as this theory. Braithwaite speaks of a model as "another interpretation of the theory's calculus," [12] and holds that "similarity in formal structure . . . is all that is required of the relationship of model to theory." [13] Nagel defines a model for a theory T as a set of true propositions with the same formal structure or calculus as T.[14] The position here is closely related to the previous claim that a model provides an interpretation for an uninterpreted formalism. According to the present claim this formalism is that of some theory.

5) A model is an analogy. Nagel uses the terms "model" and "analogy" interchangeably and classifies the Bohr model of the atom and the wave model of light with the analogy between molecules and billiard balls and the analogy between light and sound.[15] Braithwaite adopts a similar approach and cites models of molecules as linked systems of atoms and the analogy between hydrogen atoms and solar systems as examples of the same sort of thing.[16] Mary Hesse classifies the analogy between gas molecules and billiard balls with postulates about atomic particles, claiming both as examples of models.[17]

How do these claims fare when applied to the models and analogies of the previous chapter?

2. MODELS, STATEMENTS, AND INTERPRETATION

1) *A model is a set of statements ascribing properties to some object or system.* This is warranted for theoretical models and imag-

---

[11] *Language of Modern Physics*, p. 82.

[12] "Models in the Empirical Sciences," p. 225.

[13] *Scientific Explanation*, p. 225.

[14] *Structure of Science*, p. 96.

[15] *Ibid.*, Chap. 6.

[16] *Scientific Explanation*, p. 93.

[17] "Models in Physics," *British Journal for the Philosophy of Science*, 4 (1953), 198–214. In her later work, *Models and Analogies in Science* (London, 1963), Dr. Hesse does distinguish two types of models which appear to be theoretical models and analogies. Hempel (*Aspects of Scientific Explanation*) also distinguishes analogies from theoretical models.

inary models (though the latter can also be construed as the objects described by these statements), but not for representational models. The latter are objects, not statements, though of course they are described by using statements. What about analogies? These, we recall, can be construed as similarities of certain sorts or as (something like) comparisons noting these similarities. In the former sense they are not statements, but in the latter they might be characterized as such. At least comparisons can be made by making statements. Even so, it would be misleading to say that such statements simply ascribe properties to some object or system. They express the fact that similarities exist between two objects or systems.

2) *The statements that constitute the model describe some item assumed to be distinct from that of which it is a model.* This cannot be satisfied by representational models since they are not statements. What could be said is that the object called the representational model is distinct from that of which it is a model. Theoretical and imaginary models, although composed of statements, do not describe items assumed to be distinct from that of which they are models. A theoretical model of a gas describes molecules in the gas, not, say, billiard balls in a box. Maxwell's imaginary model of the electromagnetic field makes assumptions about this field, not about some different system. Analogies, when construed as (something like) comparisons, come closest to satisfying (2), but even here it would be more enlightening to say simply that the items between which the analogy is drawn are distinct.

3) *A model is designed to provide an interpretation for an uninterpreted formalism or calculus.* ("Interpretation," as in Chapter Three, is to be understood as the assignment of meanings to words or symbols.) I want to consider this claim first with respect to theoretical models. To do so it will be useful to examine the discussion offered by Nagel, who more than most representatives of this position gives detailed attention to specific examples.

On page 94 of the *Structure of Science,* Nagel writes:

> The Bohr theory of the atom . . . assumes that there are atoms, each of which is composed of a relatively heavy nucleus carrying a positive electric charge and a number of negatively charged electrons with smaller mass moving in approximately elliptic orbits with the nucleus at one of the foci. . . . The theory further assumes that there are only a discrete set of permissible orbits for the electrons, and that the diam-

eters of the orbits are proportional to h^2n^2, where h is Planck's constant . . . and n is an integer. Moreover, the electromagnetic energy of an electron in an orbit depends on the diameter of the orbit. . . .

On page 95, however, Nagel informs us that what he actually presented was not the Bohr *theory* but the Bohr *model* ("in such an exposition the postulates the theory are embedded in a model or interpretation"). The Bohr theory, we are told, is really a calculus only some of whose terms are interpreted, whereas what is presented above is not a set of "statement-forms" but full-fledged "statements at least part of whose content can be visually imagined." We can certainly grant that what Nagel presents above is the Bohr *model* (as noted in the previous chapter, what he presents is also the Bohr theory). But given Nagel's notion of a theory as a partially interpreted calculus,[18] he would argue that not only does the Bohr model have the same calculus as the Bohr theory but also that it provides an interpretation for this calculus. I want to consider this latter claim; it might be understood in a number of different ways.

a) The Bohr model as an interpreted system can be distinguished from its calculus; it happens to be one among many possible interpretations for this calculus. If this is all that is meant, I have no objection. A similar point can be made about any proposition or set of propositions. ("All metals melt" can be distinguished from the schema "All *A* is *B*" and happens to be one among many possible interpretations for this schema.) More generally, I have no objection if Nagel and others simply want to distinguish the presentation of a theory in an interpreted form from one in which only (mathematical) formulas with no meanings attached are given, where by a model they mean to be referring to a presentation of the former sort, nothing more. On the other hand, the examples cited by these authors suggest that this is not their point. References to the Bohr model, the billiard ball model, the corpuscular model of light, models of molecules as linked systems of atoms, and so forth, suggest that they mean to be describing what is characteristic of those conceptions I have called theoretical models, not what is characteristic of *any* set of (interpreted) propositions whatever. Moreover, with respect to these models the suggestion appears to be not just that they are interpreted propositions distinguishable from their respective calculi, but something more. Nagel, we observed, says

[18] See Chap. Three, sec. 4.

that the Bohr theory is a partially interpreted calculus but that when "customarily expounded" it is "embedded in a model." This might suggest the following claim.

b) The *point* of formulating and utilizing a theoretical model is to provide an interpretation for uninterpreted terms in a calculus; or at least the model is used because it constitutes such an interpretation. Nagel recognizes that this does not represent the historical order of development: he is not saying that scientists first formulate an uninterpreted or partially interpreted calculus and then supply a theoretical model. But he might be understood as saying that once a theory is conceived (no matter in what order), the theoretical model is actually utilized by the physicist to provide, or because it provides, an interpretation for the calculus (of this theory). Such a claim, however, is too strong. The physicist no more utilizes the Bohr model in order to supply an interpretation for a calculus, or because it supplies such an interpretation, than one who utters the sentence "All metals melt" does so in order to interpret the schema "All *A* is *B*," or because the sentence provides such an interpretation.

This is not to deny that the Bohr model *could* be used in certain cases to furnish interpretations. One might consider certain mathematical equations and then show what physical interpretations they have in this model. However, this context is very special, and what is envisaged is not something especially characteristic of theoretical models but holds equally for any set of propositions containing mathematical equations. Nor is this to deny that certain theoretical models have played important roles in furnishing interpretations for formulas and may be used in some instances because they furnish such interpretations. The Schrödinger wave equation in quantum mechanics was interpreted in a particle model by specifying that the square of the psi-function at a given point in space represents the probability of finding the corresponding particle in the neighborhood of that point. However, this sort of interpretative role is not characteristic only of theoretical models. The same role is often played by theories, many of which would not be classified as theoretical models. Thus, quantum statistics provides interpretations for certain terms and equations in thermodynamics. Even when a theoretical model *is* used to provide, or because it provides, an interpretation for equations, these equations will not be mere uninterpreted strings of symbols. The terms in the Schrödinger equation, for example, already have meanings, though these are fairly abstract;

the particle model is then employed to assign a new interpretation to the psi-function, which appears in this equation and is already interpreted as representing the amplitude of a matter wave at a point in space. Similarly, the Bohr model can be used to assign meaning to the term "R" appearing in Balmer's equation describing a relationship among the wavelengths of the lines in the visible region of the hydrogen spectrum.[19] Yet this term (the gas constant) has already been given a meaning independent of the Bohr model by reference to the ideal gas law. Moreover, despite the fact that a theoretical model is sometimes used to supply, or because it supplies, new interpretations for terms in certain equations, it would be misleading to consider this to be one of the principal reasons for its use, especially when considering those equations appearing in its own basic assumptions. The Bohr model is not something designed or utilized by the physicist to provide, or because it provides, interpretations new or otherwise for terms such as "elliptical orbit," "mass," or "charge," which appear in its central postulates (indeed such terms were in use prior to the model and retain their original meanings in it). Rather it is a set of assumptions that employs these (already interpreted) terms to describe the atomic structure.

A final way to construe Nagel's claim is this.

c) Although scientists do not actually utilize partially interpreted calculi, it is important to recognize the possibility of reconstructing the systems they do present in this way. If so, a theoretical model would be important insofar as it provides an interpretation for a system so reconstructed. In other words, if scientists were to present their ideas as partially interpreted calculi, then theoretical models would be utilized to serve the purpose specified. In assessing this claim the reasons for reconstructing scientific systems as partially interpreted calculi would need to be examined—something I did in Chapter Three, where criticisms were offered of such an approach. (It might be noted that for the very reasons generally given in favor of reconstructing systems in the manner proposed—reasons concerning the presence of so-called theoretical terms—many theoretical models, such as atomic and nuclear models, would themselves need to be construed as partially interpreted calculi.) For present purposes, however, it suffices to note that even if it were valuable for scientists to reconstruct their ideas as partially interpreted calculi and even if theoretical models were con-

19 See Chap. Four, sec. 2.

sidered to be interpreted systems in the required sense, the interpretative role would not be one especially characteristic of such models but would be one served by any set of scientific propositions. Any such set, after being presented as a partially interpreted calculus, could be utilized to interpret that calculus.

So far I have considered claim (3) only with reference to theoretical models. How does this claim fare when we turn to other conceptions discussed in the previous chapter?

In the case of imaginary models (viewed as sets of assumptions) the three ways of construing this claim just considered for theoretical models would be possible. But construals (a) and (c) would be open to the very same objections. So, let us consider (b), namely, that the point of formulating and utilizing a model is to provide an interpretation for uninterpreted terms in a calculus; or at least the model is utilized because it constitutes such an interpretation. Something *like* this can be said for at least some imaginary models. The point of an imaginary model of X is to indicate what X could be like if it were to satisfy conditions C. To indicate this, the model might show, among other things, how terms in C could be interpreted so that C would be satisfied by the item described in the model. Now, C might consist of formulas whose terms already have been assigned meanings, though very abstract ones; and the imaginary model might provide more concrete and fully-developed meanings for these terms. Or C might consist of formulas whose terms have been assigned no meanings, a task left for the imaginary model. In the sciences the latter situation seldom arises because rarely if ever is use made of a formalism whose terms have no meanings whatever. An example of the former situation is provided by Poincaré's imaginary model of a non-Euclidean world.[20]

One of the aims of this model can be viewed as that of providing interpretations for certain terms in Lobachevskian geometry. For example, in this model "point" is interpreted to mean point in a sphere with the features described by Poincaré. And "straight line" means shortest distance between two points in this sphere. Before developing his imaginary model, Poincaré had already provided interpretations for the terms in Lobachevsky's geometry by using what he called a dictionary that translates terms from this geometry into terms from two-dimensional Euclidean geometry. His imaginary model might be construed as expanding upon such definitions, as developing the meanings

[20] See Chap. Seven, sec. 4.

of the Lobachevskian concepts for a three-dimensional case. By doing this the model shows what something could be like if it were to satisfy Lobachevsky's geometry.

However, an imaginary model need not proceed in this way. To show what something could be like if it were to satisfy conditions C, the model need not assign meanings to terms in C. Such terms may already be interpreted, and the model may add little or nothing to their interpretations. This is so in Maxwell's mechanical model of the electromagnetic field.[21] The model is designed to show what this field could be like if it were to satisfy Newtonian principles, but it does not stipulate or develop meanings for terms in these principles. It does not show how such terms could be interpreted so that Newtonian principles would be satisfied by the mechanical system described. The model simply ascribes properties to the electromagnetic field in such a way that Newtonian principles (already interpreted independently of the model) are satisfied.

In short, claim (3), that a model is designed to provide an interpretation for an uninterpreted formalism or calculus, is too sweeping in the case of imaginary models. Some of these models will not serve this function at all. Others may provide interpretations for terms whose meanings have been only partially explained. It is certainly not typical of such models that they take terms assigned no meanings and interpret them.

The present claim is equally dubious for analogies. Consider Kelvin's analogy between heat conduction and electrostatic attraction, where certain laws governing each can be shown to be similar in form.[22] In this analogy the laws governing one phenomenon are not treated as mere uninterpreted formulas that the other laws are supposed to interpret. *Source of heat* is not proposed as a meaning for the concept *source of electricity,* or vice versa. The point is simply that the source of heat in heat phenomena is what corresponds to, what is analogous to, the source of electricity in electrostatic phenomena. What *can* be said is that analogies frequently help one to understand an interpretation already given to a term. That is, when an analogy is drawn between X and Y, thinking about Y is sometimes helpful in trying to understand the meaning of certain terms used in describing X. So employed, the

[21] See Chap. Seven, sec. 4.
[22] See Chap. Seven, sec. 1.

analogy does not assign meanings to such terms; indeed, it presupposes that meanings have already been assigned.

This completes my discussion of claim (3). However, a related claim is sometimes made, namely, that models are designed to prove the consistency of a set of assumptions. This idea may derive from mathematical logic, where a model is construed as a set in which a calculus is satisfied.[23] One begins with a calculus and attempts to show that it is logically consistent by finding an interpretation for it in some domain.

The claim that models are designed to demonstrate the consistency of a set of assumptions is definitely appropriate in the case of imaginary models. One way of describing such models is to say that they are attempting to show the supposition that X satisfies conditions C to be a *consistent* supposition.[24] For example, Maxwell was trying to show that it was possible to describe an electromagnetic field that satisfies mechanical principles only, that the supposition of such a field is at least consistent. However, in constructing a theoretical model, a representational model, or even an analogy, one is making stronger claims than this. Such conceptions are not designed to show merely the consistency of certain claims about X. Moreover, even in the case of an imaginary model, the scientist does not proceed in the manner outlined by the mathematical logician. Maxwell did not begin with an uninterpreted calculus and then show how this could be interpreted in some domain. He began with interpreted mechanics and showed how this could be applied to a mechanism imagined to constitute the electromagnetic field, a mechanism that would produce the known effects of such a field.

3. MODELS AND FORMAL STRUCTURE

4) *A model is always proposed with reference to some theory, the model having the same formal structure (the same calculus) as this theory.* This claim is subject to various interpretations:

a) Consider any (partially interpreted) calculus. This is to be called a theory. Provide interpretations for *all* terms in this calculus. The result will be a model. On this view, we obtain a model if and only

[23] See footnote 4.
[24] See Chap. Seven, sec. 4.

if we interpret a calculus. (This construal might be suggested on the basis of Nagel's definition of a model [25] and of a theory.[26] It certainly appears to be the position of Braithwaite.[27])

b) Consider anything that would be generally *recognized* as a scientific theory.[28] Such a theory as "customarily expounded" is "embedded in a model" (Nagel). That is, what is usually presented is a set of (interpreted) statements—the model. The theory itself is to be construed as the calculus for this set of statements (in which certain terms may be interpreted as designating "observables"). From this point of view, we obtain a model if and only if we interpret the calculus of something generally recognized as a scientific theory, where the interpretation will be one in terms of which that theory is usually presented. (This construal might be suggested on the basis of Nagel's discussion of the Bohr model.)

c) Consider anything that would generally be recognized as a scientific theory. We obtain a model if and only if we interpret the calculus of this theory, where such an interpretation may employ any meaningful notions whatever and may indeed generate a description of a "second system" [29] completely dissimilar physically to the system described in the theory. [This construal, which includes (*b*) but not (*a*) as a special case, might be suggested on the basis of Nagel's later discussion on pp. 108ff.]

Each of these claims implies that a model has the same formal structure as that of some theory. Yet none is acceptable if applied to theoretical or imaginary models. For one thing none provides a *sufficient* condition. Consider any arbitrary (partially interpreted) calculus. Whether by completely interpreting this calculus a theoretical or imaginary model is obtained [as claimed in (*a*)] depends upon whether or not the resulting propositions fulfill criteria for theoretical and imaginary models expounded earlier; this will not in general be assured, even if [as in (*b*) and (*c*)] the calculus in question is that of something that would generally be recognized as a scientific theory and if, in addition [follow-

[25] *Structure of Science*, p. 96.
[26] *Ibid.*, pp. 90ff.
[27] "Models in the Empirical Sciences," p. 231.
[28] That is, any *T* that is (was, might plausibly have been) had as a theory in science. (See Chap. Four, sec. 1.) Although this might constitute a fairly large class, depending upon how broadly we are willing to construe the context, it would not include every possible statement or set of statements.
[29] Nagel, *The Structure of Science*, p. 110.

ing (*b*)], the interpretation is one in terms of which that theory is usually presented. Furthermore, although (*a*) does provide a *necessary* condition for theoretical and imaginary models, it is a trivial one. Any theoretical or imaginary model (for that matter, any set of statements) is an interpretation of its own calculus. And if a theory can be constructed simply by re-interpreting some of the terms in this calculus, then any theoretical or imaginary model (any set of statements) has the same formal structure as a theory so constructed.

Claims (*b*) and (*c*), on the other hand, are by no means trivial, since they require the theory in question to be one that would generally be recognized as such and not one concocted simply by arbitrary re-interpretation of a calculus. Yet neither provides a necessary condition. There are theoretical as well as imaginary models that are not interpretations for the calculus of any theory of the sort required (for example, theoretical models of the atomic nucleus, Maxwell's imaginary model of the electromagnetic field). One might wish to claim that the partially interpreted calculi of such models themselves are theories; but if so, there would be a violation of the requirement that the theory in question be one that would generally be recognized as such; even more important, if this sort of partially interpreted calculus were to count as a theory, conditions (*b*) and (*c*) would be trivially satisfied by any set of propositions.

What, then, about analogies and representational models? There is a way to construe claim (4) so that it might be said to apply to such conceptions. (In what follows, to avoid triviality, I use the word "theory" to refer to what would generally be recognized as such in science and not to cover just any arbitrary statement or set of statements.[30])

A) We draw an analogy between *X* and *Y* in science if and only if we note that the principles governing *X* can be obtained by re-interpreting the calculus of some theory governing *Y* (and hence if and only if we note that the principles governing *X* have the same formal structure as this theory).[31]

B) We construct a representational model of *X* in science if and only if we construct something *Y* so that the principles governing *X* can be obtained by re-interpreting the calculus of some theory

---

[30] See footnote 28.

[31] Braithwaite, for example, writes that the "model is another interpretation of the theory's calculus," and that "there is a one-one correlation between the concepts of [the theory] *T* and those of [the model] *M*" ("Models in the Empirical Sciences," p. 225).

governing Y (and hence if and only if we note that the principles governing X have the same formal structure as some theory governing Y).

My claim is that (A) fails to provide a necessary or a sufficient condition for analogies in science and that (B) fails to provide a necessary or a sufficient condition for representational models. Neither supplies a necessary condition, for each is much too stringent. First, each requires *complete* formal similarity, whereas in analogies and representational models the similarity will be only *partial*. Although some of the laws involved may be formally similar, others will not be, or indeed may have no formal counterparts whether similar or dissimilar. When an analogy is drawn between an atom (as described by some set of principles, say those of the Bohr theory) and a planetary system, only certain properties of atoms (so described) and solar systems are relevant in the description of the analogy, for example, orbits with relatively large masses at center. Other properties attributed to atoms by the principles in question, for example, quantum jumps with electromagnetic radiation resulting, are in no way considered part of this analogy. When the comparison is made, such properties of atoms are ignored. Contrary to (A), in drawing the analogy the physicist is not concerned with all properties attributed to atoms by the principles in question; nor does he necessarily attempt to find a correlate for each such property in the realm of planetary systems. Conversely, various properties attributed by a theory to solar systems have no counterparts in atomic systems. Similar arguments apply to representational models.

Second, an analogy may be drawn between X and Y, or Y may be constructed as a representational model of X, even though no *theory* governing Y has been developed or even though whatever theory does govern Y is irrelevant for the analogy or representational model. Huygens had no theory about water waves when he drew an analogy between light waves and water waves. When Maxwell drew an analogy between the electric field and the tubes of incompressible fluid, his description of the latter was not a theory about incompressible fluid. Many of his assumptions were arbitrary stipulations needed to make his conception analogous to the electric field. A representational model of the solar system may be constructed of cardboard and wires, even though no theory governing cardboard and wires is relevant for the model.

Third, where an analogy is drawn between X and Y, or Y is a representational model of X, although in some cases principles may be involved that are, formally speaking, identical, in other cases this is not so. Analogies are drawn in science when principles, if any, are non-mathematical or not subject to the sort of formal axiomatization required; for example, analogies in biology between parts of birds and parts of fish. Also, analogies are drawn between X and Y despite the fact that relevant laws governing X and Y, although mathematically expressible, are not of the same form. There is an analogy between a Bohr hydrogen atom and a planetary system containing one planet even though (in an idealized case assuming circular orbits) relevant equations (energy and momentum equations that determine the orbital character) have different forms in each. The energy equation for the Bohr atom is $E_n = -\dfrac{2\pi^2 m e^4}{n^2 h^2}$, that for the planetary system is $E = -\tfrac{1}{2} G \dfrac{mM}{r}$.

Do (A) and (B) provide *sufficient* conditions for analogies and representational models in science? That is, to draw an analogy between X and Y is it sufficient to note that the principles governing X and Y are formally identical? And to construct a representational model of X is it sufficient to construct a Y such that the principles governing X have the same calculus as that of a theory governing Y? In the case of the first three types of representational model of X noted earlier, the true model, the adequate model, and the distorted model, it is not sufficient to construct something governed by principles bearing only a formal similarity to those governing X.[32] Such principles must indicate *physical* similarities between X and Y; and this will be possible only if at least some physical items (objects, properties, quantities, relationships) designated by terms in these principles are identical or similar, something not guaranteed by identity of calculi. What, then, about the fourth type of representational model, the analogue model, and what about analogies?

To begin with, to draw an analogy between X and Y it is not sufficient simply to note similarities, formal or otherwise. X and Y must be unlike in other respects; and typically, especially in science, it will be intended that X be thought of and described using Y as a basis and that this illuminate X in some way.[33] Moreover, if I describe (or build) an

---

[32] See Chap. Seven, sec. 2.
[33] See Chap. Seven, sec. 1.

object Y governed by principles similar in certain respects to those governing another object X, I have not necessarily described (or built) an analogue model of X (for example, I, as well as others, may not treat Y as something to be studied before or in place of studying X directly).[34]

What *can* be said is this. If other conditions I have specified for analogies and analogue models are satisfied, then the similarities between X and Y may be entirely formal ones. That is, there may be formally similar principles governing X and Y even though items designated by terms in these principles are, physically speaking, completely dissimilar or even though whatever physical similarities exist are irrelevant for the analogy. Although most analogies and analogue models employed in the sciences involve more than formal similarities, some involve only these. Perhaps the most important are those introduced when a certain mathematical problem arises in the course of developing a scientific theory: if this problem has already been solved in another area, its solution may be appropriated for purposes of the theory in question. Corresponding entities that generate the same mathematical problem may of course have certain identical or similar physical properties. However, it is possible that the entities, or the properties compared, are physically speaking so dissimilar, at least with respect to the relevant analogies, that the areas can be classified only as mathematically (or formally) analogous.

For example, in the development of statistical mechanics, the physicist is confronted with the following problem of combinatorial analysis: In how many different ways can n phase points—representing, for example, position and momentum coordinates of a set of gas molecules—be distributed into k cells in phase space so that the first cell contains n_1 points, the second n_2, and so on? This is a mathematical problem analogous to asking for the number of different ways in which n balls (or birthdays of n people) can be distributed into k urns (or days) in such a way that the first contains n_1 balls (or birthdays), the second n_2, and so on. The distribution of phase points in phase space and balls in urns (or birthdays throughout the year) involves equations of the same mathematical form, although the respective situations are physically speaking entirely different. Yet, rather than appeal only to abstract formulas of combinatorial analysis, the physicist may refer to

[34] See Chap. Seven, sec. 2.

mathematical analogies of this type in which the balls are said to be analogous to the phase points and the urns to the phase cells.

A different example comes from nuclear physics, where an important mathematical analogy was developed between isotopic (or isobaric) spin and ordinary spin angular momentum. It was observed that certain sets of fundamental particles (for example, protons and neutrons; positive, negative, and neutral pi-mesons) are similar in all respects except charge. Accordingly, the idea was suggested by Heisenberg that the particles in each set represent different quantum states of a single particle. A useful account is provided by physicist D. H. Wilkinson:

> The problem now arises of devising a formalism that will imply this charge-labelling and which will also tell us how many members there are in each set of particles. . . . This problem reminds us very strongly of the situation which obtains for ordinary angular momentum. This is represented by a (pseudo or axial) vector J of a certain length which can take up a limited number of orientations in a space corresponding to the quantizations of its projections along any specified axis. . . . This leads to the concept that we might represent these sets of particles formally by a new vector of length T, which can also take up a number . . . of orientations in its own space, each orientation corresponding to a different state of the particle. . . . This new vector in analogy to the angular momentum or spin vector which characterizes ordinary rotation is called the isotopic spin, and the projection of the isotopic spin along a specified axis in the new isotopic space is a measure of the charge state of the particle.[35]

Yet, Wilkinson stresses, the analogy between isotopic spin and ordinary spin is to be construed as a formal one:

> It is to be emphasized that this new parameter with which we characterize particles is only called 'spin' in analogy to ordinary angular momentum to which it bears this close formal resemblance. In using this term we have no picture of anything rotating in the conventional sense.[36]

In these cases the conditions are satisfied that generally obtain when an analogy in science is invoked. Certain similarities between other-

[35] "Towards New Concepts: Elementary Particles," *Turning Points in Physics* (Amsterdam, 1959), pp. 172–73.

[36] *Ibid.*

wise unlike things X and Y are noted (albeit only formal similarities between equations governing X and Y), attention to which enables one to think of and describe X using Y as a basis and thus to provide illumination for X. I claimed, however, that most analogies and analogue models utilized in science are based upon similarities that are not purely formal. This claim appears to be denied by proponents of the theory I am discussing. These authors hold that many if not most of the analogies and analogue models used in the sciences involve only formal similarities, or else that even if there are physical similarities between analogues, the analogy is based entirely upon formal similarities among the laws involved. I turn now to this position.

4. ANALOGIES AND FORMAL STRUCTURE

Hempel discusses the analogy between the flow of an electric current in a wire and the flow of a fluid in a pipe. He writes:

> . . . the relevant similarity or "analogy" between a model of the kind here considered and the modelled type of phenomenon consists in a *nomic isomorphism, i.e., a syntactic isomorphism between two corresponding sets of laws.*[37]

Others, such as Nagel, cite Kelvin's analogy between heat conduction and electrostatics as an example of an analogy based entirely on formal similarities.[38] The view that many analogies and analogue models are so based is suggested by scientists themselves. Maxwell emphasizes similarity *in form* between laws governing different phenomena and also suggests that Kelvin's analogy is of this sort.[39] In a book entitled *Dynamical Analogies,* dealing with analogies between electrical, mechanical, and acoustical systems, the author writes:

> The analogies as outlined in this book are formal ones due to the similarity of the differential equations and do not imply that there is any physical similarity between quantities occupying the same position in their respective equations.[40]

I have already agreed that purely formal analogies and analogue

---

[37] *Aspects of Scientific Explanation,* p. 436.
[38] See Chap. Seven, sec. 1, example (7).
[39] *Scientific Papers,* ed. W. D. Niven (New York, 1965), I, 156–57.
[40] Harry F. Olson, *Dynamical Analogies* (New York, 1947), p. 3, footnote 3.

models are employed in the sciences. What I now want to dispute is the frequency of this, more particularly the claim that analogies such as those between the flow of current in a wire and the flow of fluid in a pipe, heat conduction and electrostatic attraction, and dynamical analogies (and analogue models) involving electrical, mechanical, and acoustical systems are based entirely on formal similarities.

Consider first the analogy cited by Hempel between the flow of electric current in a wire and the flow of fluid in a pipe. (The fluid flowing in the pipe could also be considered an analogue model of the electricity flowing through the wire.) Hempel notes that the equation governing the flow of a fluid through a narrow pipe with circular inner cross section is:

$$V = \frac{c}{L}(p_1 - p_2) \qquad \text{[Poiseulle's Law]},$$

where V is the volume of fluid flowing through a fixed cross-section per unit time, c a constant, L the length of the pipe, and $p_1 - p_2$ the difference in pressure between the ends of the pipe. The law governing the flow of electricity is:

$$I = \frac{k}{L}(v_1 - v_2) \qquad \text{[Ohm's Law]},$$

where I is the quantity of charge passing through a fixed cross-section of the wire per unit time, L the length of the wire, k a constant, and $v_1 - v_2$ the potential difference between the ends of the wire.

Contrary to what Hempel suggests in the quotation above, the analogy does not depend solely on the similarity in form of these equations. In both we are dealing with a long narrow object of length L; in both we are concerned with the quantity of something that passes through a spatial cross-section of this narrow object in unit time; and in both we are concerned with the difference in the value of certain quantities between the ends of this narrow object. To draw the analogy one considers not only the formal structure of the equations but also similarities in the designata of the symbols they contain.

Indeed, if, following Hempel, all that is required to draw an analogy between two phenomena is to note a formal similarity in laws governing them, then analogy-drawing would be the simplest exercise in the world and could be done by someone entirely ignorant of physics. Such a person, thumbing through a physics text, could draw an "analogy" between the flow of fluid through a pipe and the expansion of air by heating in a constant pressure (reversible) process, since the latter is governed by the formula:

$$W = \frac{P}{m}(V_2 - V_1),$$

where W is the work done, P the pressure of the gas, m its mass, and $V_2 - V_1$ its change in volume. Or, he could draw an "analogy" between the flow of fluid through a pipe and radiation from a Bohr atom, since the latter is governed by the formula:

$$v = \frac{const}{h}(E_2 - E_1),$$

where v is the frequency of the radiation, h is Planck's constant, and $E_2 - E_1$ is the difference in energy. These purely formal resemblances, however, do not provide the basis for analogies between the phenomena in question. There is no temptation, nor would it be particularly enlightening, to think of fluid flow using, as a basis, the expansion of air in a constant pressure process or the radiation from a Bohr atom.

Another example sometimes held to involve only formal similarities is Kelvin's analogy between heat conduction and electrostatic attraction. Here the following sets of equations can be compared:

heat case	*electrical case*
$v = \dfrac{A}{r}$	$V = \dfrac{A}{r}$
$\dfrac{dv}{dr} = -\dfrac{A}{r^2}$	$\dfrac{dV}{dr} = F = -\dfrac{A}{r^2}$
$v = \displaystyle\iint \dfrac{\rho d\omega^2}{r}$	$V = \displaystyle\iint \dfrac{\rho d\omega^2}{r}$

The analogy, however, is not meant to be a purely formal one, as can be seen from the interpretations given to these formulas. In both sets of formulas a point is imagined that is a distance r units from the surface of a source (in the one case a source of heat, in the other a source of electricity); and in both, $d\omega^2$ represents an area element on the surface of this source. According to the first equation in each set, both the temperature v at a point a distance r from the heat source and the electrical potential V at a point a distance r from an electrical source

246

vary inversely as the first power of the distance from the source. According to the second set of equations, both the temperature gradient $\frac{dv}{dr}$ at a point a distance r units from a heat source, and the electrostatic force at a point a distance r units from an electrical source, vary inversely as the square of the distance from respective sources. According to the third set of equations, the temperature at a point r units distant from the surface of a source is equal to the sum (as a double integral) of the quantity $\frac{\rho d\omega^2}{r}$ for each area element $d\omega^2$ of the source, where ρ is the intensity of the source; in the electrical counterpart, ρ is the intensity of electricity at the area-element $d\omega^2$ of the source.

In short, the similarities providing the basis for this analogy are not purely formal ones but include similarities among designata of certain terms in respective sets of equations. Temperature v in the heat case is analogous to potential V in the electrical case not simply because there exist the formally similar equations $v = \frac{A}{r}$ (for heat) and $V = \frac{A}{r}$ (for electricity), but because r in both cases means the distance between a point in space and a surface of a source, where what happens at the surface will affect what happens at the point.

Nor, finally, are analogies between electrical, mechanical, and acoustical systems entirely formal either, although here the physical similarities become more abstract; one needs to retreat much further than in the previous cases to find a neutral language for describing both X and Y. Still, in electrical, mechanical, and acoustical cases there are equations concerned with changes in energy over time. In all three instances energy can be changed into heat; in the electrical and acoustical cases energy is changed into heat by the passage of some physical substance through another (in the former, by the passage of an electric current through a wire offering resistance; in the latter, by the passage of a fluid through a substance offering resistance); in the mechanical case energy is changed into heat by the passage of one substance not necessarily *through* another but in contact with it, so that there is resistance in the form of friction.[41] These physical similarities are relevant for the analogies and cannot be discerned simply by contemplating uninterpreted formulas.

Analogies and analogue models form a range of cases. In some, the

[41] See Olson, *Dynamical Analogies.*

similarities that provide the basis for the analogy or analogue model are physical similarities between a relatively large number of properties, and X and Y may be thought of as differing principally in size (for example, molecules and billiard balls). In others, the X and Y, though entirely different in almost all respects, have at least some important relational properties that are physically similar. (In Maxwell's fluid analogy for the electric field, the relationship between an electrostatic source and the force on unit charges at varying points is similar to that between a fluid source and the fluid velocity at varying points, since both relationships involve the inverse squares of the respective spatial distances.[42]) In some cases, but not those generally cited by the authors in question, and certainly not in most cases, the similarity may be a purely formal one.

5. THE IDENTIFICATION OF MODELS AND ANALOGIES

5) *A model is an analogy.* This claim would be trivial if for "model" we are supposed to substitute "analogy," that is, if the only conceptions to be classified as models are what I have called analogies. However, it is intended to hold as well for theoretical models, imaginary models, and representational models, since examples of these are cited. In these three cases such a claim, as it stands, is clearly false, so let us try to construe it more liberally. What might be involved in identifying theoretical models as analogies?

Is it perhaps being suggested that a set of assumptions constitutes a theoretical model of X if and only if it is a description of an analogue for X? This would conform with the view, suggested at one point by Nagel, that a model describes a "second system" distinct from that described in the corresponding theory. Yet if we consider the examples of theoretical models cited by Nagel and others, the above is neither a necessary nor a sufficient condition. Such models of X are not descriptions of analogues for X. The Bohr model of the atom describes atoms, not solar systems. Nor is a description of an analogue of X a theoretical model of X. The laws of heat conduction describe phenomena analogous in certain respects to those in electrostatics. Yet these laws do not constitute a theoretical model of electrostatic phenomena.

Perhaps the identification of theoretical models and analogies is

[42] See Chap. Seven, sec. 1.

meant to suggest something weaker, namely, that the formulation of a theoretical model requires, among other things, that an analogy be invoked. Even this is dubious. No doubt an analogy will frequently be utilized and perhaps incorporated into the very formulation of a theoretical model, either explicitly or implicitly ("electrons are like planets in that they revolve in elliptical orbits about an attracting object," "the planetary electron revolves about the solar nucleus"). Such use of analogy cannot fail to be noted and often proves helpful in comprehending the basic assumptions of the model. However, it is not something peculiar to theoretical models but holds for scientific hypotheses generally. Moreover, the assumptions constituting a theoretical model are frequently formulated without the aid of analogy, depending upon the level of the presentation.[43] If, then, the proposed identification is meant to suggest only that analogies *can* be important in formulating (and explaining) theoretical models, the point is well-founded (indeed, it was recognized in our earlier characterization of such models). Stronger connections of the sorts mentioned above, however, are neither necessary nor sufficient.

What has just been said of theoretical models can be repeated for imaginary models. Turning finally to representational models, the only type for which the identification of models and analogies has any plausibility is the analogue model. The latter, although not itself an analogy, is based upon one. However, it is not the case that whenever an analogy is drawn between X and Y, Y is treated as an analogue model, since in not every case is Y treated as something to be studied, considered in depth, before or in place of studying X. So even here the identification of models and analogies is unwarranted, and a much weaker claim required.

6. ON THE MERITS OF "SEMANTICAL" MODELS

I have considered the extent to which the semantical theory of models applies to conceptions discussed in Chapter Seven, and we have seen that the theory does not fare well with respect to these conceptions. Some of its champions may reply, however, that they mean to *explicate* the concept of a model, that is, to replace the present concept

[43] See, for example, Robley D. Evans, *The Atomic Nucleus* (New York, 1955), for a presentation of nuclear models that is fairly free of the use of analogies.

or concepts by a different one regarded as more satisfactory.[44] On this interpretation of the semantical theory, the fact that the models I distinguished are not semantical ones would not be too disturbing. Indeed, even if semantical models are not actually utilized in science, the semantical theory would not be refuted. How, then, should the merits of this new concept of a model be judged?

One way is to determine whether or not it is a fruitful concept, whether or not semantical models could serve important roles in science. According to proponents of this theory, models aid in formulating, developing, and understanding theories. So, in assessing the semantical concept of a model one must determine whether such models could function in the way their proponents maintain.

Let us begin with the following claim:

  i) If a set of propositions P about a group of familiar and intelligible objects has the same calculus as a certain physical theory T, that is, if P is a semantical model for T, then P provides an important aid for understanding some of the concepts in T.

To examine this claim, consider the following miniature axiomatic system, or calculus, which provides a formalization for a part of geometry dealing with line segments:

1) $(x)(x \epsilon K \supset Rxx)$
2) $(x)(y)(x \epsilon K . y \epsilon K . \supset . Rxy \supset Ryx)$
3) $(x)(y)(z)(x \epsilon K . y \epsilon K . z \epsilon K . \supset : Rxy . Ryz . \supset Rxz)$
4) $(\exists x)(\exists y)(x \neq y . x \epsilon K . y \epsilon K . \sim Rxy)$

By appropriate substitutions for K and R in the above calculus, the following sets of propositions with the same logical structure can be obtained:

  a) Every light ray is self-congruent
  b) If x and y are light rays, then if x is congruent with y, then y is congruent with x
  c) If x, y, and z are light rays, then if x is congruent with y and y is congruent with z, then x is congruent with z
  d) At least two light rays are not congruent

  e) Every swan has the same color as itself
  f) If x and y are swans, then if x has the same color as y, then y has the same color as x

[44] See Chap. Three, sec. 4.

g) If *x, y,* and *z* are swans, then if *x* has the same color as *y* and *y* has the same color as *z*, then *x* has the same color as *z*

h) At least two swans have different colors

According to the semantical theory, if propositions (*a*) through (*d*) are considered (part of) the axioms for a physical theory of spatial congruence, then propositions (*e*) through (*h*) constitute a model for (part of) this theory.[45] These propositions inform us that both spatial congruence for light rays and color equality for swans are reflexive, symmetrical, transitive, and "nonuniversal" relations. Furthermore, (*e*) through (*h*) are true and describe objects both familiar and intelligible —thus fulfilling additional requirements for models specified by some of those proposing the semantical definition.

Yet an example of this sort could not be classified as a case of "finding resemblances between new experiences and familiar facts, so that what is novel is in consequence mastered by subsuming it under established distinctions," or as one that "helps us to imagine what happens in the world by suggesting an analogy with familiar experience"— features alleged by Nagel and Hutten, respectively, to be characteristic of models. The comparison between the (partially) axiomatized theory dealing with congruence of light rays and the propositions concerning identity of color in swans affords no clarification of what sort of thing a light ray is or of the physical conditions under which two of them are congruent, even though we may possess a wealth of corresponding information about swans and their color.

However, such an example might help to provide a certain type of understanding whose nature, together with the misleading character of claim (*i*), can be appreciated by recalling a distinction introduced by the authors in question. This is the distinction between the calculus of a theory and the semantical rules that provide physical interpretations for expressions in that calculus. From the viewpoint of these authors, for the concepts in the theory to be found intelligible an understanding is required of the semantical rules as well as of the calculus. A set of

---

[45] Comparable examples of calculi with completely different interpretations can be found in Nagel, *Structure of Science,* in which a certain calculus is interpreted, on the one hand, in the realm of molecules in cells and, on the other, in the realm of probability sets; and in Ernest V. Adams, "The Foundations of Rigid Body Mechanics and the Derivation of Its Laws from Those of Particle Mechanics," *The Axiomatic Method,* ed. L. Henkin, P. Suppes, and A. Tarski (Amsterdam, 1959), in which a model for particle mechanics is provided in the domain of numbers.

propositions bearing only a structural similarity to the theory can provide illumination insofar as it aids one in understanding the calculus of that theory and hence the formal features of some of the concepts involved, these formal features being present in concepts initially more familiar and intelligible. Thus, formal notions such as reflexivity, symmetry, and transitivity might be found more intelligible if considered first in the case of color equality and then for spatial congruence.[46] (It is certainly possible that formal principles such as those involved in combinatorial analysis will be more quickly understood if applied first to balls in urns and then to molecules in gases.)

What an example of the sort above does not do is help to make intelligible the semantical rules that are supposed to relate terms such as "light ray" and "congruence" to actual physical phenomena, even though corresponding semantical rules for "swan" and "color equality" may be known and understood. The misleading aspect of claim (*i*) lies in its suggestion that the existence of a structural similarity between a given set of propositions describing familiar objects and propositions comprising a theory can help render intelligible both formal and nonformal aspects of the concepts in the theory.

On the other hand, analogies in which properties of the analogue are *physically* similar to those of objects postulated by certain principles can be of help in clarifying the nonformal aspects of concepts in these principles by suggesting physical conditions similar to those under which such concepts are applicable. The planetary analogy for the Bohr atom is useful because it suggests, and helps make intelligible, physical conditions involving attractive forces and (nearly) circular motion— conditions understood as underlying both planetary and atomic systems. The comparison in such a case depends not just on the similarity in mathematical structure of formulas in each area but very significantly on the similarity in physical interpretations given to various symbols in these formulas. Moreover, when an analogy involving physical similarities is invoked, no semantical model need be involved. As noted previously, there need not be complete or even any formal identity of principles, nor need there be a theory governing the analogue in question.

---

[46] So one might speak here of a (formal) analogy between spatial congruence and color equality but not of an analogy between light rays and swans, for the similarities in question are too removed to be regarded as important in understanding very much about light rays (or swans). See Chap. Seven, sec. 1.

The second claim I want to consider is this:

ii) Models, defined in the semantical sense, provide important guides in the formulation and extension of theories.

All proponents of the semantical definition make this claim, yet only Braithwaite attempts to provide some general indication of how models so understood could serve these roles, although he is mainly concerned with their role in extending theories. Following Braithwaite's account, suppose we begin with a theory T and construct a semantical model for it, that is, "another theory M which corresponds to the theory T in respect of deductive structure." Then, in showing how models in this sense can be used to extend theories, Braithwaite writes:

> Considering the familiar properties L_1, L_2, . . ., L_m occurring in the initial propositions of the model may suggest propositions about some of these familiar properties which would, if added to the initial propositions in the model, enable new generalizations about, e.g., B_1, B_2, B_3, to be deduced in the model. Passing then from the model to the theory will suggest that if corresponding new initial hypotheses are added to the theory, the extended theory will yield new testable generalizations about A_1, A_2, . . ., A_n [properties in the theory whose formal correlates in the model are B_1, B_2, . . ., B_n].[47]

This suggests the following general account of the manner in which semantical models can furnish guides for the formulation and development of theories. Suppose the scientist has observed certain regularities for which he desires an explanation. These regularities can be expressed by a set of laws L having a logical structure or calculus S. Suppose, further, that there is an established theory dealing with certain familiar objects, where the theorems of this theory, or a subset of them, also have the calculus S. Then in order to explain laws L, the scientist can construct a theory whose postulates have the same calculus as that of the established theory (where the latter will be a semantical model for the new theory). In this manner the scientist can use identity in logical structure as a guide in formulating a theory for the laws in question.

Similar reasoning might be offered for extending theories. Suppose the scientist has formulated a theory T and a semantical model for it in which familiar objects of type O are described by a set of laws having the same formal structure as those of the theory. Usually more information will be available about O's than is cited in the model; this

[47] "Models in the Empirical Sciences," p. 228.

additional information is expressed by means of a set of statements M. The scientist may therefore add postulates to the theory which are formal analogues of ones in M.

Either it is being claimed here that the methods described will yield theories with some initial plausibility, or else no claim is being made about the plausibility of resulting theories. A claim of initial plausibility for a theory *formulated* in the manner proposed would rest on the following assumption: if the statements in a set S_1 (for example, the established laws or theory) have the same calculus as those in a set S_2 (the constructed theory), and if the statements in S_1 are known to be true, this constitutes a reason for believing that the statements in S_2 are true, or at least for attributing some plausibility to such statements. Similarly, a claim of plausibility for a theory *extended* in the manner proposed would rest on the following assumption: if the statements in a set S_1 have the same calculus as a subset of the statements in S_2, and if S_1 and S_2 are well-confirmed, then by adding to S_1 a statement whose analogue is in S_2 we introduce a new postulate that has some measure of plausibility.

Such claims would be totally unfounded. Given an identity in logical form of two sets of statements, nothing can be inferred about the plausibility of statements in one set from a knowledge of the truth of statements in the other; for the plausibility of statements must be determined by an appeal to content and not logical form alone. A calculus may have innumerably many interpretations. The fact that one of these contains true statements is obviously no reason for thinking that the statements yielded by another interpretation are true or plausible.

Suppose, then, no claim is made about the plausibility of theories formulated and extended in the manner proposed. If not, the purely formal methods described above are no better than any entirely arbitrary device for generating theories. Indeed, if *no* requirements are made concerning plausibility many simpler methods for theory improvisation will come to mind. For example, to construct a "theory" for laws L, formulate any set of postulates T whatever and add $T \supset L$ as an additional postulate. This is readily done without producing any semantical model, and what results will satisfy the deductive criterion of explanation expounded by the authors in question. Indeed, T could readily be constructed to satisfy further requirements as well, such as empirical significance, generality, and simplicity. In this manner theories are trivially formulated and extended without any need to discover formal similarities.[48]

I have noted the unwillingness to make a plausibility claim as one alternative. Yet this is unrealistic when actual scientific contexts are considered; for normally when theoretical postulates are proposed on the basis of an analogy between these and some other principles, the former thereby gain some measure of plausibility. This does not mean that the statements describing the analogue establish the theoretical postulates; but they do at least render them initially more probable than certain others that might be constructed. This fact will not be reflected in those theories developed in the manner described above.

For these reasons claim (*ii*) is unacceptable. This does not mean, however, that attention to formal structure is irrelevant for the development of theories. Here two types of cases might be mentioned.

In the first, the scientist who is developing a theory and is confronted with a mathematical problem that has been solved in a different area appropriates this solution for use in his theory. An example noted earlier involves a problem of combinatorial analysis which appears in statistical mechanics and whose solution can be arrived at by considering, as an analogy, the distribution of balls in urns. But this sort of example is markedly different from the type of case above in which, it is contended, formal considerations can be used to generate *additional empirical assumptions*. In the combinatorial problem no such additional assumptions are being added to the theory. Instead the analogy is used to work out mathematical consequences of empirical assumptions already made.

In the second type of case the scientist does employ a mathematical analogy when generating new postulates for his theory; but in doing so he makes additional empirical assumptions that seem plausible to him on the basis of information available. In the development of statistical mechanics empirical assumptions involving probability considerations were made about gas molecules; these assumptions seemed reasonable on the basis of information about gases already known.[49] The fact that analogous probability considerations may be illustrated in the urn problem by itself lends no plausibility to the corresponding claims about molecules.

Accordingly, neither type of case supports the thesis that formal

[48] Cf. Chap. Three, sec. 2.
[49] See R. H. Fowler, *Statistical Mechanics* (Cambridge, England, 1929).

considerations are sufficient for generating new empirical postulates. The fact that a theory T and a set of true propositions M both contain equations E, and in addition M contains equations E', logically independent of E, does not by itself provide any reason for incorporating E' into T. On the other hand, those analogies in which objects are described as having properties physically similar to properties of entities in the theory can provide a plausible foundation for additional theoretical postulates; if two types of objects are described as physically similar in certain respects, this can furnish a basis for supposing that further similarities may be discovered, depending on the properties and the extent of the similarity. Yet again, and for reasons noted earlier, no semantical model need be involved in such a case.

7. CAN THERE BE A THEORY ABOUT MODELS AND ANALOGIES?

The semantical theory attempts to supply a condition both necessary and sufficient for a model or an analogy. What I have argued is that this theory fails to characterize the cases to which its proponents want to apply it. Moreover, if we were to utilize conceptions that actually satisfied the conditions of this theory, that is, semantical models, these would in general not serve the roles imputed to them by proponents of the theory.

In the light of this discussion one might ask whether there can be a theory governing analogies and models. If the question is whether there are necessary and sufficient conditions that hold for all the conceptions I have described, the answer I would give is No, for these conceptions are all different in important respects. Any set of conditions proposed will either be too broad or too narrow to pick out just the set wanted. The claim that a model or analogy is another interpretation of a theory's calculus is too narrow to be of use. Indeed, it fails to provide an adequate characterization of any of the conceptions discussed. But it is not only philosophers who have attempted to provide such general definitions. Scientists have also. Maxwell defined an analogy as "that partial similarity between the laws of one science and those of another which makes each of them illustrate the other"; [50] he seems to have meant this definition to apply not only to analogies but

[50] *Scientific Papers,* I, 156.

to imaginary models and possibly theoretical models as well. More recently the biologist Kacser, in a symposium on models and analogies in biology, defines a model as a "statement or series of statements in language." [51] Neither Maxwell's definition of an analogy nor Kacser's definition of a model suffices to pick out the appropriate class of items, Maxwell's being too narrow (even for analogies), Kacser's too broad.

If no set of necessary and sufficient conditions can be given for models and analogies, does it follow that we can say nothing about what tempts philosophers as well as scientists to classify these together? Not at all. I think there is something common to all of these, although it must be described in a fairly abstract, general, and even loose way. It will not pick out the class of items in question; it is not a condition that is both necessary and sufficient, although it may be taken to be necessary without being sufficient. In all of the cases considered we might describe the model or analogy as (or as containing) (1) a representation of X; but (2) one that is either not literal, or not faithful in all respects, or not complete, and may represent X in some "indirect" manner; and (3) one that utilizes something more or less familiar, known, understood, readily grasped, or easily experimented upon. Thus, a representational model represents X, but not completely and not necessarily literally, by utilizing something Y that is familiar or more readily grasped. In a theoretical model we represent X, but only approximately and not completely, by bringing it under, or at least utilizing parts of, some more basic theory or theories that are familiar and understood. In an imaginary model we represent X, but not in a way intended to be literal, by imagining how X could satisfy certain conditions, where either the set of conditions or the way we represent X is more or less familiar and understood. In an analogy X is represented in an indirect way by being shown to be similar in some though not all respects to a distinct item more familiar or more readily grasped.

This "common element" is not a sufficient condition, since it holds as well for items not classifiable as models or analogies (for example, diagrams, over-simplified accounts). Moreover, it employs the notion of representation to cover quite different sorts of things, for example, statements as well as objects. Furthermore, it requires the use of alternation in clauses (2) and (3) to capture all cases. Of course in each

---

[51] H. Kacser, "Kinetic Models of Development and Heredity," *Models and Analogies in Biology: Symposia of the Society for Experimental Biology* (New York, 1960), p. 14.

case our aim will be more than simply providing the sort of representation described, and the means we employ will be different.

I do not propose this as a *theory* of models and analogies. It is too meager and abstract to help us understand very much about these conceptions. A proper understanding can be had only by considering the particular characteristics of each type of conception. This is what I attempted to do in Chapter Seven. If, then, in seeking a theory of models and analogies one means to be looking for some specific set of characteristics shared by all and only models and analogies reference to which will provide considerable illumination for these devices, then, I think, one is looking in vain. If, on the other hand, one means to be looking for specific characteristics of each type of conception reference to which will provide illumination, then a theory, or theories, can be found.

INDEX

Hertz, Heinrich, 152
Hesse, Mary, 230
Hutten, Ernest H., 229, 230, 251
Huygens, Christiaan, 139, 204
Hypothetical cases, 4, 5, 10–11, 13–15, 17–19
Hypothetico-deductive system: as definition of "theory," 129–32; Positivist account, 69–71; and presentation of scientific theories, 148–53

I

Ideal gas, 19
Imaginary models, 218–21: characteristics of, 218–21; comparisons with theoretical and analogue models, 221–22; Maxwell's, 219–20; Poincaré's, 218–19, 235, 236; and the semantical theory, 230, 231, 235, 238, 239; use in proving consistency, 237
Indirect interpretation, 85–91
Inner structure: and semantical relevance, 24; and theoretical models, 213–14
Interpretation of terms, 67–119: actual, in science, 106–19 *passim;* for theoretical terms, 112–19; by use of analogy, 117–18
—Positivist account: indirect interpretation, 85–91; interpretation for observational terms, 68–69; interpretation for theoretical terms, 69, 85–91, 112–19; interpretation provided by semantical models, 231–37; partial interpretation, 85–91, 106–7
Introduction of terms: actual, in science, 106–19 *passim;* Positivist account, 67–72, 109
Isotopic spin, 243

J

Jammer, Max, 57n

K

Kacser, H., 257
Kelvin, Lord: analogy between heat conduction and electrostatics, 205, 236, 237, 246–247; model of ether, 224
Kepler, Johannes, 123, 133

Kimball, Arthur L., 58
Kinetic energy, 54, 55–56, 62–63, 192
Kinetic theory of gases, 70: Maxwell on, 143–44; partial calculus for, 227–28; Positivistic reconstruction of, 70–71
Kuhn, Thomas S., 92n, 132n

L

Light: corpuscular model of, 212
Lindsay, Robert B., 58n
Linguistic descriptions, 19: D_1, 19; D_2, 25; indefiniteness in, 24–25; models of, 27–31; and use of terms, 36–39; variations of D_1 and D_2, 26
Linsley, E. G., 206n
Lists of terms A, B, C, 2: Definitions for A, 3–46; definitions for B, 47–54; definitions for C, 54–66
Lobachevsky, N., 218, 219, 235
Logical necessity, 3–5: and analyticity, 39, 40, 41; definition of, 3; and linguistic descriptions, 19; for quantity terms, 60; for terms on List B, 47–48
Logical Positivism. *See* Positivism
Logical sufficiency, 5–6: definition of, 5; and linguistic descriptions, 19; for quantity terms, 60; for terms on List B, 47

M

Mach, Ernst, 55
Margenau, Henry, 58n
Mass, 56–57, 59–60, 63
Maxwell, Grover, 80n
Maxwell, James Clerk, 57n, 108, 109: analogy between electric field and incompressible fluid, 204–5, 208, 211; analogy for self-diffusion of gases, 117–18, 210; definition of "analogy," 256; imaginary model of electromagnetic field, 219–21; on kinetic theory, 143–44, 148; on molecules, 110, 113, 114
Mayr, E., 206n
Meaning: having meaning vs. having a meaning, 31–32; of a term, 31–33; criterion of meaningfulness. *See* Empirical significance
—changes in, and dependence upon

Designed by Arlene J. Sheer
Composed in Times Roman by the Colonial Press, Inc.
Printed offset by the Colonial Press, Inc., on P & S R
Bound by the Colonial Press, Inc., in Columbia Milbank Linen